Thomas Harriot, Christopher Columbus, Amerigo Vespucci

The Spanish letter of Columbus to Luis de Sant'Angel

.

Thomas Harriot, Christopher Columbus, Amerigo Vespucci

The Spanish letter of Columbus to Luis de Sant'Angel

ISBN/EAN: 9783337043292

Printed in Europe, USA, Canada, Australia, Japan

Cover: Foto ©ninafisch / pixelio.de

More available books at **www.hansebooks.com**

THE

SɪANISH LETTER

OF

COLUMBUS

TO

LUIS DE ᶜ ANGEL

Escribano de Racion of the Kingdom of Aragon

DATED 15 FEBRUARY 1493

REPRINTED IN REDUCED FACSIMILE, AND TRANSLATED
FROM THE

UNIQUE COPY

OF THE ORIGINAL EDITION

(PRINTED BY JOHANN ROSENBACH AT BARCELONA
EARLY IN APRIL 1493)

LATELY

in the possession of

BERNARD QUARITCH

LONDON, 15 PICCADILLY

1893

LONDON:
G. NORMAN AND SON, PRINTERS, HART STREET,
COVENT GARDEN.

PREFACE.

"THE greatest event which has happened since the creation of the world (leaving aside the incarnation and death of Him who made it) is the discovery of the Indies." Thus said Lopez de Gomara, in dedicating his history to Charles V, three hundred and forty years ago. The eloquent Spaniard was, of course, unable to realise the full import of his words, which seem to have been touched with the spirit of prophecy. Even the centuries behind him contained facts which he did not know, and which are hardly understood in our own days. There is some ground for believing that certain parts of the North American continent were visited, eight hundred years back, by Norsemen sailing from Iceland and Greenland, but we have slender means of verifying the uncritical narratives in which the story is related. Nothing came of the achievement. It began and ended like a flash of lightning, leaving the Western horizon as dark as before. Systems of civilisation, not very unlike our own earlier developments, grew up, and flourished, and died (or survived) beyond the further shores of the Atlantic while Abelard, William of Ockham, Roger Bacon, and Albertus Magnus gave their powerful intellects to the discussion *de omni scibili*, and died unaware of the existence of the vast regions of the West. We must not, however, allow that the Middle Ages were so densely ignorant as many writers have asserted. Numberless surprises for modern students lie in the perusal of forgotten books, the contents of which lend peculiar force to the phrase of the Bible— "There is nothing new under the sun."

A work called the *Image dou Monde* (a different book from the *Imago Mundi* of Pierre d'Ailly) was written towards the middle of the thirteenth century, in which one of the subjects discussed, is the spherical form of the earth and the possibility of making its circuit. The conclusion arrived at, is a conditional negative: the feat, although possible,—the time being calculated at three years, and the circumference of the earth at twenty-two thousand miles—would not be practicable by reason of physical difficulties and the changes of climate.

In the first half of the fourteenth century, the world was made acquainted, by Marco Polo, with lands beyond the ken of Ptolemy, and men who studied geography learned that an ocean bounded Asia on the East, as an ocean bounded Europe on the West. With this knowledge, a spirit of exploration was evoked which became incarnate, soon after the beginning of the fifteenth century, in Prince Henry of Portugal. The efforts of the Portuguese in that century, to reach and turn the southern limit of Africa, so as to win by sea a passage to the golden shores of India—lost since the time of Alexander the Great, save in the glimpses afforded by Arab merchants and by Marco Polo—stimulated so keenly the desire for geographical discovery, that its fascination has not yet become inoperative.

Under the influence of that spirit, a Genoese mariner whom we call Christopher Columbus, set his heart upon traversing the ocean which he imagined lay between Europe and Cathay, in order to find a Western passage to India, as the Portuguese were seeking the Eastern. His hopes were not realised, for he found what he had not sought; but his efforts were crowned with the achievement so enthusiastically lauded in the first sentence of this preface, when he discovered the West Indies on Thursday, October 11th, 1492.

One of the chapters of the *Historia de los Reyes Catolicos*, by Andres Bernaldez, a man acquainted personally with Columbus, begins as follows:—In the name of God Almighty. There was a man of Genoa, a dealer in printed books, trading in this land of Andalusia, whom they called Christoval de Colon, a man of very high intellect without much book-learning, very skilful in the art of Cosmography and of the divisions of the world; who perceived, by what he read in Ptolemy, and in other books, and by his own discernment, how and in what wise is formed the world into which we are born and in which we move. This he placed within the sphere of the heavens, so that it touches them upon no side, nor has aught of firmness to rest upon, but is only earth and water globed by heat within the hollow vault of the sky. And he considered of the way by which regions of much gold might be found, and esteemed that this world and firmament of earth and water is wholly traversable in circuit, as John of Mandeville relates; and he who should have shipping at his need, and should be willing to hold on his course by sea and by land, would assuredly be able to pass by the West in a straight line from San Vicente, and return by Jerusalem to Rome and to Seville; which would be the girdling of the whole earth and round of the globe. And he made, by his wit, a Mapa-mundi, and studied much therein; and judged that from whatever part of the ocean he should begin his passage, he could not fail to meet land, and he deemed, because he saw this, that regions of much gold would be found. Glad with his notion, and knowing that the King Don John of Portugal took much delight in discovery, he repaired thither to win his inclinations; and narrating the import of his reflexions, no credit was yielded him, because the King of Portugal had very eminent and well-trained mariners who esteemed not Colon, and who assumed that in the world there were no greater discoverers than they. Whereupon Christoval Colon betook himself to the court of the King Don Fernando and the Queen Doña Isabel, and made to them a relation of his ideas, to which they likewise gave but little heed. And he discoursed with them, and said that he was sure of what he told them; and explained to them the Mapa-mundi, so that he made them long to know of those lands. Quitting him, they summoned wise astrologers and astronomers, and courtiers skilled in cosmography, from whom they took advice. And the opinion of most of them, upon hearing the discourse of Christoval Colon, was that he spoke truth; insomuch that the King and the Queen became strongly trustful in him, and ordered that three ships should be given him at Seville, manned and victualled for the time that he required; and sent him, in the name of God and of our Lady, forth to make discoveries.—

In this chapter of Bernaldez, who proceeds to narrate the

events of the voyage as told by Columbus himself in the document written to the sovereigns—that source being indicated by several passages in the text—there is no allusion to certain circumstances which must be supplied from the *Historia de las Indias* of Bartolomé de las Casas, who was likewise a friend of the Admiral. He states that the result of the conference with philosophers, cosmographers, and astrologers, was a flat contradiction of the project of Columbus, and that "all in one voice said that it was complete folly and vanity." Dismissed and disappointed, Columbus quitted Granada and took the road for Cordova in order to carry his schemes to the French court. Here we may go on in the words of Las Casas :—

Amongst other persons who gave him aid at court, and desired that his task should be fulfilled and promoted, was Luis de Santangel, the *Escribano de Raciones*. He was as much grieved and saddened by this second and final rejection, without any hope, as though he had personally suffered it in some matter little less than life itself. Seeing Cristobal Colon thus dismissed, and being unable to endure the damage and disparagement which he deemed the sovereigns would incur, by losing the great benefits and riches which Cristobal Colon promised, if his words came true, and by letting another Christian king obtain them ; as well as the degradation of their royal authority—which was so much esteemed in the world—through the lack of spirit to venture so trifling a cost for a gain so infinite; he, trusting in God, and in his intimacy with the sovereigns, or their estimation of his fidelity and of the desire which they knew he had to serve them, went boldly to the Queen, and spoke to her thus. " Lady, the desire which I have ever had to serve the King my Lord, and your Highness, insomuch that if it were necessary I would die for your royal service—has constrained me to appear before your Highness, in order to speak upon a matter which is no concern of mine, and which I am aware lies outside of the duties or limits of my office . . . I have wondered much that your Highness did not accept an empire such as this Columbus has offered . . . this business is of such a quality that if what your Highness thinks difficult or impossible, should be proposed to another King

and should prove successful, as this man says—and to any one
who cares to understand, he gives good reasons for it—the result
would be a manifest lessening of the credit of your Highness, and
an injury to your kingdom. . . . Further, Lady, since what he
asks for now is nothing but a million [of maravedis], and as it
may be said that your Highness lets him go in order not to expend
such an amount, this would indeed be of ill report; and it is in
no wise fitting that your Highness should draw back from an
enterprise so great, even though it were much more uncertain."
The Catholic Queen, then, recognizing the good intention, and
the zeal in her service, of Luis de Santangel, said that his desire
was very pleasing to her, as well as his counsel, which she thought
good to take, but that the matter must be deferred for a time
until there should be more ease and leisure, as he could see in
what straits they were already by reason of those wars which had
been so protracted. "However, if it seem to you, Santangel,"
said the Queen, "that this man cannot brook any longer delay,
I am willing to raise, upon my own private jewels, the money
which he needs for fitting out his expedition, and arrangements
therefor may immediately be set in course." Luis de Santangel
went upon his knees, and kissed the hands of the Queen, in
gratitude for the confidence in his judgment which she evinced
by agreeing to an affair which was held so doubtful, and which
every one opposed. And he added, "Most serene Lady, there is
no need that, for this, your Highness's jewels should be pawned:
it will be but a small service I shall render to your Highness, and
to the King, my Lord, in lending the million from my own house,
but let your Highness order Columbus to be sent for, who has, I
believe, already gone." The Queen at once commanded that an
officer of the court should post after Cristobal Colon, to say that
she bade him return, and should bring him back. The alguacil
found him two leagues from Granada, at the bridge of Pinos.
Columbus returned with the officer, and was joyfully received by
Santangel. When the Queen knew that he was come, she
straightway gave order to the Secretary, Juan de Coloma, that
he should with all speed apply himself to making out the letters
of commission, and all such warrants as Columbus should think

necessary and require for his whole voyage and discovery. . . .
In conclusion, this work, so heroic and stupendous in its nature
and vastness, had to be begun with the aid of a million (of
maravedis) lent by a servant of the sovereigns, a man of no great
wealth ; whereas no eyes have seen, no ears have heard, no heart
has imagined, anything like the treasures which have since then
poured into Castile from the Indies, and been lavished away by
the Kings of Castile.—So far Las Casas.

Furnished with his commission, Columbus started for Palos,
and there entered into negociations to obtain the services of the
three brothers Pinzon, rich and renowed mariners.   The million
lent by Santangel proved insufficient for the purpose in view, and
Martin Alonso Pinzon advanced another half-million to the new
Admiral; with which Columbus was enabled to complete all his
arrangements.   Three caravels were fitted out.   In the Capitana,
Columbus himself took the command with forty men; Martin
Alonso Pinzon went as commander, with his brother Francisco as
captain, in the Pinta, the fastest sailer of the three ; and Vicente
Yañez Pinzon sailed in the Nina.

Early in the morning of the 3rd August, 1492, they weighed
anchor and started from the little island of Saltes, opposite
Huelva, in the port of Palos; and early in the morning of
Friday, the 12th October, they sighted Guanahani, which is
generally considered identical with Watling Island in the Bahamas.
The voyage had thus occupied seventy-one days; and the statement in Columbus' printed letter that it was thirty-three days is
usually supposed to be a blunder.   Such is not the case.   He
reckoned only from the time of quitting the known outposts of
Christendom, and his calculation of thirty-three days began when
his ships, lying becalmed on the 7th September between Teneriffe
and Gomera in the Canary Islands, were enabled to start on the
following day with a N.E. wind, which bore them out into the
ocean.   Thus twenty-two days of September and eleven of
October constituted what he regarded as the duration of his
passage from land to land, from Christendom to the Indies.

All the circumstances of the voyage are familiar to the world.
The chief authority is Columbus' own diary carefully written day

by day in the form of a letter to Ferdinand and Isabella. The original has long disappeared, but Las Casas, about 1520, made an abridged copy of it, occasionally giving the exact text, when he considered it impressive. This transcript still exists, and was published by Navarrete in 1825 (Coleccion, Tomo I). We also find it embodied in the *Historia de las Indias* of Las Casas, a great and invaluable work printed for the first time in 1875. Clear evidence is afforded by an examination of the text that Columbus never failed in the duty of writing his daily record, notwithstanding all the mental and physical difficulties that encompassed his enterprise. Under such circumstances, it is easy to account for the blanks that occur here and there in the transcript made by Las Casas. The handwriting of the great Genoese, at the most favourable moments, was not very clear, as we can see by the facsimiles of holograph letters in the *Cartas de Indias*. What it must have been on ship-board in a boisterous ocean, we may imagine from the errors which appear in the various printed texts of the letter now republished, which we give in a reduced facsimile from the recently discovered unique copy of the first impression. That letter seems to have originated in the following manner.

On the return of Columbus, a terrible storm arose when he was approaching the Azores. From the night of the 12th February, until after sundown on the 14th, he was driven and tossed about under bare poles, with constant expectation of shipwreck. Fearing that the sovereigns would never learn the extent of his services, and dreading that his boys at Cordova would be left beggars in a strange land, the orphans of a discredited foreigner, he resolved to commit his story to the seas. He took a sheet of parchment and traced upon it as much as he could write about his great discovery; then wrapping it in a piece of cloth, well secured, he placed it in a barrel which was flung into the ocean. From the state of the sea, and the words " todo lo qué pudo," we may conclude that the account was a very brief one, and would have been well-nigh illegible if it had ever reached the sovereigns to whom it was addressed. It is said by Ferdinand Columbus that he wrote the same letter in duplicate, and placed the second copy in another barrel, which was retained on board

2

to await the moment of the ship's dissolution; but this statement is not found in Las Casas, and is probably a distortion of the fact that Columbus wrote the two letters about to be referred to. We may confidently assert that, under the circumstances, Columbus could hardly have managed to write more than a few lines; and that consequently the barrel-letter need not be confounded with any extant piece of his composition. It is, however, very likely that the experience of the 14th of February would have set him thinking in regard to the desirability of multiplying the record of his voyage. From Wednesday morning (the 13th) till the night of Sunday (the 17th) he was unable to take any repose, and it was probably during the hours of night, when all active attention to the business of navigation was necessarily interrupted, that he applied himself to writing that compendium of his diary which we know as the letter of Columbus. However rapidly he might write, such a piece of work, regarded even as a transcript, must have occupied nine or ten hours at least, probably more. The likelihood is, that the night of the 14th and the morning of the 15th were given to the writing of the Carta al Escribano de Racion—our present letter; and that on the 17th and 18th, when the sea was a little calmer, he made or caused to be made a transcript or second copy of it, which he addressed to the Treasurer Sanchez. The latter was, as a matter of course, more neatly and correctly written than the former: the violence of the storm had abated, and there was more leisure to improve the roughness of the original, as well as avoid its defects. This is easily observable in comparing the text of the Sanchez letter, as printed for the first time by Varnhagen in 1858, with that of the present reproduction. Although, however, the fair copy of an author's draught composition is usually superior to its original, yet the Sanchez letter has not entirely escaped the fate of most copies; for there are some small matters, which have been pointed out elsewhere, in which its text is inferior to the other. Among the typographical blunders in our Santangel first edition, one small error may be particularised as showing that it followed an ill-written original. Columbus makes a statement twice—once near the beginning, and once near the end—that his outward voyage (from the Canaries) had occupied thirty-three days. In our facsimile it will be seen that the printer blundered; and gave in the first instance " ucinte," in the second " xxxiii." The cause of the error (which was corrected in the [Naples?] reprint preserved in the Ambrosian library at Milan) is easily traceable. If we examine the writing of Roman numerals by Columbus in the facsimiles given in the *Cartas de Indias*, we see at once that Columbus must have used " xxxiii." in the first place, and perhaps written the number in words in the second place. In his writing, " xxxiii." would, to inexpert eyes, look like " veynt," and was so read by the printer. This can easily be tested by any one who chooses to examine the facsimiles of the writing of Columbus, and takes the trouble to imitate his method of forming the numerals in question.

The words which express the date of the Santangel letter show that on the 15th February Columbus thought himself close to one of the Canary Islands; on the 17th he discovered that the land he saw was Santa Maria in the Azores, and he specified the fact correctly in dating the Sanchez letter on the 18th, when he was anchored close to the island and had sent a boat ashore. The weather continued very bad, with occasional mitigations, till the 22nd when an improvement set in. In the evening of the 23rd, he set sail for Spain. On the night of March 2nd, his vessel was again in great danger not far from the coast outside Lisbon; on the night of March 3rd a still more terrible storm arose in which nearly all hope of safety was abandoned; and on the morning of the 4th, he succeeded, much to the wonder of himself and the inhabitants of the coast, in entering the mouth of the Tagus. He then wrote to the King of Portugal, asking permission to enter Lisbon. On the 8th he had a letter from the King, who was at Paraiso, nine leagues away, requesting his presence there. He was received with much courtesy by the monarch, notwithstanding the ill-will of the Portuguese officials who had already begun to show hostility. On the 11th he took leave of the King, on the 12th he decided not to make his way by land to Castile, notwithstanding the proffer of facilities from Dom João; and returned that night to his ship. At 8 o'clock on the following morning, he set sail towards Seville, and early on the 15th he crossed the bar of Saltes and entered the port of Palos. According to his own statement the return voyage had occupied twenty-eight days; in which calculation he included only the space of time between the 18th or 19th January, when he knew that he was in the vicinity of Matinino, and the 16th February, when he found himself close to the Azores. From the latter date onwards, his progress was a stormy and dangerous one, and cost him twenty-three days (as he calculates) beating about "this sea." His reckoning is evidently meant to comprise the time from the 18th of February when he had anchored in the Azores to the 13th of March when he quitted Lisbon for Palos. It had been his intention to write to Ferdinand and Isabella from Lisbon (adonde acordé escrivir a sus Altezas) and we have no proof that he did not send some message announcing his return. But it is very improbable that he did so, when we know that he changed his mind on the subject of accepting Dom João's aid in travelling by land to Castile, and that he was prudently distrustful of his Portuguese friends. It is quite certain that he did not send off the Santangel letter till he reached Seville, since its postscript is dated March 14th. *A fortiori*, he would assuredly not have sent his important journal-letter to the sovereigns; and it is not likely, since he deferred the transmission of the Santangel epistle, that he would have risked the despatch of the improved copy of it which he had addressed to Sanchez. We have, besides, a reason in the date affixed to the Latin version of the latter, for supposing that it was still in his hands on March 14th.

With regard to the persons to whom Columbus addressed his compendious Letter, we have already seen good reason why his friend Luis de Santangel should have been considered a worthy recipient. As for Gabriel Sanchez, the Treasurer of Aragon, it must have been his official position which prompted the navigator to send him the second copy, or fair transcript. His good-will was a matter of no small moment to Columbus in connexion with he expected "muy poquita ayuda que sus Altezas me daran." His rank as a royal minister was higher than that of Santangel, and his power to influence the King greater. Santangel had already been a successful intermediary with the Queen; Sanchez might be won over to perform an equally useful office with the King. However well-disposed Isabella might be, however large her independence in dealing with the states of Castile, Ferdinand was, after all, the real arbiter in their united councils. That Sanchez was personally a stranger to Columbus, and a man with whom he wished to ingratiate himself, would have been a reason for addressing to him the fair copy, more carefully transcribed than the original written three days earlier and addressed to Santangel. Hence we find that the Sanchez text is better than the other, but in a few instances the Santangel letter is decidedly superior.

As already shown, the primary existing authority, in point of fulness and detail, for the history of the first voyage of Columbus, is his own Diary, in so far as it was partly transcribed and partly abridged by Las Casas. But this transcript was never published until 1825, although Herrera and others made use of it in the sixteenth century. The primary authority, in point of publication to the world, is the Santangel letter written by Columbus on the 15th of February, 1493, printed, as we have reason to conclude, in the April of that year at Barcelona, and here published in reduced facsimile. The place of secondary authority must be assigned to the Sanchez letter (written by Columbus on the 18th of February, 1493), not in its original form—since the Spanish text was printed for the first time in 1858—but in the Latin version which appeared in 1493, and which was frequently reprinted and translated afterwards. Although the Santangel letter had been twice printed,—in its *princeps* state at Barcelona, and in a second edition elsewhere (of which the Ambrosian quarto is the only extant specimen)—before the publication of the Sanchez letter in Latin; those two editions must have been carefully suppressed by authority. Otherwise we could not account for the singular fact that no allusion is made to them by any of the writers of the sixteenth century, and that their very existence was unknown till the second edition was discovered about thirty years ago in the Ambrosian library at Milan, and the first was found three years ago in Spain. There is no date of impression or printer's name upon either; but the type of the Spanish folio is that which was used by Johann Rosenbach at Barcelona in 1493-94. The Spanish quarto is evidently later, as is shown by various technical peculiarities of correction and error; but they both naturally preceded the editions of the Latin translation which was printed out of Spain—as was also indeed the Spanish quarto. The Spanish scholar Asensio, in a book upon Columbus published in 1891, asserts that the Ambrosian quarto emanated from a Seville press, and concludes that it was printed there when the discoverer had reached that city on his way from Palos to Barcelona. He forgets that Columbus was not a professional author, and that nothing would have induced him to put the letter in type before it had been delivered to the gentleman to whom it was addressed. It was a private communication, and can only have been given to the press by Santangel or one of his intimate friends then in attendance on the King and Queen at Barcelona. If the Ambrosian quarto was really printed at Seville, it must have been some weeks later than the Barcelona impression. But internal evidence shews that the quarto was printed in Italy, there being numerous instances of the substitution of the initial *j* in words requiring *i* or *y*. The Spaniards frequently used *i* for *j*, but never in any case converted an initial *i* into *j*, the two letters being differently sounded in Spain while in Italy they were homophonous.

During the last three or four years certain quartos (three in number) have made their appearance in the world, produced by typography, and purporting to be fifteenth century editions of the Spanish text. There is, however, no appearance of antiquity about them, and they are evidently clumsy attempts to reproduce the Ambrosian quarto with sufficient inexactness to pass as variant editions.

It is frequently asserted that Columbus never learned that Cuba was an island, or anything other than the coast of Cathay. But the statement made in this letter (on the 19th and 20th lines of the facsimile), shows clearly enough that he had heard and believed it to be an island, as his Indian prisoners had informed him.

SEÑOR porque se que aurei s plazer dela grãd victoria que nuestro señor me
ba dado en mi viaie vos escriuo esta por la ql sabreys como en veinte dias pasc A
las ydias cõ la armada q los illustrissimos Rey e Reyna ñros señores me dieron
dõde yo falle muy muchas Yslas pobladas cõ gente sin numero : y dellas todas
he tomado posesion por sus altezas con pregon y vãdera real estendida y non me fue
cõtradicho Ala primera q yo falle puse nonbre sant saluador a comemoracion desu alta magestad
el qual marauillosamente todo esto andadolos idios la llaman guanaham Ala segũda
puse nonbre la isla de santa maria deconcepcion ala tercera ferrandina ala quarta la isla bella
ala quinta la Ysla Juana e asi a cada vna nonbre nueuo Quando yo llegue ala Juana seg
ui io la costa della alp õniente yla falle tan grãde q pense que seria tierra firme la prouincia de
catayo y como no falle asi villas y lugares enla costa dela mar saluo pequeñas poblaciones
con lagente delas quales nopodia hauer fabla por qu: luego fuyan todos: andaua yo a de
lante por el dicho camino pensado deuo errar grãdes Ciudades o villas y al cabo de muchas
leguas visto q no hauia inouacion i que la costa me leuaua alsetentrion de adõde mi voluntad
era cõtraria porq el yuierno era ya encarnado yo tenia proposito de hazer del al austro y tan bien
el viêto medio adelãte determine deno aguardar otro tiêpo y bolui atras fasta vn señalado puer
to de adõde enbie dos hõbres por la tierra para saber si hauia Rey o grãdes Ciudades, andoui
eron tres iornadas y hallarõ ifinitas poblaciones pequeñas i gête si numero mas no cosa de regi
miento por lo qual seboluierõ yo entêdia harto de otros idios i ia tenia tomados como conti
nuamête esta tierra era Ysla y asi segui la costa della al onête ciento i siete leguas fasta dõde fa
zia fin del qual cabo vi otra Ysla al onête districta de esta diez o ocho leguas ala qual luego
puse nonbre la spañola y fui alli y segui la parte del setentrion asi como dela iuana al oriente
clxxviii grãdes leguas por linia recta del onête asi como dela iuana la qual y todas las otras
sõ fortissimas en demasiado grado y esta en estremo en ella ay muchos puertos en la costa dela
mar si cõparaciõ de otros q yo sepa en cristianos y hartos rios y buenos y grandes q es mara
villa las tierras della sõ altas y en ella muy muchas sierras y mõtañas altissimas si cõparaciõ
de la isla de çetre fra todas fermosissimas de mil fechuras y todas ãdabiles y llenas de arbole
de mil maneras i altas i parecen q llegã al cielo i têgo por dicho q iamas pierdê lafoia segun lo
puede cõpehêder q los vi tã verdes i tã hermosos como sõ por mayo en españa i dellos staua flor
ridos dellos cõ fruto i dellos en otro termino segũ es su calidad i cãtaua el ruiseñor i otros pa
xaricos de mil maneras en el mes de nouiêbre por alli dõde io ãdaua ay palmas de seis ode
ocho maneras q es admiracion verlas põr la deformidad fermosa dellas mas asicomo los
otros arboles y frutos e eruas en ella ay pinares amarauilla eay cãpiñas grãdissimas eay mi
el y de muchas maneras de aues y frutas muy diuersas enlas tierras ay muchas minas deme
tales eay gête istimabile numero Laspañola es marauilla las sierras ylas mõtañas y las vegas
ilas campiñas y las tierras tan fermosas y gruesas para plantar ysebrar pa criar ganados de to
das suertes para bedificios de villas elugares los puertos dela mar aqui no haura creencia sin
vista y delos rios muchos y grandes y bacinas aguas los mas dellos quales trae oro e los arbo
les y frutos e yeruas ay grandes differencias de aquel las dela iuana en esta ay muchas speçie
rias y grandes minas de oro y de otros metales La gente desta ysla y de todas las otras q he
fallado y hauido: ni aya hauido noticia andan todos desnudos hõbres y mugeres asi como
sus madres los pare haun que algunas mugeres se cobria vn solo lugar cõ vna foia de yer
ua o vn cosa de algodõ quepa ello fazen ellos no tienen fierro ni açero ni armas ni son
ello no por que no son gente bien dispuesta y de fermosa estatura saluo que sõ muy te
y marauilla no tiene otras armas saluo las … as delas cañas quando … cõla simiente …
qual ponen al cabo vn palillo agudo eno vnas vsa de aqllas que … vezes m…
cho a enbiar aeura dos otres hombres alguna vila pa hauer fabl … tura a …

f ... victory? despues q̃ los veyã llegar fuyan a no aguardar padre a hijo y esto no por q̃ a ni
guno se aya hecho mal antes a todo cabo ãdõde yo aya estado y podido hauer fabla les heda
do de todo lo q̃ tenia asi paño como otras cosas muchas sĩ recebir por ello cosa algũa mas
fõ asi temerosos sin remedio: verdad es q̃ despues q̃ aseguran y pierden este miedo ellos son
tanto sĩ engaño y tan liberales de lo q̃ tienẽ que no lo creerian sino el q̃ lo viese: ellos de cosa que
tẽgan pidiẽdogela iamas dizẽ de no antes cõuidã la psona cõ ello y muestran tãto amor q̃
darian los coraçones y quierẽ sea cosa de valor quien sea de poco precio luego por qual quie
ra cosica de qual quiera manera que sea q̃ sele de por ello sea cõtentos: yo defendi q̃ nofeles dĩe
sen cosas tan siniles como pedaços de escudillas rotas y pedaços de vidrio roto y cabos de agu
getas: haũ que quãdo ellos esto podiã llegar les parescia hauer la mejor ioya del mũdo. que
se acerto hauer vn marinero por vna agugeta de oro de peso de dos castellanos y medio: y otros
de otras cosas q̃ muy menos valiã mucho mas ya por blãcas nueuas dauan por ellas todo
quãto tenien haũ que fuese dos ni tres castellanos de oro o vna arroua o dos de algodõ fila
do: fasta los pedaços delos arcos rotos delas pipas tomauan y dauan lo q̃ tenian como besti
as: asi que me parecio mal: yo lo defẽdi: y daua yo graciosas mil cosas buenas q̃ yo leuaua por
que tomen amor y alliẽda desto se farã cristianos que se inclinan al amor e servicio de sus altezas
y de toda la naciõ castellana: e procurã de aiũtar de nos dar delas cosas que tenẽ en abundã
cia que nos sõ necessarias y no conocian niguna seta ni idolatria saluo que todos creen q̃ las
fuerças y el bien es en el cielo y creian muy firme que yo cõ estos nauios y gente venia del cielo y en tal
catamiento me recebian en todo cabo despues de hauer perdido el miedo y esto no procede por q̃
sean ignorantes saluo de muy sotil igenio y õbres que nauegan todas aquellas mares que es
marauilla la buena cuenta q̃ ellos dan de todo saluo por q̃ nunca vierõ gẽte vestida ni semeiã
tes nauios y luego que llege alas dichas indias en la prima isla q̃ halle tome por fuerça algunos dellos pa
ra que deprendiesen y me diese notia delo que auia en aquellas partes casi fue que luego se entẽdiõ
y nos a ellos quando por lengua o señas: y estos han aprouechado mucho oy en dia los traigo
q̃ siempre estã de proposito q̃ vẽgo del cielo por mucha cõuersaciõ q̃ ayan hauido cõtigo y estos
eran los primeros a pronunciarlo a donde yo llegaua y los otros andauan corriendo de casa e
casa y a las villas cercanas cõ bozes altas venit venit a ver la gente del cielo asi todos hõbres
como mugeres despues de hauer el coraçõ seguro de nos venia q̃ no cadaua grande ni pequeño
y todos trayan algu de comer y de beuer que dauan cõ vn amor marauilloso ellos tiene todas
las yslas muy muchas canoas a manera de fustes de remo dellas maiores dellas menores y al
gunas y muchas fõ mayores que vna fusta de dieciz cocho bãcos no sõ tan anchas porque fõ
de vn solo madero mas vna fusta no terna cõ ellas al remo porque van que no es cosa de cre
er y cõ estas nauegan todas aquellas islas q̃ sõ innumitables: y tratã sus mercaderias: algunas
destas canoas he visto cõ lxx y lxxx õbres en ella y cada vno cõ su remo en todas estas islas no
vide mucha diuersidad dela fechura dela gente ni en las costumbres ni en la lengua: saluo que
todos se entienden q̃ es cosa muy singular para lo q̃ espero q̃ determinaran sus altezas para la
cõuersaciõ dellos de nuestra santa fe ala qual sõ muy dispuestos: ya dixe como yo hauia andã do
e vii leguas por la costa dela mar por la derecha liña de õcidẽte a oriẽte por la isla iuana segũ d
qual camino puedo dezir que esta isla es maior que inglaterra y escocia iuntas por q̃ allẽde de es
tas e vii leguas me queda dela parte de poniẽte dos provincias q̃ io no he andado: la vna de
las q̃les llaman auau: adõde nasce la gẽte cõ cola las q̃les provincias no pueden tener en lõgura
menos de lo. lx. leguas segu puede entẽder destos idios q̃ yo tengo los q̃les saben todo e
las yslas esta otra española en cerco tiene mas que la españa toda desde colunya por costa de
mar hasta fuẽte rauia en vizcaya pues en vna quadra anduue: dirrui gracias leguas por rec
ta briẽ de occidente a oriẽte esta es para desear: e ... es para nunca de exar en la qual puesto
... nas tenga tom ... a possessiõ por sus altezas y todas sean mas abastadas de lo q̃ yo
... rtos se los traigo por sus altezas que dellas ...

se y puedo dezir y todas las tengo por de sus altezas qual dellas pueden disponer como y tan cõ
plidamête como delos Reynos de castilla eu esta española en ellugar mas cõuenible y mejor
comarca para las minas del oro y de todo trato asi dela tierra firme deaqua como de aquella
dealla od gran can adõde haura grãd trato e ganancia he tomado possessiõ de vna villa gran
de ala qual puse nõbre la villa de nauidad: y en ella hefecho fuerça y fortaleza que ya a estas ho
ras estara del todo acabada y he dexado en ella gente que abasta para semejante fecho cõ armas
y artellarias e vituallas por mas de vn año y fusta y maestro dela mar en todas las artes para fazer
otras y grãde amistad cõ el Rey de aquella tierra en tanto grado quese preciaua de me llamar y
tener por hermano e haû que le mudase la volûtad a hoffador esta gête el ni los suios nosabê
que sean armas y andã desnudos como yahe dicho sõ los mas temerosos que ay en el mûdo
asi que solamente la gente que alli queda es para destruir toda aquella tierra y es ysla sipeligro
de sus personas sabieu dose regir entodas estas islas me parece que todos los õbres seau cõtê
tos cõ vna muger y a su maioral o Rey dan fasta veinte: las mugeres me parece que trabaiã
mas que los õbres ni he podido entêder si tienen bienes proprios que me parecio ver q̃ a aquello
que vno tenia todos hazian parte en especial delas cosas comederas en estas islas fasta aqui
no he hallado õbres mostrudos cõmo muchos pensauan mas antes es toda gête demuy lindo
acatamiento ni sõ negros como ê guinea saluo cõ sus cabellos corredios y no se criã adõde ay
ímpeto demasiado delos rayos solares es verdad quel sol tiene alli grand fuerça puesto que es di
distinta dela liña iquinocial veinte e seis grados en estas islas adõde ay mõtañas grandes: ay tenia
a fuerça el frio este yuierno: mas ellos lo sufrê por la costumbre que cõ la ayuda delas viandas
comen cõ especias muchas y muy calientes en demasia: asi que mostruos no he hallado ni noti
cia saluo de vna ysla que es aqui en la segunda ala entrada delas yndias q̃ es poblada de vna
iente que tienê en todas las yslas por muy ferozes los quales comê carne vmana estos tiene
muchas canaus cõ las quales corretodas las yslas de india y roban y toma quanto pueden ellos
no sõ mas disformes que los otros saluo q̃ tienê en costumbre detraer los cabellos largos com
o mugeres y vsan arcos y flechas delas mismas armas de cañas cõ vn palillo al cabo por defec
to de hierro q̃ no tienê sõ ferozes entre estos otros pueblos que sõ en demasiado grado couardes
mas yo no los tengo en nada mas que a los otros estos sõ aquellos q̃ tratã cõ las mugeres
de matanino q̃ es la primera ysla partiendo despaña para las indias q̃ se falla en la qual no ay
hõbre ninguno: ellas no vsan exercicio femenil saluo arcos y frechas como los sobre dichos de cañas
y se arman y cobigan cõ launes de arambre deque tiene mucho otra ysla me seguran mayor q̃ la
española en que las personas no tienê ningû cabello. En esta ay oro sin cuento y destas y delas o
tras traigo comigo indios para testimonio: e cõclusiõ a hablar desto solamête que sea fecho este
viage que fue de corrida que pueden vdos vras altezas q̃ yo les dare oro quanto ouierê menester con
muy poquita ayuda q̃ sus altezas me daran agora especiaria y algodõ quanto sus altezas mãdarã
cargar y almastica quanta mandaran cargar: e dela qual fasta oy no se ha fallado saluo en gre
cia en la ysla de xio y el senorio la uende como quiere y ligni aloe quãto mandaran cargar y es
clauos quãtos mandarã cargar e seran destos ydolatres y creo hauer fallado ruybaruo y caue
la e otras mil cosas de sustancia fallare que hauran fallado la gête que yo alla dexo porque yo
no me he detenido ningû cabo en quãto el viento me aia dado lugar de nauegar solamête en la
villa de nauidad en quãto dexe asegurado. E bien afirmado. E ala verdad mucho mas hiziera
si los nauios me siruieran como razõ demandaua. Esto es harto y eterno dios n͂ro señor
el qual da a todos aquellos q̃ andan su camino victoria de cosas que parecen impossibles: y esta
señaladamête fuela vna porq̃ haû que destas tierras aiã hallado o escripto todo va por cõ
jectura sin allegar de vista saluo cõprendiendo a tãto que los oyêtes los mas escuchauan e
iuzgauan mas por fabla que por poca s   dello asi que pues nuestro Redentor dio esta vic
toria A nuestros Illustrisimos rey e reyna e a sus reynos famosos deta alta cosa A dõde toda

La chriftiandad deue tomar alegria:y fazer grandes fieftas:y dar gradas folènes ala fancta tri
nidad cõ muchas oraciones folènes por el tanto en̄ falcamiento que hauran en tornando fe
tantos pueblos a nueftra fancta fe :y defpues por los bienes tēporals q̃ no folamēte ala efpaña
mas atodos los chriftianos ternan aqui refrigerio y ganãcia efto fegun̄ el fecho a fi embreue
fecha enla calaue:a fobre las yflas de canaria a xv de febrero año Mil. ccccclxxxxiij.

       Fara lo que mandareys   El Almirãte

       Anima que venia dentro en la Carta.

Defpues defta efcripto:y eftãdo en mar de. Caftilla falio tanto viēto cõ migo .ful y fuefte que
me ha fecho defcargar los nauios po con̄ aqui en efte puerto delifbona oy que fue la mayor
marauilla del mundo adõde acorde efcriuir afus altezas.entodaslas ynoue de fiēpre halla
do y los tēporallcomo eu mayo adõde yo fay en xxxiiiõiaj y volui en xxviij falvo queftas tormē
tas me ãde tenido x.iij orãs corriendo por efta mar:dizen aqua todos los bõbres dfta marqua
mas ouo tan mal yuierno no ni ternas perdidas de nauestfecha ha quatorze oias de marzo:

       ESTA Carta en bio Colom Ãfcriuano Deraciõ
       De las Ŷlas Halladas en Las Ynoias:Lõtenida
       E Orã De Sus Altezas

CARTA

DE

CRISTOVAL COLON

AL ESCRIBANO DE RACION

LUIS DE SANT' ANGEL

(With the obvious typographical errors corrected.)

SEÑOR,

Porque sé que avreis plazer de la grand vitoria que nuestro
Señor me ha dado en mi viaje, vos escrivo esta por laqual sabreys
como en xxxiii dias pasé á las Indias (con la armada que los
illustrissimos Rey e Reyna nuestros Señores me dieron) donde yo
fallé muy muchas islas pobladas con gente sin numero; y dellas
todas he tomado posesion por sus Altezas con pregon, y vandera
rreal estendida, y non me fue contradicho. A la primera que yo
fallé, puse nombre Sant Salvador á comemoracion de Su alta
Magestad El qual maravillosamente todo esto ha dado: los Indios
la llaman Guanahanî. A la segunda puse nombre La Isla de
Santa Maria de Concepcion; á la tercera, Fernandina; á la quarta
La Isabela; á la quinta La Isla Juana; e asi á cada una nombre
nuevo. Quando yo llegué á la Juana, segui yo la costa della al
Poniente, y la fallé tan grande que pensé que seria Tierra firme, la
provincia de Catayo; y como no fallé asi villas y lugares en la
costa de la mar, salvo pequeñas poblaciones con la gente de las
quales no podia haver fabla porque luego fuyan todos,—andava
yo adelante por el dicho camino, pensando de no errar grandes
ciudades ó villas; y al cabo de muchas leguas, visto que no havia
inovacion, i que la costa me levava al Setentrion, de donde mi
voluntad era contraria porque el invierno era ya encarando, yo

tenia proposito de hazer dél al Austro; y tanbien el viento me dió adelante. Determiné de no aguardar otro tiempo, y volvi atrás fasta un señalado puerto, de donde enbié dos hombres por la tierra para saber si havia Rey o grandes ciudades. Andovieron tres jornadas, y hallaron infinitas poblaciones pequeñas i gente sin numero, mas no cosa de regimiento; por lo qual se bolvieron. Yo entendia harto de otros Indios que ya tenia tomados, como continuamente esta tierra era isla; e asi segui la costa della al Oriente ciento i siete leguas fasta donde fazia fin; del qual cabo, vi otra isla al Oriente, distincta de esta diez y ocho leguas á la qual luego puse nombre La Española. Y fui alli, y segui la parte del Setentrion, asicomo de la Juana, al Oriente, clxxxviii grandes leguas, por linea recta del Oriente, asicomo de la Juana; la qual y todas las otras son fertilisimas en demasiado grado, y esta en estremo. En ella, ay muchos puertos en la costa de la mar, sin comparacion de otros que yo sepa en Cristianos, y fartos rrios, y buenos y grandes, que es maravilla. Las tierras della son altas, y en ella muy muchas sierras y montañas altissimas sin comparacion de la Isla de Tenerife; todas fermosissimas de mil fechuras, y todas andables y llenas de arboles de mil maneras i altas, i parecen que llegan al cielo. I tengo por dicho que jamás pierden la foja, segun lo puedo comprehender que los vi tan verdes i tan hermosos, como son por Mayo en España. Y dellos estavan floridos, dellos con fruto, i dellos en otro termino segun es su calidad; i cantava el ruiseñor i otros paxaritos de mil maneras, en el mes de Noviembre, por alli donde yo andava. Ay palmas de seis o de ocho maneras, que es admiracion verlas por la diformidad fermosa dellas; mas asicomo los otros arboles y frutos e yervas. En ella ay pinares á maravilla, e hay campiñas grandissimas, y ay miel, i de muchas maneras de aves, y frutas muy diversas. En las tierras ay muchas minas de metales, e ay gente inestimable numero. La Española es maravilla: las sierras y las montañas y las vegas, i las campiñas, y las tierras tan fermosas y gruesas para plantar y senbrar, para criar ganados de todas suertes, para hedificios de villas e lugares. Los puertos de la mar aqui no havria crehencia sin vista, y de los rios muchos y grandes, y buenas aguas, los mas de los quales traen oro. En los arboles y frutos e yervas, ay grandes differencias de aquellas de la Juana. En esta ay muchas especierias, y grandes minas de oro y de otros metales. La gente desta ysla y de todas las otras que he fallado, y havido (ni aya havido) noticia, andan todos desnudos, honbres y mugeres, asi como sus madres los paren, haunque algunas mugeres se cobijan un solo lugar con una foja de yerva, o una cosa de algodon que para ello fazen. Ellos no tienen fierro ni azero ni armas ni so[n par]a ello, no porque no sea gente bien dispuesta y de fermosa estatura salvo que son muy te[merosos] á maravilla. No tienen otras armas, salvo las a[rm]as de las cañas quando est[an] con la simiente á [la] qual ponen al cabo un palillo agudo, e no osan usar de aquellas: que m[uchas] vezes me [ha aca]escido embiar á tierra dos o tres hombres á alguna villa para haver fabl[a, y] salir á [ellos dellos] sin numero; y despues que los veyan llegar, fuyan á no aguardar padre á hijo. Y esto no porque á ninguno se aya hecho mal, antes á todo cabo á donde yo aya estado y podido haver fabla, les he dado de todo lo que tenia, asi paño como otras cosas muchas, sin recebir por ello cosa alguna; mas son asi temerosos sin remedio. Verdad es, que despues que aseguran, y pierden este miedo, ellos son tanto sin engaño y tan liberales de lo que tienen, que no lo creerian sino él que lo viese. Ellos de cosa que tengan, pidiendosela, jamás dizen de nó; antes convidan la persona con ello, y muestran tanto amor que darian los corazones; y quier sea cosa de valor, quier sea de poco precio, luego por qualquiera cosica, de qualquiera manera que sea, que seles dé por ello, sean contentos. Yo defendi que no seles diesen cosas tan ceviles como pedazos de escudillas rotas, y pedazas de vidrio roto, y cabos de agugetas—haunque quando ellos esto podian llegar, les parescia haver la mejor joya del mundo. Que se acertó haver un marinero por una aguageta de oro de peso de dos castellanos y medio; y otros, de otras cosas que muy menos valian, mucho mas. Ya, por blancas nuevas, davan por ellas todo quanto tenian, haunque fuesen dos ni tres castellanos de oro, o una arrova o dos de algodon filado. Fasta los pedazos de los arcos rotos de las pipas tomavan, y davan lo que tenian, como bestias; asi que me pareció mal. Yo lo defendí, y dava yo graciosas mil cosas buenas que yo levava, porque tomen amor, y

4

allende desto se fagan Cristianos;—que se inclinan al amor e servicio de sus Altezas, y de toda la nacion Castellana; e procuran de ajuntar de nos dar de las cosas que tienen en abundancia, que nos son necessarias. Y no conocian ninguna seta nin idolatria, salvo que todos creen que las fuerças y el bien es en el cielo; y creian muy firme que yo, con estos navios y gente, venia del cielo; y en tal acatamiento me recebian en todo cabo, despues de haver perdido el miedo. Y esto no procede porque sean ignorantes, —salvo de muy sotil ingenio; y onbres que navegan todas aquellas mares, que es maravilla la buena cuenta qu' ellos dan de todo— salvo porque nunca vieron gente vestida ni semejantes navios. Y luego que llegué á las Indias, en la primera isla que hallé, tomé por fuerza algunos dellos para que deprendiesen y me diesen noticia de lo que avia en aquellas partes; e asi fue que luego entendieron y nos á ellos, quando por lengua o señas. Y estos han aprovechado mucho. Oy en dia los traigo, que siempre estan de proposito que vengo del cielo, por mucha conversacion que ayan havido conmigo. Y estos eran los primeros à pronunciarlo donde yo llegava, y los otros andavan corriendo de casa en casa, y a las villas cercanas, con vozes altas: Venid! venid á ver la gente del cielo. Asi todos, honbres como mugeres, despues de haver el corazon seguro de nos, venian, que no quedavan grande ni pequeño, y todos trayan algo de comer y de bever que davan con un amor maravilloso. Ellos tienen [en] todas las yslas muy muchas canoas á manera de fustas de remo, dellas maiores, dellas menores, y algunas y muchas son mayores que una fusta de diez e ocho bancos. No son tan anchas porque son de un solo madero, mas una fusta no terná con ellas al remo porque van que no es cosa de creer; y con estas navegan todas aquellas islas que son innumerables, y tratan sus mercaderías. Algunas destas canoas he visto con lxx y lxxx [h]onbres en ella, y cada uno con su remo. En todas estas islas no vide mucha diversidad de la fechura de la gente, ni en las costumbres, ni en la lengua salvo que todos se entienden; que es cosa muy singular para lo que espero que determinaran sus Altezas para la conversacion dellos de nuestra santa fe, á la qual son muy dispuestos. Ya dixe como yo havia andado cvii leguas por la costa de la mar, por la derecha

linea de Occidente á Oriente, por la isla Juana; segun el qual
camino puedo decir que esta isla es maior que Inglaterra y
Escocia juntas; porque, allende destas cvii leguas, me queda de
la parte de Poniente dos provincias que yo no he andado,—la una
de las quales llaman Avan, donde nacen la gente con cola—las
quales provincias no pueden tener en longura menos de l ó lx
leguas, segun puedo entender destos Indios qu[e] yo tengo, los
quales saben todas las yslas.   Esta otra Española en cierco tiene
mas que la España toda desde Co[libre en Cata]luña por costa
de mar fasta Fuenteravia en Viscaya; pues en una quadra anduve
clxxxviii grandes leguas por recta linea de Occident[e] á Oriente.
Esta es para desear; e v[ista] es para nunca dexar.   En la qual,
—puesto [que de to]das tenga tomada possession por sus Altezas,
y todas sean mas abastadas de lo que yo sé y puedo dezir y todas
las tengo por de sus Altezas quales dellas pueden disponer como
y tan conplidame[n]te como de los reynos de Castilla—en esta
Española, en el lugar mas convenible y meior comarca para las
minas del oro, y de todo trato asi de la tierra firme de acá, como
de aquella de allá del gran Can, donde havrá grand trato e
ganancia, he tomado possession de una villa grande, á la qual
puse nonbre la villa de Navidad; y en ella he fecho fuerza y
fortaleza—que ya á estas horas estará del todo acabada—y he
dexado en ella gente que basta para semejante fecho, con armas y
artellarias, e vituallas por mas de un año, y fusta y maestro de la
mar en todas artes para fazer otras: y grand amistad con el Rey
de aquella tierra en tanto grado que se preciava de me llamar y
tener por hermano.   E aunque le mudase la voluntad á offender
esta gente, el ni los suios no saben que sean armas, y andan
desnudos.   Como ya he dicho, son los mas temerosos que ay en
el mundo; asi que solamente la gente que allá queda es para
destruir toda aquella tierra; y es ysla sin peligro de sus personas
sabiendo se regir.   En todas estas islas me parece que todos los
[h]onbres sean contentos con una muger, i a su maioral, ó rey,
dan fasta veynte.   Las mugeres me parece que trabaxan mas que
los [h]onbres.   Ni he podido entender si tenian bienes propios;
que me pareció ver que aquello que uno tenia, todos hazian parte,
en especial de las cosas comederas.   En estas islas, fasta aqui, no

he hallado [h]onbres monstruos, como muchos pensavan ; mas
antes es toda gente de muy lindo acatamiento, ni son negros
como en Guinea, salvo con sus cabellos correntios ; y no se crian
donde ay inpeto demasiado de los rayos solares. Es verdad qu'
el sol tiene alli grand fuerça puesto que es distinta de la linea
equinocial veinte e seis grados. En estas islas donde ay montañas
grandes, ahi tenia fuerça el frio este ynvierno ; mas ellos lo
sufren por la costumbre con la ayuda de las viandas que comen con
especias muchas y muy calientes en demasía. Asi que monstruos
no he hallado, ni noticia, salvo de una ysla que es aqui la segunda
á la entrada de las Yndias, que es poblada de una gente que tienen
en todas las yslas por muy ferozes, los quales comen carne humana.
Estos tienen muchas canoas con las quales corren todas las yslas
de India, roban y toman quanto pueden. Ellos no son mas
difformes que los otros, salvo que tienen en costumbre de traer
los cabellos largos como mugeres, y usan arcos y flechas de las
mismas armas de cañas con un palillo al cabo por defecto de fierro
que no tienen. Son ferozes entre estos otros pueblos que son en
demasiado grado cobardes, mas yo no los tengo en nada mas
que á los otros. Estos son aquellos que tratan con las mugeres
de Matinino, que es la primera ysla partiendo d'España para las
Indias que se falla ; en la qual no ay honbre ninguno. Ellas no
usan exercicio femenil, salvo arcos y flechas, como los sobre
dichos de cañas ; y se arman y cobijan con laminas de arambre
de que tienen mucho. Otra ysla me aseguran mayor que la Española en que las personas no tienen ningun cabello. En esta ay
oro sin cuento, y destas y de las otras traigo co[n]migo Indios
para testimonio. E[n] conclusion, á fablar desto solamente que
sea fecho este viage que fue asi de cor[r]ida, que pueden ver sus
Altezas q[ue] yo les daré oro quanto [h]ovieren menester, con
muy poquita ayuda que sus Altezas me daran ; agora [e]speciaria
y algodon quanto sus Altezas mandaran cargar, y almastica quanta
mandaran cargar—e de la qual fasta [h]oy no se ha fallado salvo
en Grecia en la ysla de Xio, y el Señorio la vende como quiere —; y
lignumaloe quanto mandaran cargar, y esclavos quantos mandaran
cargar,—y seran de los ydólatras ; y creo haver fallado ruybarbo
y canela. E otras mil cosas de sustancia fallare que havran fallado

la gente que yo allá dexo. Porque yo no me he detenido [en] ningun cabo en quanto el viento me aya dado lugar de navegar; solamente en la villa de Navidad en quanto dexé asegurado e bien asentado. E á la verdad mucho mas ficiera si los navios me sirvieran como razon demandava. Esto es harto: y [*gracias á ?*] eterno Dios nuestro Señor el qual da á todos aquellos que andan su camino victoria de cosas que parecen imposibles—y esta señaladamente fue la una; porque aunque destas tierras ayan fablado ó escripto, todo va por conjectura sin alegar de vista; salvo comprendiendo á tanto que los oyentes los mas escuchavan e juzgavan mas por fabla que por poca cosa dello. Asi que pues nuestro Redemtor dió esta victoria a nuestros illustrisimos Rey e Reyna, e á s[us] reynos famosos, de tan alta cosa, donde toda la Christiandad deve tomar alegria, y fazer grandes fiestas, y dar gracias solennes á la sancta Trinidad, con muchas oraciones solennes por el tanto enxalçamiento que havran en tornandose tantos pueblos á nuestra sancta fe, y despues por los bienes temporales que no solamente á la España mas á todos los Christianos, ternan aqui refrigerio y ganancia. Esto segun el fecho, asi en breve.

Fecha en la caravela sobre las yslas de Canaria á xv de Febrero, año Mil. cccclxxxxiii.

Fará lo que mandareys.

EL ALMIRANTE.

Nema que venia dentro en la carta.

Despues desto escripto, estando en mar de Castilla, salió tanto viento conmigo, sul y sueste, que me ha fecho descargar los navios; pero cor[r]i aqui en este puerto de Lisbona [h]oy, que fue la mayor maravilla del mundo, donde acordé escrivir á sus Altezas. En todas las Yndias he siempre hallado los temporales como en Mayo. Adonde yo fuy en xxxiii dias, y volvi en xxviii, salvo qu' estas tormentas me[h]an detenido xxiii dias corriendo por esta mar. Dizen acá todos los honbres de la mar q[ue] jamás [h]ovo tan mal ynvierno, no ni tantas perdidas de naves.

8

Fecha á quatorze dias de Marzo.

Esta carta enbió Colom al Escrivano de Racion, de las
Islas halladas en las Indias, contenida á otra de sus Altezas.

NOTE.

The preceding letter is on two folio leaves, or four pages, of which page 1 has forty-seven lines, page 2 forty-eight lines, page 3 forty-seven, and page 4 sixteen lines. The extra line on page 2 is almost illegible and seems to have undergone an attempt at obliteration by the printer himself. Its substance (with two small variations) is repeated on the first line of page 3. The Letter has no external mark of the date of impression, or of the place where it was printed. However, as already stated, the typographical character enables us to assert that Juan de Rosenbach printed it at Barcelona. The assertion is rendered conclusive by a number of Catalanisms in spelling which disfigure the text, and expose the hand of a Catalonian type-setter.

Four leaves of contemporary paper are stitched with it, and have been no doubt its companions for nearly four hundred years. Of those four leaves the first and second are glued together, and the whole four, as we may perceive from looking at the first of them, have served as "end-paper" and "fly-leaves" in a book in which the Letter was preserved from the year 1497 until some curious hand extracted it. There is writing on all the four leaves. The matter which fills the third and fourth was written evidently in Bruges in 1497; the matter contained in the first and second (pp. 1-3) is in the same hand, but has a direct Spanish interest.

The latter is a life of Saint Leocadia who was martyred in Toledo in A.D. 304. It is headed thus:

Incipit Confessio Sancte Leochade Virginis qu obiit in civitate Tholetana sub ydus Decembris sub Datiano preside.

The first words of the text are: "In temporibus illis dum post corporeum Salvatoris adventum."

The other two leaves are less imperfect than those, and are endorsed

App ᵒ intposita p. dnm Archiducem ad habitum Concilium.

It is a rather important document,—the Appellatio or Appeal presented to the Archduke Philip sitting in public court in his hall at Bruges, on the 12th May, 1497, by Johannes Rousselli, Lord of Hernetes, Procurator General or Fiscal of his Highness, against the harsh and exorbitant imposition of imperial taxes upon the people of the Low Countries. The mode adopted by certain tyrannical officials to increase the revenue (and benefit themselves both directly and indirectly) by enhancing levies and forestalment of dues, had terribly injured the states and caused many persons to fly the country. Even the rightful heads of ecclesiastical foundations had been in many places ejected by ignorant and avaricious strangers; and the condition of things called for such resistance to tyranny as St. Paul had prescribed.—Redress of grievances was promised by the Archduke. His pledge and the proceedings of the Council were witnessed in this formal document by

> Gerardus Numan, Audientiarius,
>
> Laurentius de Blitil, Grifiarius Ordinis Velleris,
>
> Johannes de Longavilla⎫
> Bartholomeus Le Fevre ⎬ ordinary Secretaries,
> Hugo Le Cocq   ⎪
> Johannes Le Borgne   ⎭

and many other counsellors and secretaries whose names are not given.

In connexion with this curious adjunct to the unique Columbus letter, we may state that the Archduke Philip and his consort Juana visited Toledo in 1502, and presented to the Cathedral, *una reliquia grande de la gloriosa Virgen Leocadia, Padrona de aquella ciudad*. This statement, taken from the *Primacia de Toledo* of Castegon y Fonseca, printed in 1645, helps to account for the conjunction of the Leocadia legend and the Bruges Council decree in the manuscript leaves prefixed to the Columbus letter.

This is a suitable occasion to mention the fact that the letter here given in facsimile was in my possession for over two years, but has now taken a permanent resting-place in the fittest home that could be found for it. It forms part of the treasures in the great Lenox library of New York, where it will be carefully preserved as the first printed document relating to the New World.

LITERAL TRANSLATION

OF

THE FIRST EDITION OF COLUMBUS'
SPANISH LETTER
TO LUIS DE SANT' ANGEL.

SIR,

As I know that you will have pleasure of the great victory which our Lord hath given me in my voyage, I write you this, by which you shall know that, in *twenty*[1] days I passed over to the Indies with the fleet which the most illustrious King and Queen, our Lords, gave me: where I found very many islands peopled with inhabitants beyond number. And, of them all, I have taken possession for their Highnesses, with proclamation and the royal standard displayed; and I was not gainsaid. On the first which I found, I put the name Sant Salvador, in commemoration of His high Majesty, who marvellously hath given[2] all this: the Indians call it Guanaham.[3] The second I named the Island of Santa Maria de Concepcion, the third Ferrandina, the fourth, *Fair Island*,[4] the fifth La Isla Juana; and so for each one a new name. When I reached Juana, I followed its coast westwardly, and found it so large that I thought it might be the mainland province of Cathay. And as I did not thus find any towns and villages on the sea-coast, save small hamlets with the people whereof I could not get speech, because they all fled away forthwith, I went on further in the same direction, thinking I should not miss of great cities or towns. And at the end of many leagues, seeing that there was no change, and that the coast was bearing me northwards,

[1] *veinte*, typographical blunder for *xxxiii*. It is corrected in the Ambrosian quarto.

[2] *Andado* in text, blunder for *ha dado*.

[3] *Guanaham*, blunder for *Guanahani*.

[4] *Isla bella*, blunder for *Isabela*.

whereunto my desire was contrary since the winter was already confronting us,[1] I formed the purpose of making from thence to the South, and as the wind also blew against me, I determined not to wait for other weather and turned back as far as a port agreed upon ; from which I sent two men into the country to learn if there were a king, or any great cities. They travelled for three days, and found innumerable small villages and a number-less population, but nought of ruling authority; wherefore they returned. I understood sufficiently from other Indians whom I had already taken, that this land, in its continuousness, was an island ; and so I followed its coast eastwardly for a hundred and seven leagues as far as where it terminated ; from which headland I saw another island to the east, ten or[2] eight leagues distant from this, to which I at once gave the name La Spañola. And I proceeded thither, and followed the northern coast, as with La Juana, eastwardly for a hundred and *seventy*[3]-eight great leagues in a direct easterly course, as with La Juana. The which, and all the others, are most strong[4] to an excessive degree, and this extremely so. In it, there are many havens on the sea-coast, incomparable with any others that I know in Christendom, and plenty of rivers so good and great that it is a marvel. The lands thereof are high, and in it are very many ranges of hills, and most lofty mountains incomparably beyond the Island of Centrefrei ;[5] all most beautiful in a thousand shapes, and all accessible, and full of trees of a thousand kinds, so lofty that they seem to reach the sky. And I am assured that they never lose their foliage; as may be imagined, since I saw them as green and as beautiful as they are in Spain during May. And some of them were in flower, some in fruit, some in another stage according to their kind. And the nightin-gale was singing, and other birds of a thousand sorts, in the month of November, round about the way that I was going. There are palm-trees of six or eight species, wondrous to see for their

[1] *Encarnado* in original for *encarado* or *encarando*.
[2] Ten or eight (diez o ocho) ought to be eighteen (diez e ocho).
[3] Should be "eighty."
[4] Fortissimos, should be fertilisimos: most fertile.
[5] Ought to be Tenerife.

beautiful variety; but so are the other trees, and fruits, and plants therein. There are wonderful pine-groves, and very large plains of verdure, and there is honey, and many kinds of birds, and many various fruits. In the earth there are many mines of metals; and there is a population of incalculable number. Española is a marvel; the mountains and hills, and plains, and fields, and the soil, so beautiful and rich for planting and sowing, for breeding cattle of all sorts, for building of towns and villages. There could be no believing, without seeing, such harbours as are here, as well as the many and great rivers, and excellent waters, most of which contain gold. In the trees and fruits and plants, there are great diversities from those of Juana. In this,[1] there are many spiceries, and great mines of gold and other metals. The people of this island, and of all the others that I have found and seen, or not seen,[2] all go naked, men and women, just as their mothers bring them forth; although some women cover a single place with the leaf of a plant, or a cotton something which they make for that purpose. They have no iron or steel, nor any weapons; nor are they fit thereunto; not because they be not a well-formed people and of fair stature, but that they are most wondrously timorous.[3] They have no other weapons than the stems of reeds in their seeding state, on the end of which they fix little sharpened stakes. Even these, they dare not use; for many times has it happened that I sent two or three men ashore to some village to parley, and countless numbers of them sallied forth, but as soon as they saw those approach, they fled away in such wise that even a father would not wait for his son. And this was not because any hurt had ever done to any of them :— on the contrary, at every headland where I have gone and been able to hold speech with them, I gave them of everything which I had, as well cloth as many other things, without accepting aught therefor—; but such they are, incurably timid. It is true that since they have become more assured, and are losing that terror, they are artless and generous with what they have, to such

[1] i.e. Hispaniola. [2] y havido ni aya havido noticia.
[3] A few lines are a little defective, and portions of words lost.

a degree as no one would believe but him who had seen it. Of anything they have, if it be asked for,[1] they never say no, but do rather invite the person to accept it, and show as much lovingness as though they would give their hearts. And whether it be a thing of value, or one of little worth, they are straightways content with whatsoever trifle of whatsoever kind may be given them in return for it. I forbade that anything so worthless as fragments of broken platters, and pieces of broken glass, and strap-buckles, should be given them; although when they were able to get such things, they seemed to think they had the best jewel in the world, for it was the hap of a sailor to get, in exchange for a strap, gold to the weight of two and a half castellanos, and others much more for other things of far less value; while for new blancas[2] they gave everything they had, even though it were [the worth of] two or three gold castellanos, or one or two arrobas[3] of spun cotton. They took even pieces of broken barrel-hoops, and gave whatever they had, like senseless brutes; insomuch that it seemed to me ill. I forbade it, and I gave gratuitously a thousand useful things that I carried, in order that they may conceive affection, and furthermore may be made[4] Christians; for they are inclined to the love and service of their Highnesses and of all the Castilian nation, and they strive to combine in giving us things which they have in abundance, and of which we are in need.[5] And they knew no sect, nor idolatry; save that they all believe that power and good-ness are in the sky, and they believed very firmly that I, with these ships and crews, came from the sky; and in such opinion, they received me at every place where I landed, after they had lost their terror. And this comes not because they are ignorant: on the contrary, they are men of very subtle wit, who navigate all those seas, and who give a marvellously good account of every-thing—but because they never saw men wearing clothes nor the

---

[1] pidiendogela, for pidiendosela.   [2] Copper-coins.

[3] An arroba = 25 lbs.   [4] se faran. for se fazan, or se fagan.

[5] This sentence continues to be subjunctive after the word "Christians," in the Sanchez-letter of Varnhagen, and the word aiuntar, here translated "com-bine" is there ayudar = to aid.

like of our ships. And as soon as I arrived in the Indies, in the first island that I found, I took some of them by force, to the intent that they should learn [our speech] and give me information of what there was in those parts. And so it was, that very soon they understood [us] and we them, what by speech or what by signs; and those [Indians] have been of much service. To this day I carry them [with me] who are still of the opinion that I come from heaven [as appears] from much conversation which they have had with me. And they were the first to proclaim it wherever I arrived; and the others went running from house to house and to the neighbouring villages, with loud cries of "Come! come to see the people from heaven!" Then, as soon as their minds were reassured about us, every one came, men as well as women, so that there remained none behind,[1] big or little; and they all brought something to eat and drink, which they gave with won-drous lovingness. They have in[2] all the islands very many canoes, after the manner of rowing-galleys, some larger, some smaller; and a good many are larger than a galley of eighteen benches. They are not so wide, because they are made of a single log of timber, but a galley could not keep up with them in rowing, for their motion is a thing beyond belief. And with these, they navigate through all those islands which are numberless, and ply their traffic. I have seen some of those canoes with seventy, and eighty, men in them, each one with his oar. In all those islands, I saw not much diversity in the looks of the people, nor in their manners and language; but they all understand each other, which is a thing of singular towardness for what I hope their Highnesses will determine, as to making them conversant with our holy faith, unto which they are well disposed. I have already told how I had gone a hundred and seven leagues, in a straight line from West to East, along the sea-coast of the Island of Juana; accord-ing to which itinerary, I can declare that that island is larger than England and Scotland combined; as, over and above those hundred and seven leagues, there remains for me, on the western side, two provinces whereto I did not go—one of which they call

---

[1] *cadavan* for *quedaban*.   [2] *en* omitted.

15

Avan, where the people are born with tails—which provinces cannot be less in length than fifty or sixty leagues, according to what may be understood from the Indians with me, who know all the islands. This other, Española, has a greater circumference than the whole of Spain from Co*libre in Catal*unya,[1] by the sea-coast, as far as Fuente Ravia in Biscay; since, along one of its four sides, I went for a hundred and eighty-eight great leagues in a straight line from West to East. This is [a land] to be desired,—and once seen,[2] never to be relinquished—in which (—although, indeed, I have taken possession of them all[3] for their Highnesses, and all are more richly endowed than I have skill and power to say, and I hold them all in the name of their Highnesses who can dispose thereof as much and as completely as of the kingdoms of Castile—) in this Española, in the place most suitable and best for its proximity to the gold mines, and for traffic with the continent, as well on this side as on the further side of the Great Can, where there will be great commerce and profit,—I took possession of a large town which I named the city of Navidad.[4] And I have made fortification there, and a fort (which by this time will have been completely finished) and I have left therein men enough for such a purpose, with arms and artillery, and provisions for more than a year, and a boat, and a [man who is] master of all sea-craft for making others; and great friendship with the King of that land, to such a degree that he prided himself on calling and holding me as his brother. And even though his mind might change towards attacking those men, neither he nor his people know what arms are, and go naked. As I have already said, they

[1] The eleven letters in italics are omitted from the text.

[2] The word *vista* deficient in consequence of a hole in the paper.

[3] A few letters deficient in consequence of the paper being torn. It is curious that the words from "have skill. "down to "as com[pletely]" are printed twice. In the first instance, the line which comprises them is extra-regular at the bottom of page 2, and is so blurred and broken that its duplicate presentation (with a slight variant) at the top of page 3, seems to be a deliberate repetition.

[4] *Navidad* is the same as *Natividad*: he reached the spot on Christmas-day, 1492.

are the most timorous creatures there are in the world, so that the men who remain there are alone sufficient to destroy all that land, and the island is without personal danger for them if they know how to behave themselves. It seems to me that in all those islands, the men are all content with a single wife; and to their chief or king they give as many as twenty. The women, it appears to me, do more work than the men. Nor have I been able to learn whether they held personal property, for it seemed to me that whatever one had, they all took share of, especially of eatable things. Down to the present, I have not found in those islands any monstrous men, as many expected, but on the contrary all the people are very comely; nor are they black like those in Guinea, but have flowing hair; and they are not begotten where there is an excessive violence of the rays of the sun. It is true that the sun is there very strong, notwithstanding that it is twenty-six degrees[1] distant from the equinoctial line. In those islands, where there are lofty mountains, the cold was very keen there, this winter; but they endure it by being accustomed thereto, and by the help of the meats which they eat with many and inordinately hot spices. Thus I have not found, nor had any information of monsters, except of an island which is here[2] the second in the approach to the Indies, which is inhabited by a people whom, in all the islands, they regard as very ferocious, who eat human flesh. These have many canoes with which they run through all the islands of India, and plunder and take as much as they can. They are no more ill-shapen than the others, but have the custom of wearing their hair long, like women; and they use bows and arrows of the same reed-stems, with a point of wood at the top, for lack of iron which they have not. Amongst those other tribes who are excessively cowardly, these are ferocious; but I hold them as nothing more than the others. These are they who have to do with the women of Matremonio[3]—which is the first island that is encountered in the passage from Spain to the Indies—in

---

[1] Instead of *grados* = degrees, the text has (by a typographical error) *grädes*.
[2] The word *en* = in precedes "the second" in the text.
[3] So in the text; it should be Matinino.

which there are no men. Those women practise no female usages, but have bows and arrows of reed such as above mentioned; and they arm and cover themselves with plates of copper of which they have much. In another island, which they assure me is larger than Española, the people have no hair. In this, there is incalculable gold; and concerning these and the rest I bring Indians with me as witnesses. And in conclusion, to speak only of what has been done in this voyage, which has been so hastily performed, their Highnesses may see that I shall give them as much gold as they may need, with very little aid which their Highnesses will give me; spices and cotton at once, as much as their Highnesses will order to be shipped, and as much as they shall order to be shipped of mastic,—which till now has never been found except in Greece, in the island of Xio,[1] and the Seignory[2] sells it for what it likes; and aloe-wood as much as they shall order to be shipped; and slaves as many as they shall order to be shipped,—and these shall be from idolators. And I believe that I have discovered rhubarb and cinnamon, and I shall find that the men whom I am leaving there will have discovered a thousand other things of value; as I made no delay at any point, so long as the wind gave me an opportunity of sailing, except only in the town of Navidad till I had left things safely arranged and well established. And in truth I should have done much more if the ships had served me as well as might reasonably have been expected. This is enough; and [thanks to] eternal God our Lord who gives to all those who walk His way, victory over things which seem impossible; and this was signally one such, for although men have talked[3] or written of those lands, it was all by conjecture, without confirmation from eyesight, importing just so much that the hearers for the most part listened and judged that there was more fable in it than anything actual, however trifling. Since thus our Redeemer has given to our most illustrious King and Queen, and to their famous kingdoms, this victory in so high a matter, Christendom should take gladness therein and make

---

[1] Chios, or Scio.   Of Genoa.
[3] By a typographical blunder, *fallado* is found in the text, instead of *fablado*.

great festivals, and give solemn thanks to the Holy Trinity for the great exaltation they shall have by the conversion of so many peoples to our holy faith; and next for the temporal benefit which will bring hither refreshment and profit, not only to Spain, but to all Christians. This briefly, in accordance with the facts. Dated, on the caravel, off the Canary Islands, the 15 February of the year 1493.

At your command,

THE ADMIRAL.

POSTSCRIPT WHICH CAME WITHIN THE LETTER.

After having written this [letter], and being in the sea of Castile, there rose upon me so much wind, South and South-West, that it has caused me to lighten the vessels, however, I ran hither to-day into this port of Lisbon, which was the greatest wonder in the world; where I decided to write to their Highnesses. I have always found the seasons like May in all the Indies, whither I passed in thirty-three days, and returned in twenty-eight, but that these storms have delayed me twenty-three days running about this sea. All the seamen say here that there never has been so bad a winter, nor so many shipwrecks.

Dated the 14th of March.

Columbus sent this letter to the Escrivano de Racion. Of the islands found in the Indies. Received with another for their Highnesses.

G. NORMAN AND SON, PRINTERS, HART STREET, COVENT GARDEN, LONDON.

THE

LATIN LETTER

OF

COLUMBUS

PRINTED IN 1493

AND ANNOUNCING THE DISCOVERY OF

AMERICA

REPRODUCED IN FACSIMILE, WITH A PREFACE

———————

LONDON

BERNARD QUARITCH

15 PICCADILLY

1893

LONDON :

G. NORMAN AND SON, PRINTERS, HART STREET,

COVENT GARDEN.

INTRODUCTION.

THE Latin letter of Columbus, although plainly indicated in its heading as a translation, was for centuries considered to be the only authentic account of his voyage derived from his own pen. The existence of the Spanish original in a printed text of the period was for the first time made known in 1856, when the quarto now in the Ambrosian library came to light, and it is only three years since the discovery of the still earlier Spanish folio, which has been acquired by the Lenox library from Mr. Quaritch. The importance of the Latin letter as a collateral and (in some instances) corrected document will not easily pass away; collectors and libraries will still bid enormous prices for such rare copies of any of the four editions which appeared in 1493, as may turn up from time to time.

The facsimile of the Latin letter now offered to the public is unaccompanied by an English version, because that work has already been done several times, notably by Mr. Eames of the Lenox library a few months ago ; and also because the translation appended to the facsimile of the Spanish folio announced on the wrapper of the present letter, will serve as a translation for either. Nothing therefore remains to be said here except a few words with regard to the origin, dates, and succession of the first four editions of the Latin Columbus.

The Spanish folio was printed at Barcelona in April, 1493, probably before the middle of that month. The transmission of copies from the Peninsula to the rest of Europe was not effected in the same manner as at present, when railway communication has made Paris the immediate recipient of Spanish traffic. Its ordinary course was by sea to Naples, where the dynasty of Aragon was reigning and where the languages of Catalonia, Valencia, and Castille were familiarly used. It was perhaps about the 22nd or 23rd of April, that the Barcelona letter reached Naples, and it was probably in that city, not in Spain, that the Spanish quarto of the Ambrosian library was reprinted from the Barcelona folio of the Lenox library. As for the Latin letter, its origin was slightly different. Columbus had addressed separate copies of the same narrative to two persons—the first to his friend Luis de Santangel, King Ferdinand's financial secretary, the second (which, from the very fact that it was secondary, contained some corrections and some errors) to Gabriel Sanxis, the Treasurer of Aragon. As the text in both was almost identical, there was no occasion to print the one addressed to Sanxis after that to Santangel had issued from the press of Johann Rosenbach at Barcelona. In any case, for whatever reason, the Spanish text so inscribed was never printed until Varnhagen gave it from a manuscript in 1858. But it was a copy, undoubtedly in MS., of the Sanxis letter, which reached the hands of Leandro de Cosco in Naples somewhere about the 23rd or 24th of April, 1493, and was rendered by him into Latin in the version which was printed four times in 1493, and has been frequently reprinted since. This Leandro was a subject of the kingdom of Aragon as his appellation shows, Cosco being a small town in Lerida not far from Balaguer. The natural jealousy between Aragon and Castille accounts for his evidently wilful omission of Isabel's name in the heading of his translation. He presented the work to Leonardus, Bishop of the Neapolitan see of Monte Peloso, a prelate of Catalonian birth, whose family name appears elsewhere Latinised as "de Carninis," but who called himself "Leonardus de Corbaria," because his native place was Corbaria (now called Corbière), a town on the frontiers of Aragon and Roussillon. The Bishop, who was no less patriotic and prejudiced than Leandro, carried the translation to Rome with

him, and, having added to it some verses enthusiastically
laudatory of his sovereign Ferdinand (but ignoring the Queen
of Castille, to whom Columbus was so much indebted, and
whom he never forgot in writing about " Their Highnesses "),
he gave it to Stephan Planck to print. Planck, who was a
priest as well as a printer, produced an impression (in small
quarto size, four leaves with thirty-four lines to each full page)
which was published early in May, 1493. [One copy of that
edition is in the Lenox library; another in the Boston library.]
In the usual course of transmission to the North, which was
almost always from Rome to Cologne, by the river-way from
Basel, a copy of Planck's first edition reached the latter city and
was there reprinted with pictorial illustrations in wood-engraving
(in small quarto size, ten leaves, with twenty-seven lines to each
full page). This Basel edition is very rare, and the only perfect
copy known is in the Lenox library. Two reprints of the same
text were also published in Paris by Gui Marchant; both probably
in 1493 but dateless. Before this time, Planck had been
reproved by Castilians in Rome for having produced a book
so pointedly injurious to the credit of Queen Isabel. He
therefore printed a second edition (small quarto, four leaves,
thirty-three lines to each full page) in which Leander's words
" invictissimi Fernandi Hispaniarum Regis " were altered to
" invictissimorum Fernandi et Helisabet Hispaniarum Regum,"
Isabel and Ferdinand, although wife and husband, being equally
sovereigns, the one of Castille and Leon, the other of Aragon.
The name of the Treasurer, which had appeared in Planck's first
edition as Raphael Sanxis, by error for Gabriel Sanxis, was
altered, correctly from Raphael to Gabriel, but incorrectly from
Sanxis to Sanchis. The Catalonian name Sanxis (pronounced
Sanshis) had a Castilian correlative in Sanchez, and if it was
necessary to make a Castilian of the Treasurer he ought to have
been transmuted into Gabriel Sanchez. But the Castilianisers
evidently objected merely to Ferdinand *solus* and to the Aragonese
x in Sanxis; so that Planck's second edition when it came out had
still the Catalonian *i* after the Castilian *ch*. Hence when another

edition was required, later in the same year, it was printed by Franck or Silber of Rome (who called himself Eucharius Argenteus) with two further corrections. "Fernandi et Helisabet" became "Fernandi *ac* Helisabet" and "Sanchis" was turned into "Sanches"; and a word on the third page, which is "noverant" in the other three editions, is properly corrected into "neverant." Generally, however, Silber's edition is less intelligently printed than the others, and the best of the four is, on the whole, the one here given in facsimile. Silber's edition is the only one of the four which is dated and inscribed. Planck's two editions and the Basel edition, bear neither name nor date. Silber's has his name "Argenteus" with place and date given as "Rome . . . M . cccc . xciij". It is in small quarto, four leaves, with forty lines to each full page; and a copy is to be found in the Lenox library at New York.

¶ Epiſtola Chꝛiſtofoꝛi Colom: cui etas noſtra multũ debet: de
Jnſulis Jndie ſupꝛa Gangem nuper inuẽtis. Ad quas pergren⸗
das octauo antea·menſe auſpiciis ⁊ ere inuictiſſimoꝝ Fernãdi ⁊
Beliſabet Hiſpaniaꝝ Regũ miſſus fuerat: ad magnificum dñm
Gabꝛielem Sanchis eoꝛundẽ ſereniſſimoꝝ Regum Teſaurariũ
miſſa: quã nobilis ac litteratus vir Leander de Coſco ab Hiſpa
no idiomate in latinum cõuertit tertio kalˢ Maii· M·cccc·rciij
pontificatus Alerandri Serti Anno pꝛimo·

Quoniam ſuſcepte pꝛouintie rem perfectam me ꝓſecutum
fuiſſe gratum tibi foꝛe ſcio: bas conſtitui erarare: que te
vniuſcuiuſcꝗ rei in hoc noſtro itinere geſte inuenteꝗ ad⸗
moneant: Tricelimotertio die poſtꝗ Gadibus diſceſſi in mare
Jndicũ perueni: vbi plurimas inſulas innumeris habitatas ho⸗
minibus repperi: quarum omnium pꝛo feliciſſimo Rege noſtro
pꝛeconio celebꝛato ⁊ verillis ertenſis contradicente nemine poſ⸗
ſeſſionem accepi: pꝛimeꝗ earum diui Saluatoꝛis nomen impo⸗
ſui: cuius fretus aurilio tam ad banc: ꝗ ad ceteras alias perue⸗
nimus·Eam ⱶo Jndi Guanabanin vocant·Aliarũ etiam vnam
quanꝗ nouo nomine nuncupaui: quippe aliã inſulam Sancte
Marie Conceptionis· aliam Fernandinam· aliam Byſabellam·
aliam Joanam· ⁊ ſic de reliquis appellari iuſſi·Cum pꝛimum in
eam inſulam quam dudum Joanam vocari diri appulimus: iu⸗
rta eius littus occidentem verſus aliquantulum pꝛoceſſi: tamꝗ
eam magnam nullo reperto fine inueni: vt non inſulã: ſed conti
nentem Chatai pꝛouinciam eſſe crediderim: nulla tñ videns op
pida municipiaue in maritimis ſita confinibˀ pꝛeter aliquos vi
cos ⁊ pꝛedia ruſtica: cum quoꝝ incolis loqui nequibam·quare ſi
mul ac nos videbant furripiebant fugam · Pꝛogrediebar vltra:
eriſtimans aliquã me vrbem villaſue inuenturũ·Deniꝗ videns
ꝗ longe admodum pꝛogreſſis nihil noui emergebat: ⁊ bmõi via
nos ad Septentrionem deferebat: ꝗ ipſe fugere eroptabã: terris
etenim regnabat bꝛuma: ad Auſtrumꝗ erat in voto cõtendere:

nec minus venti flagitantib? succedebāt constitui alios nō ope
riri successus:τ sic retrocedens ad portū quendā quem signaue/
rām sum reuersus:vnde duos boies et nostris in terrā misi: qui
inuestigarēt esset ne Rex in ea prouincia vrbesue alique. Di per
tres dies ambularūt inuenerūtcḡ inumeros populos τ babita/
tiones:paruas tñ τ abscḡ vllo regimine. quapropter redierunt.
Interea ego iam intellexeram á qbusdam Indis quos ibidē sui
sceprā quó bmōi prouincia insula quidem erat:τ sic perrexi ori
entem rersus eius semp stringēs littora vscḡ ad miliaria cccxxii
vbi ipsius insule sunt extrema:binc aliā insulam ad oriētē pro
speri distante ab bac Joana miliarib? liiii.quā protiuus Dispa
nam dixi:in eamcḡ concessi τ direxi iter quasi per Septentrionē
quemadmodum in Joana ad orientez miliaria dlxiiii que dicta
Joana τ alie ibidē insule ḡ̄fertilissime existunt. Dec multis atcḡ
tutissimis τ latis nec aliis quos vncḡ viderim cōparandis por/
tibus est circundata multi maximi τ salubres banc interfluunt
fluuii multi quocḡ τ eminentissimi in ea sunt montes Omnes
be insule sunt pulcherrime τ variis distincte figuris:puie:τ ma/
xima arboꝝ varietate sidera lambentiū plene:quas nuncḡ foliis
priuari credo. Quippe vidi eas ita virentes atcḡ decoras ceu mē
se Maio in Dispania solent esse:quaꝝ alie florētes alie fructuo/
se:alie in alio staru fni vniuscuiuscḡ qualitatē vigebant: garrie/
bat philomela τ alii passeres varii ac inūmeri mēse Nouembris
quo ipse per eas deambulabā. Sunt preterea in dicta insula Joa
na septē vel octo palmaꝝ genera ḡ proceritate τ pulcbritudine
quēadmodū cetere oēs arbores:berbe:fructuscḡ nr̄as facile exu/
perāt. Sūt τ mirabiles pin? agri τ prata vastissima:varie aues:
varia mella:variacḡ metalla ferro excepto. In ea aūt quā Dispa
nam supra diximus nuncupari maximi sunt mōtes ac pulcbri: va
sta rura nemora campi feracissimi seri pascicḡ τ ꝥdendis edifici
is aptissimi portuū in bac insula cōmoditas τ prestantia flumi
nū copia salubritate admixta boim:ḡ nisi quis viderit:credulita
tez superat. Dui? arbores pascua τ fructus multū ab illis Joane

differunt·Hec preterea Hispana diuerso aromatis genere·auro·
metallisq; abundat·cuius quidem τ oium aliaꝝ quas ego ridi τ
τ quaꝝ cognitionē babeo incole vtriusq; sexus nudi semper ince
dunt quēadmodū edunt in lucem:preter aliquas feminas:q̄ fo⸗
lio frondeue aliqna aut bombicino velo pudenda operiunt: q̄
ipse sibi ad id negocii parant·Carent ii oēs(vt supra diꝛi)quo⸗
cūq; genere ferri·carēt τ armis vtpote sibi ignotis nec ad ea sūt
apti:nō ꝓpter corporis deformitatem cū sint bene formati : sed
qa sunt timidi ac pleni formidine·gestant tn̄ pro armis arundi⸗
nes sole pustas:in quaꝝ radicib; bastile quoddā ligneū siccū et
in mucronem attenuatū figunt·necq; iis audēt iugiter vti: nā se
pe euenit cū miserim duos vel tris boies ex meis ad aliquas vil
las vt cū eaꝝ loquerent̄ incolis:exiisse agmen glomeratū ex Jn
dis:τ vbi nr̄os appropinquare videbant fugā celeriter arripuis⸗
se despretis a patre liberis τ econtra·τ boc nō q̄ cuipiam eoꝝ dā
num aliq̄ vel iniuria illata fuerit:imo ad quoscūq; appuli τ qui
bus cū verbum facere potui:quicq̄d babebā sum elargitꝰ: pan
num aliaq; pmulta nulla mibi facta versura: sed sunt natura pa
uidi ac timi⸗di·Cereꝝ vbi se cernunt turos oī metu repulso: sunt
admodum simplices ac bone fidei τ in oib? que babēt liberalisse
mi:roganti q̄ possidet inficiat̄ nemo:quin ipsi nos ad id poscē
dū inuitāt·Maximū erga oēs amorē preseferunt:dant queq; ma
gna pro paruis:minima lꝫ re nibiloue ꝑtenti.ego artn̄ ꝓhibui ne
tā minīa τ nulli? precii bisce darent̄ :vt sunt lancis· parapsidū·
vitriq; fragmenta·itē claui ligule·quanꝫ si boc poterāt adipisci
videbat̄ eis pulcherrima mūdi possidere iocalia·Accidit·n·quē
dam nauitam tantū auri pōdus babuisse pro vna ligula quanti
sunt tres aurei solidi·τ sic alios pro aliis minoꝛis precii;ꝑsertim
pro blanquis nouis:quibusdā nūmis aureis:ꝑ qb? babēdis da
bant quicquid petebat vēditor: pura vnciam cū dimidia τ duas
auri:vel triginta τ quadraginta bombicis pondo: quā ipsi iam
nouerant·itē arcuum·amphoꝛe·bydrie·dolilꝗ fragmenta bom
bice τ auro tanꝗ bestie comparabant·quod quia iniquum sane

erat vetus:dediqʒ eis multa pulchꝛa ꞇ grata que mecū ꞿulerā nul
lo interueniente pꞛemio ꞿt eos mihi facilius ꝓciliarem fierentqʒ
ᴣpicole ꞇ ꞿt ſint pꞛoni in amoꞛem erga Regē Reginā pꞛincipēꞯ
ȵoſtros ꞇ ꝟniuerſas gentes Ȝiſpanie ac ſtudeant perquirere coⸯ
aceruare eaꝙ nobis tradere quibꝰ ipſi affluunt ꞇ nos magnopeⸯ
re indigemus·ȵullam ȷȷ noꞛunt idolatriam:imo firmiſſime creⸯ
dūt oēm ꞿim:oēm potentiam:oīa deni ꝕ bona eſſe in celo : meꝙ
ȷnde cum his nauibus ꞇ nautis deſcēdiſſe:atqʒ hoc animo ꝟbiqʒ
fui ſuſceptus poſtꝙ metum repulerant·ȵec ſunt ſégnes aut ruⸯ
des:quin ſummi ac perſpicacis ingenii:ꞇ homines qui tranſſreⸯ
eant mare illud nō ſine admiratiōe ꝟniuſcuiuſꝙ rei ratiōē redⸯ
dunt:ſed nunꝙ ꝟiderūt gentes reſtitas neqʒ naues hmōi·ᶒgo
ſtatim atqʒ ad mare illud perueni e pꞛima inſula quoſdā Ꞁndos
ꝟiolenter arꞛipui:qui ediſcerent a nobis ꞇ nos pariter docerent
ea quoꝶ ipſi in iiſce partibus cognitionem habebant : ꞇ eꞅ toto
ſucceſſit:nam bꞛeui nos ipſos:ꞇ ȷȷ nos tum geſtu ac ſignis: tum
ꝟerbis intelleꞅerunt:magnoꝙ nobis fuere emolumento: ꞿeniūt
modo mecum qui ſemper putant me deſiluiſſe e celo:quáuis diu
nobiſcum ꞿerſati fuerint hodieꝙ ꞿerſentur·et ȷȷ erant pꞛimi qui
ȷd quꞅcunꝙ appellabamus nuntiabant:alii deinceps aliis claⸯ
ta ꞿoce dicentes:Ꝟenite ꞿenite ꞇ ꝟidebitis gētes ethereas·Quā
ob rem tam femine ꝙ ꝟiri:tam impuberes ꝙ adulti : tā iuuenes
ꝙ ſenes depoſita foꞛmidine paulo ante ꝓcepta nos certatim ꞿiſe
bant magna iter ſtipante caterua:aliis cibum:aliis potum affeⸯ
rentibus maximo cum amoꞛe ac beniuolentia incredibili·Ȝabet
ꝟnaqueꝙ inſula multas ſcaphas ſolidi ligni: ꞇ ſi anguſtas·lonⸯ
gitudine tń ac foꞛma noſtris biremibus ſimiles:curſu aūt ꞿeloⸯ
cioꞛes·Reguntur remis tantūmodo·Ȝaꝶ quedaꝫ ſunt magne:
quedam parue:quedā in medio conſiſtūt·Plures tń biremi que
remiget duodeuiginti tranſtris maioꞛes:cū quibus in oēs illas
inſulas:que innumere ſunt:traȷicitur· cumꝙ iis ſuam mercatuⸯ
ram exercent ꞇ inter eos comertia fiunt·Ꜳliquas ego harum biⸯ
remiū ſeu ſcaphaꝶ ꝟidi ꝗ ꝟehebant ſeptuaginta ꞇ octuaginta re

miges·In omnibus iis insulis nulla est diuersitas inter gentis
effigies:nulla in moribus atꝙ loquela : quin oēs se intelligunt
adinuicem:que res perutilis est ad id ꝗ serenissimos Reges no
stros exoptare precipue reoꝛ:scʒ eoꝛ ad sctãm xp̃i fidem ꝑuersio
nem·cui ꝗdem quantũ intelligere potui facillimi sunt et proni·
Dixi quẽadmodũ sum progressus antea insulam Jo⸗nam per re
ctum tramitem occasus in orientem miliaria·cccxxii·sm quã viã
ꞇ interuallum itineris possum dicere banc Joanam esse maioreʒ
Anglia ꞇ Scotia simul·nãꝙ vltra dicta·cccxxii passuũ milia in
ea parte que ad occidentem prospectat due:quas nõ petii: super
sunt prouincie quaꝛ alterã Jndi Anan vocant cuius accole cau
dati nascuntur·Tendunt in longitudineʒ ad miliaria·clxxx·vt
ab bis quos vebo mecũ Jndis percepi:qui oĩs basceallent insu⸗
las·Dispane ꝟo ambitꝰ maioꝛ est tota Dispania a Colonia vsꝙ
ad fontem rabidum·Dincꝙ facile arguit ꝗ quartum eius latus
quod ipse per rectã lineã occidentis in orientem traieci miliaria
continet·dxl·Dec insula est affectanda ꞇ affectata nõ spernenda
in qua ꞇ si aliaꝛ oĩm vt dixi pro inuictissimo Rege nostro solen
niter possessionem accepi:earũꝙ imperium dicto Regi penitus
cõmittitur:in oportuniori tñ loco atꝙ omni lucro et cõmertio
condecenti cuiusdã magne ville:cui Natiuitatis dñi nomen de⸗
dimus:possessionem peculiariter accepi : ibiꝙ arcem quandam
erigere extemplo iussi:que modo iam debet esse pacta:in qua bo
mĩnes qui necessarii sunt visi cũ omni aɪmoꝛ genere ꞇ vltra an
num victu oportuno reliqui·Jtem quandã carauellã ꞇ pro aliis
construendis tam in bac arte ꝗ̃ in ceteris peritos: ac eiusdẽ in⸗
sule Regis erga eos beniuolentiam ꞇ familiaritatē incredibileʒ
Sunt enim gentes ille amãbiles admoduni ꞇ benigne:eo ꝗ Rex
predictus me fratrẽ suũ dici gloriabaꞇ·Et si aīum rei ocarent et
tis qui in arce manserunt nocere relint:nequeunt: qa armis ca
rent:nudi incedũt ꞇ nimiũ timidi:ideo dictã arcem tenētce dun
taxat pñt totã eam insulam nullo sibi imminēte discrimine popu⸗
lari:dummõ leges quas dedimꝰ ac regimen nõ excedãt·Jn oĩbꝰ

lis infulis vt intelleri quifq; vni tm ꝓlugi acquiefcit:pꝛeter pꝛin
cipes aut reges:qbus viginti hic licet. Femine magis q̃ viri la/
boꝛare videntur.nec bene potui intelligere an habeãt bona pꝛo
pꝛia:vidi enim q̃ vnus habebat aliis impartiri:pꝛefertim dapes
obfonia ꞇ hmõi. Aullum apud eos monftrũ reperi vt pleriq; eri/
ftimabant:fed hoies magne reuerentie atq; benignos. Aec funt
nigri velut ethiopes. habent crines planos ꞇ demiffos. non de/
gũt vbi radioꝛ folaris emicat caloꝛ:ꝓmagna nanq; hic eft folis
vehementia:pꝛopterea q̃ ab equinoctiali linea diftat. Ubi viden
tur gꝛadus fer ꞇ viginti er montiũ cacuminibꝰ. Maximũ quoq;
viget frigus:fed id qdem moderantur Jndi tum loci cõfuetudi
ne. tum rerũ calidiffimaꝛ quibꝰ frequenter ꞇ lururiofe vefcunt
pꝛefidio. Jtacq; mõftra aliqua nõ vidi:neq; eoꝛ alicubi habui co
gnitionem.excepta quadã infula Charis nuncupata: que fecun
da er Dfpania in Jndiam tranffretantibꝰ exiftit.quã gens que
dam a finitimis habita ferocioꝛ incolit. Di carne humana vefcũ
tur. Dabent pꝛedicti biremiũ genera plurima qbus in oĩs Jndi/
cas infulas traiiciunt. depꝛedant. furripiunt quecũq; pñt. Aihil
ab aliis differunt nifi q̃ gerũt moꝛe femineo longos crines. vtũ
tur arcubꝰ ꞇ fpiculis arundineis f̈ris vt dirim̃ in groffioꝛi par
te attenuatis haftilibꝰ. ideoq; habent feroces:quare ceteri Jndi
inerbaufto metu plectunt̃:fed hos ego nihili facio plus q̃ alios
Di funt q̃ coheunt cũ quibufdã feminis:que fole infulã Mateu
nin pꝛimã er Difpania in Jndiã traiicientibꝰ habitant. De aut
femine nullũ fui ferus opus exercent:vtuntur enim arcubus et
fpiculis ficut de eaꝛ ꝓiugibus diri muniunt fefe laminis eneis
quaꝛ marima apud eas copia exiftit. Aliã mihi infulã affirmãt
fup ꝃdicta Difpana maioꝛẽ:eius incole carẽt pilis. auroq; inter
alias potiffimũ eruberat. Duius infule ꞇ aliaꝛ quas vidi hoies
mecũ poꝛto qui hoꝛ que diri teftimoniũ perhibẽt. Deniq; vt no
ftri difceffus ꞇ celeris reuerfionis compendiũ ac emolimentum
bꝛeuibus aftringã hoc polliceo::me noftris Regibus inuictiffi
mis paruo coꝛ fultũ aurilio:tantũ auri daturũ quantũ eis fue/

rīt opus.tm̄ vero aromatum·bombicis·masticis:q̄ apud Chium
duntarat inuenitur· tantūcp ligni aloes· tantum seruox bydo/
latrarum:quantum eozum maiestas voluerit erigere· itꝫm reus
barbarum τ alia aromatum genera que ii quos in dicta arce reli
qui iam inuenisse atcp inuenturos eristimo · qh̄quidem ego nul
libi magis sum mozatus nisi quantum me coegerunt venti:pzeꞌ
terꝗ in villa Aatiuitatis:dum arceȝ condere τ tuta oı̄a esse pzo
uidi.Que τ si marima τ inaudita sunt:multo tn̄ maioza fozent
si naues mibi vt ratio erigit subuenissent·Uep multūac mira
bile boc:nec nostris meritis cozrespondens:sed sancte Chzistia
ne fidei:nostrozumcp Regum pietati ac religioni: quia quod bu
manus consequi nō poterat intellectus:id b manis cōcessit di
uinus·Solet enim deus seruus suos:quicp sua pzecepta diligūt
τ in impossibilibus eraudire:vt nobis in pzesentia contigit:qui
ea consecuti sumus que bactenus moztalium vires minime atti
gerant:nam si barū insulax quipiam aliquid scripserunt aut lo
cuti sunt:omnes per ambages τ cōiecturas·nemo se eas vidisse
asserit·vnde pzopꝫ videbatur fabula·Igitur Rer τ Regina pzin
cepscp ac eox regna feliciss.ma cunctecp ali꞉ Chzistianox pzouin
cie Saluatozi dn̄o nostro Jesu Chzisto agamꝰ gratias: qui tan
ta nos victozia munerecp donauit:celebzentur pzocessiones·per
agantur solennia sacra:festacp fronde velentur delubza· erultet
Chzistus in terris quemadmodum in celis erultat:quom tot po
pulozum perditas ante bac animas sa'uatum iri pzeuidet· Lete
mur τ nos:cum pzopter eraltationem nostre fidei· tum pzcpter
rerum tempozalium incrementa:quox non solum Aispania sed
vniuersa Chzistianitas est futura particeps· Aec vt gesta sunt
sic bzeuiter enarrata.Uale·Ulisbone pzidie Jdus Martii·

Chzistofozus Colom Oceane classis Pzefectus·

¶ Epigramma · R · L · de Corbaria Episcopi Montispalusil.
  Ad Inuictissimum Regem Hispaniarum.

Iam nulla Hispanis tellus addenda Triumphis
  Atq; parum tantis viribus orbis erat·
Nunc longe Eois regio deprensa sub vndis·
  Auctura est titulos Betice magne tuos:
Vnde repertori merito referenda Colombo
  Gratia: sed summo est maior habēda deo·
Qui vincenda parat noua Regna tibicq sibicq
  Tecq simul fortem prestat τ esse pium·

DESIGN ILLUSTRATING VESPESCCI'S DISCOVERY OF AMERICA.

AN ORIGINAL DRAWING BY STRADANUS, ABOUT 1580

THE FIRST FOUR

VOYAGES

OF

AMERIGO VESPUCCI

REPRINTED IN FACSIMILE

AND

TRANSLATED

From the rare original edition (Florence, 1505-6).

LONDON

BERNARD QUARITCH

15 PICCADILLY

1893

LONDON :
G. NORMAN AND SON, PRINTERS, HART STREET,
COVENT GARDEN.

PREFACE.

THE name of the Florentine is imperishably recorded in that of the New World. We all know that it was not he who invented the word America, and that no portion of the wrong inflicted on Columbus attaches to Vespucci. Formerly, however, it was not unusual to find him abused as a base supplanter who had maliciously stolen the glory of his fellow-countryman. That feeling has not wholly passed away even from the minds of those who ought to be exempt from prejudice. While acquitting Vespucci on the charge of theft, they raise a fresh indictment against him for forgery. It is to be hoped that the second accusation will be dropped in time like the first; and that the world will learn to speak of the Florentine in the words of Columbus "Amerigo Vespucci . . is a very worthy man ; fortune has been adverse to him as to many others. His labours have not benefited him so much as justice would require." This testimony was written by Columbus to his son Diego in February, 1505, a date which is significant in connexion with the allegations made by Humboldt and others to the discredit of Vespucci. His " Four Voyages "—that is, his first four voyages to the New World, are described by himself as having taken place in 1497-98, 1499-1500, 1501, and 1503-04 ; the first two in the Spanish service, the other two in that of the King of Portugal. The impugners of his veracity assert that the first voyage was made with Alonso de Hojeda in 1499, not in 1497, and that his account of it is wilfully falsified and garbled so that he might magnify himself by concealing the names of the men under whom he sailed, and by giving an exaggerated idea of the work done. It would follow, as a matter of course, that the second voyage was wholly fictitious, and that the third and fourth ought to be called second and third. Then it is said that the " Quatuor Navigationes " was first published in 1507—an assumption to be corrected below—and that, consequently, Amerigo had no longer the fear of Columbus (dead in 1506) before his eyes when he uttered his fabricated narrative.

The fact is that Vespucci's first published Epistola contains a clear reference to three voyages which he had already made, two of them " ex mandato serenissimi Hispaniarum regis." As he wrote that letter before June, 1503, and as all bibliographers agree that it was printed (in a Latin form) three or four times in 1503 (although the first dated edition did not appear till 1504) and several times in 1504-5, Columbus must have been well aware of Vespucci's pretensions at the date (1505) when he recommended him as a worthy man who " has ever had a desire to do me pleasure." This circumstance suffices to upset a portion of the anti-Vesputian case. It gives absolute proof that in 1502-3 the facts and dates given in the book of 1507 had been publicly announced by or for Vespucci; and the absence of all contemporary denial enables us to accept his account as equally veracious with the narratives of other explorers. Confused and ill-written we must allow it to be ; for although Vespucci had been educated by his own uncle as a fellow-pupil with Pier Soderini (the future head of the Florentine republic), he became in later days, probably through companion- ship with the Spanish and Portuguese seamen, almost unfit to handle a literary pen. The " Lettera " now reproduced gives ample evidence of that fact, being written in rude and ungrammatical language, jargonised by the admixture of Spanish or Portuguese words and idioms. Such as it is, however, we must regard it as the only genuine piece of sustained composition which Vespucci has left; the Epistola being extant only in a Latin version, and the well-written letters published by Italian editors in the last and the present century, being admittedly supposititious and modern.

The great interest which attaches to Vespucci's first voyage lies in the probability that he sailed along the entire coast of the Mexican gulf as far as the point of Florida, and some distance up the shores of what is now Carolina. A side-light is thrown upon the subject by the map of the New World which appeared in the Latin Ptolemy of 1513, and which had been in the wood-engraver's hands six years earlier. That map, we have some reason to suspect, was derived from Vespucci's design. It is, in fact, called "the Admiral's map" by the editor of Ptolemy, and has, on the strength of that name, been assigned rather to Columbus or Cabral than to Vespucci. It gives to the continental shores behind and above Cuba a conformation which agrees tolerably with the actual outline of the coast from Central America to Florida; and only a very special pleader can persuade us that it is meant for anything else. Columbus, although he was a map-maker, did not possess sufficient knowledge to have designed that particular map; Cabral was a nobleman and soldier, who had neither the knowledge nor the skill required. Only Vespucci remains, and only in the narrative of his first voyage can we find any hint of such a course of exploration as would furnish the chartographer with the necessary details. As a commander of one of the ships in the Portuguese expedition of 1503-4, he would probably be regarded among foreigners as a Portuguese admiral.

The "Lettera" was printed, as the type indicates, by Gian Stefano di Carlo di Pavia at Florence not earlier than 1505, and not later than 1516. As a matter of demonstrable fact, it must have appeared in the former year. The substance has been familiar to the world since the publication of the Latin translation in 1507, but the Italian text seems to have virtually dropped out of sight from the time of its appearance down to the middle of the last century, when Bandini met with a single copy. Even now only five copies are recorded: one is in the British Museum, a second in the Biblioteca Palatina at Florence, a third belonged to Varnhagen and is perhaps now in Brazil, a fourth was in the Capponi library at the beginning of this century; and the fifth (from which the present reproduction is derived) is in the library which belonged to the late Charles Kalbfleisch of New York. Thus it has been practically inaccessible and unknown to the world; while the faulty Latin version frequently reprinted and translated since 1507 has, in its blunders, furnished the anti-Vesputians with arguments which a sight of the actual Italian original could have nullified.

Amerigo Vespucci is always said to have been born on the 9th March, 1451, but I suspect an error in the date. 1461 would harmonise better with his position as a student in 1476, when he wrote a boyish letter in Latin to his father. His uncle Giorgio Antonio Vespucci, a friend of Savonarola, was his tutor, and one of his fellow-pupils was that Pier or Pietro Soderini who became in 1502 the Gonfaloniere or Chief of the republic of Florence. He had friends likewise among the Medici, to whose expulsion from the city in 1502 Soderini owed his elevation to that dignity. Vespucci remembered them both in the after years, since he sent several letters to his patron, Lorenzo di Pier Francesco dei Medici (of which only one, the Latin Epistola, has survived) and addressed his "Lettera" to Soderini. He was despatched to Cadiz by Lorenzo di Pier in 1492, on business of the Medici banking-house, and he seems to have remained there trading or speculating on his own account after the object of the mission had been attained. He was employed by the Spanish sovereigns in 1496 to complete a contract which had been undertaken by the naval outfitter, Berardi (now dead), for the supply of some ships to the king. Ferdinand was engaged in a speculation of his own, and Vespucci took service on one of the four vessels which were sent out by the king for adventure in the New World, and which started from Cadiz on May 10th, 1497. His function was probably that of astronomer and chartographer, under the command of Vincente Yañez Pinzon and Juan Diaz de Solis, although he does not mention their names, but writes as if he were himself master of one of the ships. He returned to Cadiz on October 15th, 1498. The account of the voyage is anthropological rather than geographical. From the distances traversed and the latitudes specified (usually with exaggeration) he seems to have reached Honduras on the 4th July and thenceforward to have sailed along the coast—nearly always in sight of it—in a direction necessarily verging northward, for 870 leagues (as he computed, which would ordinarily be equal to 3480 miles, but

his leagues, like those of Columbus, were always meant to represent three miles) until he turned back in the August of the
following year.   Only two geographical names are mentioned in
this long voyage : the province of Lariab and the island of Ity.
Neither can be identified, but the former was perhaps in the
region of Vera Cruz, and the latter cannot have been the
island of Ha-iti, since it was reached in a seven days' voyage
E.N.E. from the continental coast.   It may have been Lucayo.

He went out again in an expedition of three ships led by
Alonso de Hojeda, which started from Cadiz on May 16th, 1499.
He reached Brazil on June 27th, and sailed along the northern
coast line of South America as far as Venezuela ; then proceeding
northward from the islands of St. Margaret and Curaçao, followed
his commanders to San Domingo.   Vespucci stayed there for
two months and a half, during which time he must have seen
Columbus, to whom he alludes as being then on the island.   He
returned to Cadiz on September 8th.

Towards the close of 1500, Vespucci was induced to transfer
his services to Dom Manoel of Portugal, and on May 10th, 1501,
sailed in an expedition of three ships to the South American
coast.   On the 17th August he touched at Cape St. Roque, and
then turned southwards, reaching Bahia on November 1st, and
the harbour of Rio on January 1st, 1502.   The object aimed at in
this voyage seems to have been to find a south-western passage,
as it had been in the two preceding to discover a north-west
passage.   When they failed somewhere in the latitude of La
Plata, Vespucci struck out southwardly into the ocean until at
52 degrees S.L. he thought it time to return.   On May 10th he
reached Sierra Leone and arrived in Lisbon on September 7th.
It was about the close of the year when he wrote the letter to
Lorenzo di Pier Francesco dei Medici, which is so well known in
its Latin form, the Italian original having perished.   We know
who was the translator—Fra Giovanni del Giocondo, of Verona,
then residing in Paris—but we do not know how the original got
into his hands, although Vespucci's reference to his friend
Giuliano del Giocondo, at the beginning of his account of the
third voyage, suggests an explanation.   This Latin Epistola
was printed several times in 1503 and 1504, the first edition

being probably the undated Paris one by Jehan Lambert. It circulated so widely, and became so well known, that the fame of Vespucci began to overshadow that of Columbus. The Florentine thus became accidentally the rival and supplanter of the Genoese, but had himself no part in shaping the circumstances. Neither he nor Columbus ever published a narrative by any personal exertion or desire. Each of them wrote letters which passed from the hands of their recipients into those which consigned them to the press. The Epistola is not an account of Vespucci's third voyage, as it is usually considered, but a sort of gossipy, anthropological account of the savages he had seen in the New World, with a special reference to some portion of his third voyage. Ramusio regarded it as a summary of two voyages. It was probably Vespucci's intention at some time to publish his journal—which at that time he called his " Tre Giornate," but, in 1504, after his return from the fourth voyage, " Le Quattro Giornate." From the nature of his references to it, that journal must have been a much ampler and more exact record of his wanderings than we possess otherwise, and was apparently illustrated with charts and drawings. We venture to express a hope that the manuscript may yet be found in some Spanish hiding place.

On the 10th of May (or June), 1503, he sailed again from Lisbon, and was very unsuccessful, but left twenty-four men with provisions in a fort at Cape Frio (near Rio Janeiro), and returned to Lisbon, which he reached on June 18th, 1504. This was far from being the last of his American voyages, but it was the last he had accomplished, when, on September 4th of that year, he wrote the long "Lettera" here reproduced, giving an account of his four expeditions. In its printed form, it is addressed to an individual of high rank in Florence concerned in the government of the State, whom he reminds of their early association as pupils under Fra Giorgio Vespucci. This individual, to whom he forwarded his letter by the hands of Benvenuto di Domenico Benvenuti, is clearly revealed by that circumstantial evidence as Pier Soderini, the anti-Medicean Gonfaloniere of Florence. The autograph letter must naturally have borne his name; why this is omitted in the printed book can only be guessed at. The publisher was apparently Pietro Pacini di Pescia, an adherent of the Medici party, and therefore adverse to Soderini. None of the books which were issued by him during the reign of Soderini contained any of the formal dedications to the Gonfaloniere which were used by other contemporary publishers at Florence, and it was probably he who suppressed Soderini's name. The letter got into his hands, perhaps, in the form of a copy made by Benvenuti. Gian Stefano di Pavia, mentioned above, who set it in type, was Pacini's printer from 1505 to 1513, but was not in the habit of setting down his own name till the latter year. His imprint appears for the first time, along with Pacini's name, in the " Giostra di Giuliano dei Medici," which came out in 1513 after Soderini's death and the restoration of the Medici; but three of the books produced by Pacini in 1505 are in Gian Stefano's types, identical with those of the " Lettera." Gian Stefano used the same types still in 1516 when he printed Corsali's letter about East India, but the woodcut design on the title of Vespucci's Lettera belonged to Pacini and had been used by him as far back as 1493. The honorific title with which Vespucci addresses Soderini throughout the Lettera is *Vostra Magnificentia*, everywhere except in the first instance abbreviated into *Vostra Mag.* or *V. M.* This is a point to be noted, in connexion with the following circumstances.

One of the members of the St. Dié gymnasium (or college) was Jean Basin de Sendacour, who in 1503 was in Paris and conveyed thence a copy of Vespucci's Epistola to his friends at St. Dié, chief among whom were Gautrin Lud, Nicolas Lud, Philesius (Ringmann) and Hylacomylus (Waldseemüller), men who were busy in reviving the scientific literature of the ancients. It was probably he, or Philesius, who had the good fortune to obtain a copy of the " Lettera " some time before 1507. One of them translated it, or got it translated, into French; and from the French version a Latin translation was made, as Lud stated, by Basin. The translator into French was of course ignorant of the name of the potentate to whom the original was addressed, since the Lettera bore no indication of it; and the Latiniser, receiving the letter along with some maps from his sovereign, Duke René of Lorraine, King of Sicily and Jerusalem, was misled into the blunder of supposing that *V. M.* and *Vostre Mag.* stood for *Vostre Majesté* and were addressed to René. It is singular that his eyes were not opened by the allusion to " our school-companionship under Fra Giorgio," since any such association in boyhood between the Florentine seaman and the sovereign prince of Lorraine would have been an impossibility. The letter was printed thus in Latin, with a factitious address to René, at the end of the Cosmographiæ Introductio, by Waldseemüller on the 25th April, 1507. Numerous reprints followed, and thus Vespucci's narrative was made known to the world through a second-hand Latin translation disfigured with several blunders and omissions, and beginning with an initial falsification; while the original passed completely into oblivion. The rarity of the latter may have arisen from an early attempt by Vespucci's friends to suppress any token of what might seem a deviation from loyalty to his patrons the Medici. The copy which had reached Lorraine in a French guise served to arouse the admiration of Waldseemüller so strongly that, in the text of the Cosmographia, he declared that the New World (instead of being called simply *Mundus Novus* as Vespucci had proposed) ought to bear the name of America, and his words have prevailed for all time. Yet Vespucci's own text was unknown, even at Vicenza and Milan within a couple of years after it was printed. The famous *Paesi nuovamente retrovati* (a compendious collection of voyagers' narratives) printed in 1507, 1508, 1512, 1517, 1519, and 1521, comprises the matter of the Epistola and the Lettera, not in their original form, but in retranslations from the Latin.

It is well therefore that the *New World* for which Vespucci proposed this name, and to which others gave his own, should receive a true reproduction of his text, so that he may no longer be held responsible for the errors of the Lorrainers. The present publication is intended to supply that want. The text is given in facsimile by a process which ensures its correctness, and the translation is made with literal exactness. The work has not been done before so completely : there are errors even in Varnhagen's edition of the text, and his translation, while not sufficiently literal, is also marked by several faults.

Lettera di Amerigo vespucci delle isole nuouamente trouate in quattro suoi viaggi.

MAGNIFICe do
mine.Dipoi del
la humile reue,
rentia & debite récōmenda
tioni &c̃. Potra essere che
uostra Magnificentia simara
uigliera della mia temerita/
et usada uostra sauidoria/cō
tāto absurdamēte io mimuo
ua a scriuere a uostra Mag.
la psente lettera tāto plissa:
sappiendo che di cōtinuo uo
stra Mag. sta occupata nelli
alti consigli & negotii sopra
elbuon reggimēto di cotesta
excessa Repub.Et mi terra nō solo presumptuoso/sed etiam
perotioso/in pormi a scriuere cose nō conuenienti a uostro
stato,/ne dilecteuoli/& cō barbaro stilo scripte/& fuora do,
gni ordine di humanita:ma la cōfidentia mia che tengho nel
le uostre uirtu & nella uerita del mio scriuere/che son cose nō
sitruouano scripte ne pli antichi ne p moderni scriptori/co
me nel pcesso conoscera V.M.ẽifa essere usato.La causa prin
cipale ch̃ mosse a scriuerui/fu p ruogho del psente aportato
re/che sidice Benuenuto Benuenuti nostro fiorētino/molto
scruitore secōdo che sidimostra/di uostra Mag.& molto ami
co mio:elquale trouandosi qui in questa citta di Lisbona/mi
prego che io facessi parte a uostra Mag.delle cose per meuiste
in diuerse plaghe del mondo/per uirtu di quattro uiaggi che
ho facti in discoprire nuoue terre:edua per mando del Re di
Castiglia don Ferrādo Re.vi.per el gran golfo del mare ocea
no uerso loccidente:et laltre due p mandato del poderoso Re
don Manouello Re di Portogallo/uerso laustro:Dicendomi
che uostra Mag.nepiglierebbe piacere/& che in q̃sto speraua
scrutrui:ilperche midisposi a farlo:pche mirendo certo ch̃ uo
stra Mag.mittene nel numero de suoi seruidori/ricordādomi
come nel tempo della nostra giouētu ui ero amico/& hora
seruidore:& andando a udire eprincipii di grāmatica sotto
la buona uita & doctrina del uenerabile religioso frate di.S.
Marco fra Giorgio Antonio Vespucci:econsigli & doctrina
delquale piacesse a Dio che io hauessi seguitato:che come dice

el petrarcha / Io farei altro huomo da quel ch'io fono. Quo
modocunq̃ fir / non midolgho: perche fempre mifono dile
ctato in cofe uirtuofe: et anchora che quefte mia patragne nõ
fiano connenienti alle uirtu uoftre / uidito come dixe Plinio
a Mecenate / Voi folauate in alcun tẽpo pigliare piacere del
le mie ciancie: anchora che uoftra Mag.ftia del continuo occu
pata nepublici negotii / alchuna hora piglierete di fcanfo di
confumare un poco di tempo nelle cofe ridicule / o dilecteuo
li: et come ilfinocchio ficonftuma dare in cima delle dilecte
uoli uiuande p difporle a miglior digeftione / cofi potrete p
difcanfo di tante uoftre occupationi mãdate a leggere quefta
mia lettera: perche ui apartino alcun tanto della continua cu
ra & affiduo penfamẽto delle cofe publiche: et fe faro ꝓliffo /
ueniam peto Mag.fignor mio. Voftra Mag.fapra / come el
motiuo della uenuta mia in quefto regno di Spagna fu p tra
ctare mercatantie: & come feguiffi in q̃fto propofito circa di
quattro anni: nequali uiddi & conobbi ediuariati mouimẽ
della fortuna: & come promutaua quefti beni caduci & tranfi
torii: & come un tẽpo tiene lhuomo nella fommita della ruo
ta: & altro tẽpo lo ributta da fe / & lo priua debeni che fipof
fono dire impreftati: di modo che conofciuto elcontinuo tra
uaglio che lhuomo pone in conquerirgli / con fottometterfi
a tanti difagi & pericoli / deliberai lafciarmi della mercancia
& porre elmio fine in cofa piu laudabile & ferma: che fu che
midifpofi dandare a uedere parte del mondo / & le fue mara
uiglie: & aquefto mi fiofferfe tempo & luogo molto oportu
no: che fu / chel Re don Ferrando di Caftiglia hauẽdo a man
dare quattro naui a difcoprire nuoue terre uerfo loccidente /
fui electo per fua alteza che io fuffi in effa flocta per adiutare
a difcoprire: et partimo del porto di Calis adi.16.di maggio
1497. et pigliãmo noftro cãmino per el gran golfo del mare
oceano: nelqual uiaggio ftẽmo 18.mefi: & difcoprimo molta
terra ferma & infinite ifole / & gran parte di effe habitate: che
dalli ãtichi fcriptori nõ feneparla di effe: credo pche nõ nheb
bono notitia: che fe ben miricordo / in alcuno ho lecto / che
teneua che q̃fto mare oceano era mare fenza gente: et di que
fta opinione fu Dante noftro poeta nel.xxvi.capitolo dello
inferno / doue finge la morte di Vlyxe: nelqual uiaggio uidi
cofe di molta marauiglia / come intẽdera uoftra Mag. Come
difo pra dixi / partimo del porto di Calis quattro naui di con

&. ma: & cominciámo noftra nauigatione diritti alle ifole fortunate / che oggi' fi dicono la gran Canaria / che fono fituate
nel mare oceano nel fine dello occidente habitato / pofte nel
terzo clyma: fopra lequali alza elpolo del Septentrione fuora
delloro orizonte, 27. gradi & mezo: & diftáno da quefta citta
di Lifbona 280. leghe / per eluento infra mezo di / & libeccio:
doue citenémo octo di / prouedendoci dacqua & legne & di
altre cofe neceffarie: et di qui / facte noftre orationi / cileuámo
& démo le uele alueto / cominciádo noftre nauigationi pel po
nente / pigliando una quarta di libeccio: & táto nauicámo / cñ
al capo di 37 giorni fumo a tenere una terra / cõ la giudicámo
effere terra ferma: laquale difta dalle ifole di Canaria piu alto
occidente a circha di mille leghe fuora dello habitato drento
della torrida zona: perche trouámo elpolo del feptentrione al
zare fuora del fuo orizonte 16. gradi / & piu occidétale che le
ifole di Canaria / fecõdo che moftrauano enoftri inftrumenti
74. gradi: nelquale anchorámo con noftre naui ad una legha
& mezo di terra: & buttámo fuora noftri battelli / & ftipati di
gente & darme: fumo alla uolta della terra / & prima che giu-
gneffimo ad epfa / hauémo uifta di molte géte che andauano
alungho della fpiaggia: di che cirallegrámo molto: & la trouámo effere gente difnuda: moftrorono hauer paura di noi:
credo pche ciuiddono ueftiti / & daltra ftatura: tucti. firirraffe-
no ad un monte / & cõ quári fegnali facémo loro di pace & di
amiſtà / nõ uollon uenire a ragionaméto con effo noi: di mo
do che gia uenédo la nocte & pche le naue ftauano furte i luo
go pericolofo / per ftare in cofta braua & fenza abrigo / accor
dámo laltro giorno leuarci di qui / & andare a cercare dalcun
porto / o infenata: doue afficuraffimo noftre naui: & nauigá-
mo per el maeftrale / che cofi ficorreua la cofta fempre a uifta
di terra / di continuo uiaggio ueggédo gente perla fpiaggia:
tanto cñ dipoi nauigati dua giorni / trouámo affai ficuro luo
go ple naui / & furgémo a meza legha di terra / doue uedémo
moltiffima gente: & quefto giorno medefimo fumo a terra co
battelli / & faltámo i terra ben 40. huomini bene a ordine: &
le genti di terra tuttauia fi moftrauano fchifi di noftra conuer
fatione: et nõ potauamo tanto afficurarfi che ueniffino a par
lare cõ noi: et quefto giorno tanto trauagliámo con dar loro
delle cofe noftre / come furono fonagli & fpecchi / cente / fpal
line & altre frafche / che alcuni di loro fi afficurorono & uen-

nono a tractare con noi:et facto cō loro buona amiſta /uenen
do la nocte / ci diſpedimo di loro / & tornámoci alle naui:et ʼal
tro giorno come ſali lalbaʼ /uedēmo che alla ſpiaggia ſtauano
Infinite genti / & haueuano con loro le loro donne & figliuoli:
ſumo a terra / & trouámo che tucte ueniuano cariſchate di loro
mantenimenti / che ſon tali / quali in ſuo luogho ſidira:et pri
ma che giugneſſimo in terra / molti di loro ſigittorono a nuo
to / & ciuennono a riceuere un tiro di baleſtro nel mare / che ſo
no grandiſſimi notatori / con tanta ſicurta / come ſe haueſſino
con eſſo noi tractato lungo tempo:et di queſta loro ſicurta pi
gliámo piacere. Quanto di lor uita & coſtumi conoſcēmo / fu
che del tucto uanno diſnudi / ſi li huomini come le dōne / ſen
za coprire uergogna neſſuna / nō altrimenti che come ſaliron
del uentre di lor madri. Sono di mediana ſtatura / molto ben
proporrionati:le lor carni ſono di colore che pende in roſſo co
me pelo di lione:et credo ch, ſe gliandaſſino ueſtiti / ſarebbon
bianchi come noi : nō renghono pel corpo pelo alcuno / ſaluo
che ſono di lunghi capelli & neri / & maxime le donne / che le
rendon formoſe:nō ſono di uolto molto belli / pche tengono
eluiſo largo / che uoglion parere altartaro:nō ſi laſciano creſce
re pelo neſſuno nelle ciglia / ne necoperchi delli occhi / ne in
altra parte / ſaluo che quelli del capo:che tengono epelli p bru
ta coſa:ſono molto leggieri delle loro perſone nello andare &
nel correre / ſi li huomini come le donne:che nō tiene in conto
na donna correre una legha / ò due / che molte uolte le uedē
mo:et in qſto leuon uantaggio grandiſſimo da noi chriſtiani:
nuotano fuora dogni credere / & miglior le donne che gli huo
mini:pche li habbiamo trouati & uiſti molte uolte due leghe
drento in mare ſenza appoggio alcuno andare notando. Le lo
ro armi ſono archi & ſaette molto ben fabricati / ſaluo cō non
tengon ferro / ne altro genere di metallo forte:et in luogo del
ferro pongono denti di animali / o di peſci / ò un fuſcello di le
gno forte arſicciato nella puncta:ſono tiratori certi / che doue
uogliono / danno:et in alcuna parte uſano queſti archi le don
ne:altre arme tenghono / come lance toſtate / & altri baſtoni
con capocchie beniſſimo lauorati. Vſono di guerra infra loro
con gente che non ſono di lor lingua molto crudelmente / ſen
za perdonſare la uita a neſſuno / ſe non per maggior pena

Quando uanno alla guerra / leuon con loro le donne loro: nõ
perche guerreggino / ma perche leuon lor drieto el manteni∕
mento: che lieua una donna addosso una caricha / che non la
leuera uno huomo / trenta / o quaranta leghe: che molte uolte
le uedēmo. Nõ costumano Capitano alchuno / ne uanno con
ordine / che ognuno e / signore di se: et la causa delle lor guer∕
re nõ e / per cupidita di regnare / ne di allarghare etermini lo
ro / ne per codisia disordinata / saluo che per una anticha ini∕
mista / che per tempi passati e / suta infra loro: et domandati
perche guerreggiauano / non ci sapeuono dare altra ragione /
se nõ che lo faceuon p uendicare la morte de loro antepassati /
o de loro padri: questi non tenghono ne Re / ne Signore / ne
ubidiscono ad alcuno / che uiuono in lor propria liberta: & co
me simuouino per ire alla guerra e / che quando enimici háno
morto loro / o preso alchuni di loro / si leua el suo parente piu
uecchio / & ua predicando per le strade che uadin con lui a uen∕
dicare la morte di quel tal parente suo: et cosi simuouono per
compassione: nõ usono Iustitia / ne castigano el mal factore: ne
el padre ne la madre nõ castigano e sigliuoli / & p marauiglia
o nõ mai uedēmo far questione infra loro: mostronsi semplici
nel parlare / & sono molto malitiosi & acuti in quello che loro
cuple: parlano poco / & cõ bassa uoce: usono e medesimi accenti
come noi / pche formano le parole o nel palato / o ne denti / o
nelle labbra: saluo che usano altri nomi alle cose. Molte sono le
diuersita delle lingue / che di 100. in 100. leghe trouámo muta∕
mento di lingua / che nõ sintendano luna con laltra. El modo
del lor uiuere e / molto barbaro / perche nõ mangiano a hore
certe / & tante uolte quante uogliono / et non si da loro molto
che la uoglia uengha loro piu a meza nocte cõ di giorno / che
a tucte hore mangiano: el lor mangiare e / nel suolo senza toua
glia / o altro panno alcuno / perche tengono le lor uiuande o
in bacini di terra che lor fanno / o in meze zucche: dormono in
certe rete facte di bambacia molto grande sospese nell aria: et
ancora che q̃sto lor dormire paia male / dico cõ e / dolce dormi
re in epse: & miglior dormauamo in epse che ne coltroni. Son
gente pulita & netta de lor corpi / per táto continouar lauarsi
come fanno: quando naziano con riuerentia el uentre / fanno
ogni cosa per non essere ueduti: & tanto quanto in questo sono

netti & fchifi / nel fare acqua fono altretanto fporci & fēza uer
gogna:pérche ftando / parlando con noi fenza uolgerfi / o uer
gognarfi lafciano ire tal brutteza / che in quefto non tengho/
no uergogna alchuna:non ufano infra loro matrimonii: cia/
fchuno piglia quante donne uuole:et quando le uuole repu/
diare / le repudia / fenza che gli fia tenuto ad ingiuria / o alla
donna uerghogna / che in quefto tanta liberta tiene la donna
quanto lhuomo:non fono molto gelofi / & fuora di mifura lu
xuriofi / & molto piu le donne che glhuomini / che filafcia per
honefta dirui lartificio che le fanno per contar lor difordina/
ta luxuria:fono dōne molto generatiue / & nelle loro pregneze
non fenfono trauaglio alchuno:eloro parti fon tanto leggieri
che parturito dun di / uanno fuora per tucto / & maxime a la/
uarfi a fiumi / & ftanno fane come pefci:fono tanto difamora/
te & crude / che fe fi adirono con lor mariti / fubito fanno uno
artificio con che famazzano la creatura nel uentre / & fi fcon/
ciano / & a quefta cagione amazano infinite creature:fon don
ne di gentil corpo molto ben proportionate / che non fiuede
neloro corpi cofa / o membro mal facto:et anchora che del tut
to uadino difunde / fono donne in carne / & della uergogna lo
ro non fiuede quella parte che puo imaginare chi non lha ue
dute / che tucto incuoprono cō le cofcie / faluo quella parte / ad
che natura non prouidde / che e / honeftamente parlando / el
pectignone. In cōclufione nō tenghon uergona delle loro uer
gogne / non altrimenti che noi tegniamo moftrare el nafo &
la boccha:p marauiglia uedrete le poppe cadute ad una don/
na / o p molto partorire eluentre caduto / o altre grinze / che
tucte paion cħ mai parturiffino: moftrauanfi molto defidero
fe di congiugnerfi con noi chriftiani. In quefte gente nō cono/
fcēmo che teneffino legge alchuna / ne fipoffon dire Mori / ne
Giudei / & piggior cħ Gentili: perche nō uedēmo cħ faceffino
facrificio alchuno: nec etiam non tencuono cafa di oratione:
la loro uita giudico effere Epicurea:le loro habitationi fono in
comunita:& le loro cafe facte ad ufo di capáne / ma fortemen
te facte / & fabricate con grandiffimi arbori / & coperte di fo/
glie di palme / ficure delle tempefte & de uenti:& in alcuni luo
ghi di táta largheza & lungheza / che in una fola cafa trouámo
che ftauano 600. anime:& populatione uedēmo folo di tredici

cafe / doue ftauano quattro mila anime: di octo in dieci anni
mutano le populationi: & domádaro perche lo faceuano: per
caufa del fuolo che di gia per fudiceza ftaua infecto & corropto
&che caufaua dolentia necorpi loro / che ciparue buona ragio
ne: leloro riccheze fono penne di uccelli di piu colori / o pa
ternoftrini che fanno doffi di pefci / o in pietre biáche / o uerdi
lequali fimettono ple gote & ple labbra & orechi: & daltre mol
te cofe cō noi i cofa alcuna nō le ftimiamo: non ufano cōmer
tio / ne comperano / ne uendono. In conclufione uiuono / &
ficontentano con quello che da loro natura. Le riccheze che in
quefta noftra Europa & in altre parti ufiamo / come oro / gioie
perle & altre diuitie / non le tenghono in cofa neffuna: et an
chora che nelle loro terre lhabbino / non trauagliano per ha
uerte / ne le ftimano. Sono liberali nel dare / che per maraui
glia ui nieghano chofa alchuna: et per contrario liberali nel
domandare / quando fi monftrano uoftri amici: per el mag
giore fegno di amifta / che ui dimonftrano / e / che ui danno.
le donne loro / & le loro figliuole / & fi tiene per grandemen
te honorato / quando un padre / o una madre traendoui una
fua figliuola / anchora che fia moza uergine / dormiate con
lei: et in quefto ufano ogni termine di amifta. Quando muo
iono / ufono uarii modi di exequie / & alchuni glinterrano
con acqua & lor uiuande alchapo / penfando che habbino a
mangiat: non tenghono / ne ufono cerimonie di lumi / ne di
piangere. In alcuni altri luoghi ufono el piu barbaro & inhu
mano interramento: che e / che quando uno dolente / o in
fermo fta quafi che nello ultimo paffo della morte / efuoi pa
renti lo leuano in uno grande bofcho / & corichano una di
quelle loro reti / doue dormono / ad dua arbori / & di poi lo
mettono in epfa / & li danzano intorno tuctó un giorno: et
uenendo la nocte / gliponghono alcapezzale acqua con altre
uiuande / che fi poffa mantenere quattro / o fei giorni: & dipoi
lo lafciano folo / & tornonfi alla populatione: et fe lo infer
mo fi adiuta per fe medefimo / & mangia / & bee / & uiua / fi
torna alla populatione / & lo riceuono efuoi con cerimonias
ma pochi fono quelli che fchampano: fenza che piu fieno uifi
tati / fimuiono / & quello e / la loro fepultura: et altri molti co
ftumi tenghono / che per prolixita non fi dicono. Ufono nel
le loro infermitadi uarii modi di medicine / tanto differenti

dalle noftre / che cimarauigliauamo come neffuno fcampaua: &
che molte uolte uiddi / ch ad uno infermo di febre quãdo la te
neua in augumẽto / lo bagnauano cõ molta acqua fredda dal
capo alpie: dipoi gli faceuano un gran fuoco atorno / faccen-
dole uolgere & riuolgere altre due hore tãto che lo canfauano
& lofciauano dormire / & molti fanauano: con quefto ufano
molto la dieta / che ftino tre di fenza mãgiare / & cofi elcauarfi
fangue / ma nõ del braccio / faluo delle cofcie & de lombi & del
le polpe delle gambe: alfi prouocano el uomito con loro herbe
che fimettono nella bocca: & altri molti rimedii ufano / che fa
rebbe lungho a contargli: peccano molto nella flegma & nel
fangue a caufa delle loro uiuande / che el forte fono radici di
herbe & fructe & pefci: nõ tengono femente di grano / ne daltre
biade: & alloro comune ufo & mãgiare ufano una radice duno
arbore / dellaquale fanno farina & affai buona / & la chiamano
luca / & altre che la chiamano Cazabi / & altre ignami: man
gion pocha carne / faluo che carne di huomo: che fapra uoftra
Magnificentia / che in quefto fono tanto inhumani / che tra-
paffano ogni beftial coftume: perche fimangiono tutti eloro ni
mici che amazzano o pigliano / fi femine come mafchi / con
tanta efferita / che a dirlo pare cofa brutta: quãto piu a uederlo
come miaccadde infinitiffime uolte / & i molte parti uederlo:
& fimarauigliorono udendo dire a noi che nõ ci mangiamo
noftri nimici: et quefto credalo per certo uoftra Mag. fon tãto
glialtri loro barbari coftumi / che elfacto adire uien meno: et
pche in quefti quattro uiaggi ho uifte tante cofe uarie a noftri
coftumi / midifpofi a fcriuere un zibaldone / che lo chiamo le
quattro giornate: nelquale ho relato la maggior parte delle co
fe che io uiddi / affai diftinctamẽte / fecondo che miha porto el
mio debile ingegno: elquale anchora nõ ho publicato / perche
fono di tanto mal ghufto delle mie cofe medefime / che non ren
gho fapore in epfe che ho fcripto / ancora che molti miconfor
tino alpublicarlo: in epfo fiuedra ogni cofa p minúto: alfi che
non mi allarghero piu in quefto capitolo: perche nel proceffo
della lettera uerremo ad molte altre cofe che fono particulari:
quefto bafti quanto allo uniuerfale. In quefto principio non
uedẽmo cofa di molto proficto nella terra / faluo alchuna di-
moftra doro: credo che lo caufaua / perche nõ fapauamo la lingua: che inquanto alfito & difpofitione della terra / non fipuo
migliorare: acchordãmo di partirci / & andare piu inanzi co-

seggiando di continuo la terra:nellaquale facémo molte ica,
le / & hauémo ragionamenti con mol.a gente: & alfine di certi
giorni Fimm. . nere uno porto / doue leuámo grandiffimo
pericol· · piacque allo Spirito. s. .aluarci:& fu in quefto mo
do. Fumo aterra in un porto / doue trouamo una populatione
fondata fopra lacqua come Venetia:erano circa 44. cafe gran
de ad ufo di capáne fondate fopra pali groffiffimi / & teneuano
le loro porte / o entrate di cafe ad ufo di ponti leuatoi: & duna
cafa fipoteua correre p tutte / a caufa de ponti leuatoi che gitta,
uano di cafa in cafa: & come le gente di effe ciuedeffino / moftra
rono hauere paura di noi / & difubito alzaron tutti eponti: &
ftando a uedere quefta marauiglia / uedémo uenire per elmare
circa di 22. Canoe / che fono maniera di loro nauili / fabricati
dun folo arbore:equali uénono alla uolta dé noftri battelli / co
me fimarauigliaffino di noftre effigie & habiti / & fi tennon
larghi da noi: & ftando cofi / facémo loro fegnali chi ueniffino
a noi / afficurándoli con ogni fegno di amifta: & uifto che non
ueniuano / fumo a loro / & non ci afpectorono:ma fi furono a
terra / & con cenni cidixeno che afpectaffimo / & che fubito tor
nerebbono: & furono drieto a un monte / & nő tardoron mol
to:quádo tornorono / menauan feco 16. fanciulle delle loro / &
intraron con effe nelle loro Canoe / & fi uénono a batrelli: & í
clafchedun battello nemiffon 4. che tanto cimarauigliámo di
quefto acto / quanto puo penfare V. M. & loro fimiffono cő le
loro Canoe infra noftri battelli / uenendo cő noi parlando:di
modo che lo giudicámo fegno di amifta: & andando in quefto
uedémo uenire molta gente p elmare notando / che ueniuano
dalle cafe.: & come fi ueniffino appreffando a noi fenza fofpe,
ctó alcuno / in ǧfto fimoftrorono alle porte delle cafe certe don
ne uecchie / dando grandiffimi gridi & tirandofi ecapelli / mo
ftrando triftitia:p ilche cifeciono fofpectare / & ricorrémo cia,
fcheduno alle arme: & í un fubito le fanciulle chi tenauamo ne
battelli / figittorono almare / & quelli delle Canoe fallargoron
da noi / & cominciaron cő loro archi a faettarci: & quelli chi ue
niano a nuoto / clafcuno traeua una lancia di baffo nellacqua
piu coperta che poteuano:di modo che conofciuto eltradimēto
cominciámo nő folo cő loro a difenderci / ma afpramēte a of,
fendergli / & fozobramo cő li battelli molte delle loro Almadie
o Canoe / che cofi le chiamano / facémo iftragho / & tucti figit
torono anuoto / laffando difmanparate le loro canoe / cő affai

lor danno fi furono notando aterra:morſron diloro circa 14.
o 20. & molti reſtoron feriti:& de noſtri furon feriti 4. & tucti
ſcamporono gratia di Dio:pigliãmo due delle fanciulle & dua
huomini:& fumo allelor caſe / & entrãmo in epſe / & in tut
te non trouãmo altro cõ due uecchie & uno ĩfeimo:togiiēmo
loro molte coſe / ma di pocha ualuta:& non uolēmo ardere lo
ro le caſe / perche ci pareua caricho diconſcientia: & tornãmo
alli noſtri battelli con cinque prigioni:& fumoci alle naui / &
mettēmo a ciaſchuno depreſi un paio di ferri in pie / ſaluo che
alle moze:& lanocte uegnente ſifuggirono le due fanciulle &
uno delli huomini piu ſottilmēte del mõdo:& laltro giorno ac
cordãmo di ſalire di q̃ſto porto & andare piu inanzi:andãmo
di cõtinuo allungho della coſta / hauēmo uiſta dunaltra gente
che poreua ſtar diſcoſto da quella. 80.leghe:& la trouãmo mol
to differēte di lingua & di coſtumi:accordãmo di ſurgere / & an
dãmo cõ li battelli aterra / & uedēmo ſtare alla ſpiaggia gran
diſſima gente / che poteuano eſſere alpie di 4000.anime:& co
me fumo giunti cõ terra / nõ ci aſpectorono / & ſimiſſono a fug
gire p'eboſchi / diſmamparando lor coſe:ſaltãmo ĩ terra / & fu
mo per un cãmino che andaua alboſcho:& ĩ ſpatio dun tiro di
baleſtro trouãmo le lor trabacche / doue haueuon facto gran
diſſimi fuochi / & due ſtauano cocendo lor uiuãde & arroſten
do di molti animali & peſci di molte ſorte:doue uedēmo che ac
roſtiuano un cerro animale cõ pareua un ſerpēte / ſaluo cõ nõ
teneũa alia: & nella apparenza tãto brutto / che molto cĩmara
uiglãmo della ſua fierezza:Andãmo coſi p le lor caſe/o uero tra
bacche / & trouãmo molti di queſti ſerpēti uiui / & eron legati
pe piedi / & teneuano una corda allointorno del muſo /cõ nõ
poteuono aprire la bocca /come ſiſa a cani alani / pche nõ mor
dino:eron di tanto fiero aſpecto / che neſſuno di noi nõ ardiua
di torne uno / penſando cõ eron uenenoſi:ſeno di grandeza di
uno cauretto & di lũghezza braccio uno & mezo:tēgono epiedi
lunghi & groſſi & armati cõ groſſe unghie:tengono la pelle du
ra & / & ſono di uarii colori:elmuſo & faccia tengon di ſerpēte:
& dal naſo ſimuoue loro una creſta come una ſegha / che paſſa
loro p elmezo delle ſchiene infino alla ſommita della coda:in
cõcluſione gligiudicãmo ſerpi & uenenoſi / & ſegli mãgiauanc:
trouãmo che faceuono pane di peſci piccho|i che pigliauon del
mare / con dar loro prima un bollore / amaſſarli & farne paſta
di eſſi/o pane / & li arroſtiuano inſulla bracie:coſi li mangia

mano;prouamolo / & trouāmo che era buono:teneuono tante
altre forte di mangiari / & maxime di fructe & radice / chē fareb
be cosa largha raccontarle p minuto; & uisto che la gente non
riueniua / accordāmo nō tocchare ne torre loro cosa alcuna per
miglior aßicurarli: & laßamo loro nelle trabacche molte delle
cose nostre in luogo che le poteßino uedere / & tornamoci p la
nocte alle naui: & laltro giorno come uenißse eldi / uedēmo al
la spiaggia īfinita gente: & fumo a terra: & anchora che di noi
fimostraßino paurosi / tutta uolta si aßicurorono a tractare cō
noi / dandoci quāto loro domādauamo: & mostrandosi molto
amici nostri / cidixeno cō q̄lle erono le loro habitationi / & che
eron uenuti quiui p fare pescheria: & cipregorono che fußimo
alle loro habitationi & populationi / pche ciuoleuano riceuere
come amici: & simißeno a tanta amista acausa di dua huomini
che tenauamo con eßo noi presi / perche erano loro nimici:di
modo che uista tanta loro importunatione / facto nostro consi
glio / accordāmo 28.di noi christiani andare cō loro bene aor
dine / & cō fermo proposito / se neceßario fuße / morire:et di
poi che fumo stati qui quasi tre giorni / fumo cō loro per terra
drento: & a tre leghe della spiaggia fumo cō una populatione
daßai gente & di poche case / pche nō eron piu che noue:doue
fumo riceuuti cō tante & tante barbare cerimonie / che nō ba
sta la penna a scriuerle:che furono con li balli & canti & pianti
mescolati dallegreza / & con molte uiuande: & qui stēmo lano
cte:doue ci offerseno le loro dōne / chi nō cipotauamo difende
re da loro: & dipoi deßere stati qui la nocte & mezo laltro gior
no / furon tanti epopuli che per marauiglia ciueniuano a uede
re / che erano senza conto: & li piu uecchi cipregauano chi fußi
mo con loro ad altre populationi / che stauano piu drento in
terra / mostrando di farci grādißimo honore:per onde accor
damo di andare: & nō ui sipuo dire quanto honore cifeciono:
& fumo a molte populationi / tanto che stēmo noue giorni nel
uiaggio / tāto cō di gia inostri christiani cō eron restati alle naui
stauano cō sospecto di noi: & stando circa 18.leghe drēto infra
terra / deliberāmo tornarcene alle naui: & alritorno era tāta la
gente si huomini come dōne che uennon cō noi infino al ma
re / che fu cosa mirabile:& se alcuno de nostri sicāsaua del ca
mino / cileuauano in loro reti molto discansataměte: & alpaß
sare delli fiumi / che sono molti & molto grandi / con loro ar
tificii cipaßauano tanto sicuri / che nō ieuauamo pericolo alcu

no / & molti di loro ueniuano carichi delle cose che ci haue/
uon date / che eron nelle loro reti per dormire / & piumaggi
molto ricchi / molti archi & freccie / infiniti pappagalli di ua
rii colori: & altri traeuano con loro carichi di loro manteni/
menti / & di animali:che maggior marauiglia uidiro / che per
bene auenturato fireneua quello / che hauendo a passare una
acqua / cipoteua portare adosso: et giuncti che fumo a ma/
re / uenuto nostri battelli / entràmo i epsi:et era ráta la calcha
che loro faceuano p entrare nelli battelli / & uenire a uedere
le nostre naui / chi cimarauigliauamo: & con li battelli leuàmo
di epsi quanti potèmo / & fumo alle naui / & tanti uènono a
nuoto / che citenèmo per impacciati per uederci tanta gente
nelle naui / che erano piu di mille anime tucti nudi & senza
arme: marauigliauonsi delli nostri apparecchi & artifici / &
grandeza delle naui:et con costoro ciaccadde cosa ben da ri/
dere / che fu / che accordàmo di sparare alcune delle nostre ar
tiglierie / & quando sali eltuono / la maggior parte di loro p
paura figittorono a nuoto nõ altrimenti che sifanno li ranoc
chi cõ stanno alle prode / che uedendo cosa paurosa / sigitton/
nel pantano / tal fece quella gente: & quelli che restoron nelle
naui / stauano tanto temorosi / che cenepentimo di tal facto:
pure li assicuràmo con dire loro che cõ quelle armi amazaua/
mo enostri nimici:et hauèdo folgato tucto elgiorno nelle na
ui / dicèmo loro che sene andassino / perche uelauam parti/
re la nocte / & cosi sipartiron da noi cõ molta amista / & amo
re sene furono a terra. In questa gente / & in loro terra conob
bi & uiddi tanti deloro costumi & lor modi di uiuere / che nõ
curo di allargharmi in epsi: perche sapra V.M. come in cia/
scuno delli miei uiaggi ho notate le cose piu marauigliose: &
tutto ho ridocto in un uolume in stilo di geografia: & le inti/
tulo le quattro giornate: nellaquale opera sicontiene le cose p
minuto / & per anchora nõ sene data fuora copia / perche me
necessario conferirla. Questa terra e popularissima / & di gea
te piena / & dinfiniti fiumi / animali pochi: sono simili a no/
stri / saluo Lioni / Lonze / cerui / Porci / capriuoli & dani: &
questi ancora renghono alcuna disformita: nõ tèghono caual
li ne muli / ne cõ reuerentia afini / ne cani / ne di sorte alcuna
bestiame peculioso / ne uaccino: ma sono rári li altri animali
che tèghono / & tucti sono saluatichi / & di nessuno siseruono
per loro seruitio / che nõ siposson contare. Che diremo daltri

b.i.

uccelli ! che son tanti & di tante sorte & colori di penne / che e/
marauiglia uederli. La terra e/molto amena & fructuosa / pie
na di grandissime selue & boschi: & sempre sta uerde/che mai
non perde foglia. Le fructe son tante/che sono fuora di nume
ro/ & difforme altucto dalle nostre. Questa terra sta dentro del
la torrida zona giuntamente/ o di basso del pararello/ che de-
scriue eltropico di Cancer:doue alza eipolo dello orizonte 23
gradi nel fine del secondo clyma . Vennonci a uedere molti
pepoli / & si marauigliauano delle nostre effigie & di nostra
blancheza: & ci domandoron donde uenauamo: & dauamo
loro ad intēdere / che uenauamo dal cielo / & che andauamo a
uedere el mōdo / & lo credeuano. In questa terra ponēmo son
te di baptesimo: & infinita gente sibaptezo / & cichiamauano
in lor lingua Carabi / che uuol dire huomini di gran sauido-
ria. Partimo di questo perto:& la prouincia sidice Lariab:&
nauigāmo allungo della costa sempre a uista della terra / tan
to che corrēmo dessa ꝗ 70. leghe tutta uia uerso el maestrale /
faccendo per epsa molte scale / & tractando con molta gente:
& in molti luoghi rischartāmo oro / ma non molta quanti-
ta / che assai facēmo in discoprire la terra / & di sapere che te
neuano oro. Erauamo gia stati 13. mesi nel uiaggio: & di gia
enauili & li apparecchi erono molto cōsumati / & li huomini
ansati:acchordāmo di comune consiglio porre le nostre na
ui amonte / & ricorrerle per stancharle / che faceuano molta
acqua / & calefatarle & brearle dinuouo / & tornarcene per la
uolta di Spagna:et quādo questo deliberāmo / stauamo giun
ti con un porto elmiglior del mondo:nelquale entrāmo con
le nostre naui:doue trouamo infinita gente:laquale con mol
ta amista ciriceue: & in terra facēmo un bastione con li nostri
battelli & con tonelli & botte & nostre artiglierie / che gioca-
uano per tucto:et discarichate & alloggiare nostre naui / le ti-
ramo in terra / & le correggēmo di tucto quello che era necessario: & la gente diterra ciderte grādissimo aiuto:& di con
tinuo ciprouedeuono delle loro uiuande:che in ꝗsto porto po
che ghustāmo delle nostre / che cifeciono buon giuoco:perche
tenauamo elmantenimento per la uolta pocho & tristo:doue
stēmo 37. giorni :et audāmo molte uolte alleloro populatio
ni:doue cifaceuono grandissimo honore: et uolendoci parti
re per nostro uiaggio / cifeciono richiamo di come certi tempi dellanno ueniuano perla uia di mare / questa lor terra una
gente molto crudele / & loro uimici:& con rtadimenti /o con

forza amazauano molti di loro / & fellmangiauano: & alcu
ni capriuauano / & glileuauan presi alle lor case / o terra: & cō
apena sipoteuono defendere da loro / faccendoci segnali che
erano gente di isole / & poteuono stare drento in mare 100. le
ghe: et con tanta affectione cidiceuano questo / che lo credé
mo loro: & promettémo loro di uendicarli di tanta ingiuria:
& loro restoron molto allegri di ǧsto: et molti di loro si offer
sono di uenire con esso noi / ma nō gliuolémo leuare per mol
te cagioni / saluo che neleuámo septe / cō conditione che si ue
nissimo poi in Canoe: perche nō ciuolauamo obligare a tor
narli a loro terra: & furon contenti: et cosi cipartimo da que
ste genti / lassandoli molto amici nostri: et rimediate nostre
naui / & nauigando septe giorni alla uolta del mare p euen
to infra greco & leuante: et alcapo delli septe giorni riscon
trámo nelle isole / che eron molte / & alcune populate / & al
tre deserte: & surgémo con una di epse: doue uedémo molta
gente che la chiamauano Iti: et stipati enostri battelli di buo
na gente / & in ciaschuno tre tiri di bombarde / fumo alla uol
ta di terra: doue trouámo stare alpie di 400. huomini & mol
te dōne / & tucti disnudi come epassati. Eron di buon corpo:
& ben pareuano huomini bellicosi: perche eronō armati di lo
ro armi / che sono archi / saette & lance: et la maggior parte
di loro teneuano tauolaccine quadrate: & di modo sele pone
uano / che non glimpediuono el trarre dello archo: et come
fumo a circha di terra con li battelli ad un tiro darcho / tutti
saltoron nellacqua a tirarci saette / & difenderci che non sal
tassimo i terra: & tutti eron dipincti ecorpi loro di diuersi colo
ri / & impiumati cō penne: & cidiceuano le lingue cō con noi
erano / che quādo cosi simostrauano dipincti & ipiumati / che
dauon segnale diuoler cōbattere: & tāto perseueroron i defen
derci la terra / che fumo sfforzati a giocare cō nostre artiglie
rie: et come sentirono el tuōno / & uidono de loro cader morti
alchuni / tucti sitraisseno alla terra: per onde facto nostro cōsi
glio / accordámo saltare i terra 42. di noi: & se cispectassino /
combatter con loro: cosi saltati i terra cō nostre armi / loro si
uennono a noi / & combattemo a circha duna hora / cō poco
uantaggio leuámo loro / saluo cō enostri balestrieri & spingar
dieri ne amazauano alcuno / & loro ferron certi nostri: & que
sto era / pche nō ci aspectauano nō altiro di lancia ne di spa
da: et tanta forza ponémo al fine / che uenimo al tiro delle

spade / & come ghustaſſino le noſtre armi / ſimiſſono in fuga
per emonti & boſchi / & ci laſcioron uincitori del campo con
molti di loro morti & aſſai feriti: & per queſto giorno non tra
uagliámo altriméti di dare loro drieto / perche ſtauamo mol
to affaticati / & cene tornámo alle naui con tanta allegreza
de ſepte huomini che con noi eron uenuti / che nõ capriuano
in loro: & uenendo laltro giorno / uedémo uenire per la terra
gran numero di gente / tutta uia con ſegnali di battaglia ſo/
nando corni / & altri uarii ſtrumenti che loro uſan nelle guer
re: & tucti dipincti & impiumati / che era coſa bène ſtrana a
uederli: ilperche tucte le naui fecion conſiglio / & fu delibera
to poi che queſta gente uoleua con noi nimicitia / che fuſſimo
a uederci con loro / & di fare ogni coſa per farceli amici: in ca
ſo che nõ uoleſſino noſtra amiſta / che li tractaſſimo come ni/
mici / & che quáti nepoteſſimo pigliare di loro / tucti fuſſino
noſtri ſchiaui: et armatici come miglior potauamo / fumo al
la uolta di terra / & non cidifeſono el ſaltare in terra / credo per
paura delle bombarde: & ſaltámo í terra 4.7. huomini in quat.
tro ſquadre / ciaſchun Capitano con la ſua gente: & fumo alle
mani con loro: & dipoi duna lungha battaglia morti molti
di loro / glimettémo í fuga / & ſeguimo lor drieto fino a una
populatione / hauédo preſo circa di 2 40. di loro / & ardémo
la populatione / & cenetornámo con uictoria & con 2 4 6. pri
gioni alle naui / laſciando di loro molti morti & feriti / & de
noſtri nõ mori piu che uno / & 22. feriti / cõ tucti ſcamporo/
no / dio ſia ringratiato. Ordinámo noſtra partita / & li ſepte
huomini che cinque ñe eroñ feriti / preſono una Canoe del
la iſola / & cõ ſepte prigioni che démo loro / quattro dõne &
tre huomini / ſene tornorono allor terra molto allegri / mara
uigliádoſi delle noſtre forze: & noi alſi facémo uela p Spagna
cõ 222. prigioni ſchiaui: & giugnemo nel porró di Calis adi
14. doctobre 1498. doue fumo ben riceuuti / & uendémo no
ſtri ſchiaui. Queſto e / quello che miacchádde in queſto mio pri
mo uiaggio di piu notabile.

ℂ Finiſce elprimo Viaggio.

ℂ Comincia elſecondo.

Q Vanto alſecondo Viaggio / & quello che in epſo uiddi
piu degn‹ di memoria, e‹ quello che qui ſegue. Partimo
del porto di Calis tre naui di côſerua adì 16. di Maggio 1499
& cominciámo noſtro cámino adiritti alle iſole del cauo uer‐
de / paſſando a uiſta della iſola di gran Canaria: et tanto na‐
uigámo / che fumo a tenere ad una iſola / che ſidice liſola del
fuoco: et qui facta noſtra prouiſione dacqua & di legne / pi‐
gliámo noſtra nauigatione per illibeccio: & in 44. giorni fu
mo ·a tenere ad una nuoua terra: & la giudicámo eſſere terra
ferma / & continua con la diſopra ſi fa mentione: laquale eſſi
tuata drenro della torrida zona / & fuora della linea equino‐
ctiale alla parre dello auſtro: ſopra laquale alza el polo del me
ridione ¨4. gradi fuora dogni clyma: & diſta dalle decte iſole
per eluêro libeccio 400. leghe: & trouámo eſſere equali egior
ni con ‘e nocte: oche fumo ad epſa adì 27. di Giugno / quan
do elſole ſta circa del tropico di Cancer: laqual terra trouámo
eſſère tucta annegata & piena di grandiſſimi fiumi. In queſto
principio nô uedémo gente alcuna: ſurgémo con noſtre naui
& buttámo fuora enoſtri battelli: fumo con epſi a terra / & co
me dico / la trouámo piena di grandiſſimi fiumi / & annegata

b.iii.

per grandiſſimi fiumi che trouámo:& la cõmettémo in molte
parti / per uedere ſe poteſſino entrare p epſa:& per le grandi
acque ch tracuono eſiumi / con quáto trauaglio potémo / nõ
trouámo luogho che non fuſſi annegato:uedémo per eſiumi
molti ſegnali di come la terra era populata:& uiſto ch p que
ſta parte non la potauamo entrare / accordámo tornarcene al
le naui / & di cõmetterla p altra parte:& leuatámo noſtre an-
chore / & nauicámo infra leuante & ſcilocho / coſteggiando
di continouo la terra / che coſi ſicorreua / & in molte parti la
cõmettémo in ſpatio di 40.leghe:& tucto era tempo perdu-
to:trouámo in queſta coſta che le correnti del mare erano di
tanta forza / che non cilaſciauano nauigare / & tucte correua-
no dallo ſcilocho almaeſtrale:di modo che uiſto tanti incon-
uenienti per noſtra nauicatione / facto noſtro cõſiglio / accor
damo tornare la nauicatione alla parte del maeſtrale: & tanto nauicámo allungho della terra / che fumo a tenere un bel-
liſſimo porto:elquale era cauſato da una grande iſola / che ſta
ua allentrata / & drento ſi faceua una grandiſſima inſenata:&
nauicando p entrare in epſo / prolungando la iſola / hauémo
uiſta di molta gente: et allegraticí / uidirizzámo noſtre naui
per ſurgere doue uedauamo la gente / ch potauamo ſtare piu
almate circa di quattro leghe:et nauicando in queſto modo /
hauémo uiſta duna Canoe / che ueniua cõ alto mare: nellaqua
le ueniua molta gente:& accordámo di hauerla alla mano: &
facémo la uolta con noſtre naui ſopra epſa con ordinè ch nòi
non la perdeſſimo:& nauicando alla uolta ſua con freſco tem
po / uedémo che ſtauano fermi co remi alzati / credo per ma
rauiglia delle noſtre naui:& come uidono che noi ci andauamo apreſſando loro / meſſono eremi nellacqua / & comincio-
rono a nauicare alla uolta di terra:& come í noſtra cõpagnia
ueniſſe una carouella di 44.tonelli molto buona della uela /
ſipuoſe a barlouento della Canoe:& quando lẽparue tempo
darriuare ſopra epſa / allargo li apparecchi / uenne alla uol
ta ſua / & noi alſi:et come la carouelletta pareggiaſſe con lei
& nõ la uoleſſi inueſtire / la paſſo / & poi rimaſe ſotto uento:
& come ſiuedeſſino a uantaggio / cominciarono a far forza
co remi p fuggire:& noi che trouámo ebatrelli per poppa gia
ſtipari di buona gente / penſandó ch la piglierebbono:& tra
uagliorono piu di due hore / & infine ſe la carouelletta in al-

era uolta non tornaua fopra epfa / la perdauamo: & come fi
uiddeno ftrecti dalla carouella & da batelli / tucti figittarono
almare / che poteuono effere. 7 o. huomini: & diftauano da ter
ra circa di due leghe: & feguédoli co batelli / in tutto elgiorno
nõ nepotémo pigliare piu ch dua / che fu p acerto: glialtri tut
ti fi furono a terra a faluaméro : & nella canoe reftarono 4.
fanciulli: equali non eron di lor generatione / che li traeuano
prefi dallaltra terra: & li haueuano caftrati / che tucti eron fen
za membro uirile / & con la piaga frefcha: di che molto ci ma
rauigliámo: & meffi nelle nauiu cidixeno per fegnali / che li
haueuon caftrati p mangiarfeli: & fapémo coftoro erano una
gente / che fidicono Camballi / molto efferati / chi mangiono
carne humana. Fumo con lenaui / leuando con noi la Canoe
per poppa alla uolta di terra / & furgémo a meza legha: & co
me aterra uedeffimo molta gente alla fpiaggia / fumo co bat
telli a terra / & leuámo con epfo noi edua huominini che pigliámo: & giuncti in terra / tucta la géte fifuggi / & fimiffeno
pe bofchi: & allarghámo uno delli huomini / dandogli molti
fonagli / & che uolauamo effere loro amici: elquale fece molto
bene quello li mandamo / & traffe feco tucta la gente / che po
teuono effere 400. huomini / et molte dõne: equali uennono
fenza arme alchuna adonde ftauamo con li batelli: et facto
con loro buona amifta / rendémo loro laltro prefo / et mandamo alle naui perla loro Canoe / et la rendémo loro. Quefta
Canoe era lungha 26. paffi / et largha due braccia / et tucta
dun folo arbore cauato / molto bene lauorata: et quando la
hebbono uarata in un rio / et meffala in luogho ficuro / tucti
fifuggirono / et nõ uollon piu praticare con noi / che ciparue
tucto barbaro acto / che glǐgiudicámo gente di pochafede &
di mala conditione. A coftoro uedémo alcun pocho doro che
teneuano nelli orecchi. Partimo di qui / & entrámo drento nel
la infenata: doue trouámo táta gente / che fu marauiglia: con
liquali facémo in terra amifta: & fumo molti di noi con loro
alle loro populationi molto ficuramente / & ben riceuuti. In
quefto luogho rifchattámo 140. perle / che cele detton p un fo
naglio / & alcun poco doro / che celodauano di gratia: et í que
fta terra trouámo che beuano uino facto di lor, fructe & femente ad ufo di ceruogia / & biancho & uermiglio: & el migliore era facto di mirabolani / & era molto buono: et man-

gtámo infiniti di epfi / che era eltempo loro.E / molto buona fructa / faporofa alghufto / & falutifera alcorpo. La terra
e / molto abondofa deloro mantenimenti / et la gente di buo
na conuerfatione / et la piu pacifica che habbiamo trouata in
fino aqui. Stémo in quefto porto 17.giorni con molto placere:et ogni giorno ciueniuano a uedere nuoui populi della ter
ra drento / marauigliandofi di noftre effigie & bianchezza / &
de noftri ueftbi & atme / & della forma & grandezza delle na
ui.Da quefta gente hauémo nuoue di come ftaua una gente
piu alponente chi loro / che erano loro nimici / che teneuano
infinita copia di perle:et che quelle che loro teneuano / eron
che le haueuan lor tolte nelle lor guerre:et cidixeno come le
pefchauono / & in che modo nafceuano / et li trouámo effere
con uerita / come udira uoftra Magnificentia. Partimo di que
fto porto / et nauicámo perla cofta:per laquale di continuo ue
dauamo fumalte con gente alla fpiaggia:et alcapo di molti
giorni fumo a tenere in un porto / ad caufa di rimediare ad
una delle noftre naui / ché faceua molta acqua:doue trouámo
effere molta gente:con liquali non potémo ne per forza ne
per amore hauer conuerfatione alchuna:et quando andauamo a terra / cidifendeuano afpramête la terra:et quando piu
non poteuano / fi fuggiuano per li bofchi / & non ciafpectauano.Conofciutoli táto barbari / cipartimo diqui:et andan
do nauicando / hauémo uifta duna ifola / che diftaua nel ma
re 15leghe daterra:& acchordámo di andare a uedere fe era
populata.Trouámo in epfa la piu beftial gente & la piu brut
ta che mai fiuedeffe / & era di quefta forte. Erano di gefto & ui
fo molto brutti:& tucti teneuano le ghote piene di dreato di
una herba uerde / che di continuo la rugumauano come bêftie / che apena poteuon parlare / & ciafchuno teneua alcollo
due zucche fecche / che luna era piena di ĝlla herba che teneuano i boccha / & laltra duna farina biácha / che pareua geffo
in poluere / & di quádo in quando con un fufo cñ teneuano
inmollandolo cô la boccha / lo metteuano nella farina:dipoi
felo metteuano in boccha da rutta dua le bande delle ghore:
infarinandofi lherba che teneuano in boccha:& ĝfto faceuano molto aminuto:et marinigliati di tal cofa / nô potauamo
intédere ĝfto fecreto / ne ad cñ fine cofi faceuano. Quefta gen
te come ciuidono / uennono a noi tanto familiarmête / come

ſe haueſſimo tenuto con loro amiſta tandando con loro per la
ſpiaggia parlando / & deſideroſi di bere acqua freſcha / ci fe
ciono ſegnali che nõ la teneuano / & confereuon di quella lo
ro herba & farina / di modo che ſtimámo per diſcrettione che
q̃ſta Iſola era pouera dacqua / & ch per difenderſi dalla ſete / te
neuano quella herba in boccha / & la farina per quello medeſi
mo. Andámo per la iſola un di & mezo ſenza ch mai trouaſſi
mo acqua uiua: & uedémo che lacqua che ebeeuano / era di ru
giada ch cadeua di nocte ſopra certe foglie / ch pareuano orce
chi di aſino / & empienonſi dacqua / & di queſta beeuano era
acqua optima: & di queſte foglie nõ ne haueuono in molti luo
ghi. Nõ teneuano alcuna maniera di uiuande / ne radice / co
me nella terra ferma: & la lor uita era con peſci che pigliauon
nel mare / & di queſti teneuano grandiſſima abundantia / &
erano grádiſſimi peſcatori: & ci preſentorono molte tortughe
& molti gran peſci molto buoni: le lor donne nõ uſauon tene
re lherba in boccha come glhuomini / ma tucte traeuono una
zuccha con acqua / & di quella beeuano. Nõ teneano popula
tione ne di caſe ne di capáne / ſa uo che habitauano di baſſo
in fraſchati / che li defendeuano dal Sole / & nõ da lacqua: che
credo poche uolte ui pioueua in quella Iſola: quando ſtauano
almare peſchando / tucti teneuano una foglia molto grande
& di tal largheza / che uiſtauon di baſſo dréto alle ubra / & la
ficchauano in terra: & come elſole ſiuolgeua / coſi uolgeuano
la foglia; & i queſto modo ſi difendeuano dal Sole. Liſola con
tiene molti animali di uarie ſorte: & beano acqu di pantani
& uiſto che nõ teneuano proſicto alcuno / ci partimo / & fumo
ad unaltra Iſola: & trouámo che in epſa habitaua gente molto
grande: fumo ludi in terra / per uedete ſe trouaremo acqua
freſca: & nõ penſando che liſola fuſſi populata per non ueder
gente / andando alungho della ſpiaggia / uedemo pedate di
gente nella rena molto grádi: & giudicámo ſe ſalire membra
riſpondeſſino alla miſura / che ſarebbono huomini grandiſſi
mi: & andando in queſto rincontrámo in un camino che an
daua per la terra drento: & acchordámo noue di noi: & giu
dicámo che liſola per eſſer picchola / nõ poteua hauere in ſe
molta gente: e pero andámo per epſa / per uedere che gente
era queſta: & dipoi che fumo iti circa di una legha / uedémo
in una ualle cinque delle lor capáne / che ci pareuon diſpopo
late: & fumo ad epſe / & trouámo ſolo cinque donne / & due

uecchie & tre fanciulle di tanto alta statura / che per maraul.
glia le guardauamo:& come ciuiddono / entro lor táta pau/
ra / che non hebbono animo a fuggire:& le due uecchie ci co
minciorono con parole a conuitare / ctaendoci molte cose da
mangiare / & messonci in una capána: & eron di statura mag
giori che uno grande huomo / che ben sarebbon gráde di cor
po:come fu Francesco de gliaibizi / ma di miglior proportio
ne:di modo che stauamo tutti di proposito di torne le tre fan
ciulle per forza / & per cosa marauigliosa trarle a Castiglia:
et stando i questi ragionamenti / cominciorno a entrare per
la porta della capána ben 36.huomini molto maggiori che
le donne:huomini tanto ben facti / che era cosa famosa a ue
dergli:equali cimissono in tanta turbatione, / che piu tosto sa
remo uoluti essere alle naui / ch ctrouarci cõ tal gente. Traeua
no archi grandissimi / & freccie con gran bastoni con capoc
chie: & parlauano infra loro dun suono / come uolessino ma/
nomecterci:uistoci in tal pericolo / facémo uarii cõsigli infra
noi:alchuni diceuano che i casa sicominciasse a dare in loro:
& altri che alcampo era migliore:& altri che diceuano che nõ
cominciassimo la quistione infino a tanto che uedessimo quel
lo che uoleiino fare:et acchordámo del salir della capanna / &
andarcene dissimulatamente al cámino delle naui:& cosi lo
facémo:et preso nostro cámino / cenerornámo alle naui:loro
ci uénon drieto tuttauia a un tiro di pietra / parlando infra lo
ro:credo ch non men paura haueuon di noi / che noi di loro:
perche alcuna uolta ciripofauamo / & loro alsi senza appres
farsi a noi, / tanto che giugnémo alla spiaggia doue stauano
cbatrelli aspectandoci: & entrámo i epli: & come fumo larghi
loro saltorono / & citirorono molte saccre:ma pocha paura te/
nauamo gia di loro:sparámo loro dua tiri di bombarda piu p
spauétarsi che per far loro male: & tutti altuono fuggirono al
monte: & cosi cipartimo da loro / ch elparue scampare duna pe
ricolosa giornata. Andauano del tucto disnudi come li altri.
Chiamo questa isola / lisola de giganti a causa di lor grande/
za: & andámo piu inanzi prolungando la terra:nellaquale ci
accadde molte uolte combattere con loro per non ci uolere la
sciare pigliare cosa alchuna di terra: & gia che stauamo di uo/
lonta di tornarcene a Castiglia:perche erauamo stati nel ma
re circha di uno anno / & tenauamo poco n antenimento / &
elpoco damnato a causa delli gran caldi che passamo: perche

da che partimo per llfole del cauo uerde infino aqui / di conti
nuo hauauamo nauicato p la torrida zona / & due uolte atra /
uerfato perla linea equinoctiale:che come difopra dixi / fumo
fuora di epfa 4.gradi alla parte dello auftro: & qui ftauamo in
14.gradi uerfo elfeptetrione. Stando in qfto cofiglio / piacque
allo Spirito fancto dare alchuno difcanfo a tanti noftri tra /
uagli:che fu / che andando cerchando un porto per racchon /
ciare noftri nauilii / fumo a dare con una gente:laquale ci ri
couette con molta amifta: & trouamo che teneuano grandiffi
ma quatita di perle orientali & affai buone:co quali ciritene /
mo 47.giorni: & rifcatamo da loro 119.marchi di perle con
molta pocha mercantia:che credo nó cicoftorono el ualere di
quaranta ducati: pche quello che demo loro / nó furono fe nó
fonagli & fpecchi / & conte / dieci palle & foglie di octone:che
p uno fonaglio daua uno quate perle teneua. Da loro fapemo
come le pefcauano / & donde: & cidettono molte oftriche / nel
lequali nifceuono;rifcatamo oftrica i nellaquale ftaua di na /
fcimento 130.perle / & altre di meno:quefta delle 130.mitol
fe la Regina: & altre miguardai nó le uedeffe. Et ha da fapere
V.M.che fe le perle non fono mature / & da fe non fifpiccha /
no / nó perftanno:perche fidamnano prefto:& di quefto neho
uifto experientia:quando fono mature / ftanno drento nella
oftrica fpicchate & meffe nella carne:et qfte fon buone:quan /
to male teneuano / che la maggior parte erono roche & mal
forate:tutta uia ualeuano buon danari:pche fiuendeua elmar
cho. .et alcapo di 47.giorni lafciamo la gente molto
amica noftra. Partimoci / & perla neceffita del mantenimento
fumo a tenere allifola dantiglia / che e/quefta che difcoperfe
Chriftophal colombo piu anni fa:doue facemo molto man /
tenimeto: & ftemo duo mefi & 17.giorni:doue paffamo mol
ti pericoli & trauagli con li medefimi chriftiani che in quefta
ifola ftauano col Colombo:credo per inuidia:che per nó effe /
re prolixo / li lafcio di racchontare. Partimo della decta ifola
adi 22.di Luglio: & nauicamo i un mefe & mezo: & entramo
nel porto di Calis / che fu adi 8.di Septempre di di / elmio fe
condo uiaggio:Dio laudato.

℃ Finito elfecondo Viaggio:

℃ Comincia el terzo.

STAndomi dipoi in Sibylla / riposandomi di tanti mia
trauagli / che i questi duo uiaggi haueuo passati / & con
uolonta di tornare alla terra delle perle:qñdo la fortuna nõ
contenta de miei trauagli / che nõ so come uenissi in pensa
mento a questo serenissimo Re don manouello di portogallo
eiuolersi seruire di meter stando in Sibylia fuori dogni pen
samento di uenire a Portogallo / miuéne un messaggiero cõ
lettera di sua real corona / cne introgaua ch io uenissi a Lisbo
na a parlare cõ sua alteza / promettédo farmi merzedes. Nõ
fui aconsigliato che uenissi:expedii el messaggiero / dicendo
che stauo male / & che quando stessi buono / & che sua alteza
siuolesse pure seruire di me / che farei quanto mi mandasse.Et
uisto che non mi poteua hauere / accñordo mandare per me
Giuliano di Bartholomeo del Giocondo stante qui in Lisbo
na / con commissione che in ogni modo mitraessi. Venne el
detto Giuliano a Sibylia:perla uenuta & tuogho delquale
foi forzato a uenire / che fu tenuta a male la mia uenuta da
quanti miconoscieuano:perche mipartii di Castiglia / doue mi
era facto honore / & il Re miteneua i buona possessione:peg
gior fu / che mipartii susaiutato hospiteter appresentaromi
inanzi a quello Re / mostro hauer placere di mia uenuta:&
mipriego chi fussi in compagnia di tre sue naue / che stauano

preste p andare a difcoprire nuoue terre:& come un ruogo ŭ.
Re e/mando / hebbi aconfentire a quáto mirogaua:et pardnfe
di q̃fto porto di L'iibona tre naui di conferua adl. io. di Maggio
1.401.& pigliámo noftra derrota diritti alla ifola di gran Cana
ria:& pafiamo fenza pofare a uifta di epfa:& di qui fumo cofteg
giando la cofta dafrica p la parte occidétale:uella quale cofta fa
.ë:uo noftra pefcheria a una forte pefci / che fi chiamano Parchi:
doue ci ditenémo tre giorni:& di qui fumo nella cofta dethiopia
ad un porto che fidice Befechicce / die fta dentro dalla torrida zo
na:fopra laquale álza elpolo del feptentrione 14.gradi & mezo
fituato nel primo clyma:doue ftémo.11.giorni i piguano acqua
& legne:pche mia iniéttone era di marmgare uctío lauftro p el
golfo atlantico.Pardimo di q̃fto porto di ethiopia / & nauicámo
p el libeccio / pigliando una quarta del mezo di , tanto che in 67.
giorni fumo a tenere a una terra che ftaua nel decto porto 700.
leghe uerfo libecc o:& i quelli 67.giorni leuámo el peggior té
po / che mai leuaffe huomo che nauicaffe nel mare / per molti
aguazei & turbonate & tormëte che cidettono:pche tumö i té
po molto cöttario / acaufa che elforte di noftra nauicatione fu di
córinouo giunta con la linea equinoctiale / che nel mefe di Giu
gno erinuerno:& trouámo el di con la nocte effere equale:& tro
uámo lombra uerfo mezo di cötinouo:piacq̃ adio moftrarci
terra nuoua / & fu adi 17.dagofto:doue furgémo a meza legha:
& buttámo fuora noftri battelli:et fumo auedere la terra / fe era
habitata da gente i & che tale era:& trouámo effere habitata da
gete i ch'erano peggiori ch'animali:pero V.M.intendera i q̃fto
principio nö uedémo gente / ma ben conofcémo ch'era popula
ta p molti fegnali che i epfa uedémo:pigliámo la poffeffione di
epfa p quefto fereniffimo Re:laquale trouámo effere terra molto
amena & uerde / & di buona apparentia:ftaua fuora della linea
egnoctionale uerfo lauftro 4.gradi:et per quefto ci ditornámo
ll e naui:et pche renauamo gran neceffita dacqua & di legne /
accordámo laltro giorno di tornare a terra per prouedere del ne
ceffario:et ftando i terra / uedémo uua gëte nella fommita dun
monte / che ftauano mirando / & nö ufauono defcédere abaffo:
i :ano difnudi / & del medefimo colore & factione che erano li
altri paffati:et ftando cö loro trauagliando / perche ueniffino a
parlare con epfo noi / mai nö li potémo afficurare / che nö fi fi
durono di noi:et uifto la loro obftinatione / & di gia era tardi /
cenetornámo alle naui / lafciando loro in terra molti fonagli
c.i.

& fpecchi / & altre cofe a uifta loro:et come fumo larghi al ma
re / difcefeno del mõte / & uennon p le cofe laffamo loro / faccẽ
do di epfe grã marauiglia:& p ãffo giorno nõ ci puedẽmo fe nõ
dacqua:laltra mactina uedemo delle naue cõ la gẽte di terra face
uon molte fumate:& noi penfando che ci chiamaffino / fumo a
terra / doue trouámo ch erano uenuti molti populi / & tutta uia
ftauano larghi di noi:& ci accẽnauano ch fuffimo cõ loro p la ter
ra drento:p onde fimoffeno dua delli noftri xpiani a domádare
elcapitano ch deffe loro licentia / che fiuoleuano metref a picolo
di uolere andare cõ loro i terra / p uedere cõ gente erano / & fe
teneuano alcuna riccheza / o fpetieria / o drugheria:& tanto pre
gorono / cõ elcapitano fu cõtento:& meffonfi a ordine cõ molte
cofe di rifcatto / fipartiron da noi cõ ordine / ch nõ fteffino piu
di 4.giõni a tornare:pche táto gliafpecteremo:& pfon lor cami
no p la terra / & noi p le naui afpectádoli:& quafi ogni giõno ue
niua gẽte alla fpiaggia / & mai nõ ci uollon parlare:et ilfeptimo
giorno andamo i terra / & trouamo che haueũõ tracto cõ loro le
lor dõne:et come faltaffimo i terra / glhuomini della terra man
dorono molte delle lor dõne a parlar cõ noi:& uifto nõ fi afficu
rauano / accordámo di mádare a loro uno huomo de noftri / cõ
fu un giouane ch molto faceua lo fforzo:& noi p afficurarlo / en
trámo nelli battelli:& lui fifu p le dõne:& come giũfe a loro / gli
feciono un grã cerchio itorno / toccandolo / & mirandolo fi ma
tauigliauano:et ftando i ĝfto / uedẽmo uenire una dõna del mõ
te / & tracua un grã palo nella mano:& come giunfe dõde ftaua
elnoftro xpiano / li uenne p adrieto:& alzato elbaftone / glidette
tam grãde elcolpo / ch lo diftefe morto i terra / i un fubito le al
tre dõne lo pfono pe piedi / & lo ftrafcinorono pe piedi uerfo el
mõte:& li huomini faltorono uerfo la fpiaggia / & cõ loro archi
& faette a faettarci:et poson la noftra gente i tanta paura furti
cõ li battelli fopra le fatefce / che ftauano in terra / che p le molte
freccie ch cimetteuano nelli battelli / neffuno accertaua di piglia
re larme:pure difparámo loro 4.tiri di bõbarda / & nõ accerto
rono / faluo ch udito eltuono / tutti fuggirono uerfo el mõte / &
doue ftauano gia le dõne faccẽdo pezi del xpiano / & ad un gran
fuoco che haueũõ facto / lo ftauano arroftẽdo a uifta noftra / mo
ftrãdoci molti pezi / & mãgiandofeli:et li huomini faccendoci
fegnali cõ loro cenni d come hauer morti li altri duo xpiani / &
mangiatofeli:el che cipefo molto / ueggẽdo cõ li noftri occhi la
crudelta che faceuan del morto / a tutti noi fu ingiuria intollerã

bile:& ftando di propofito piu di 40.di noi di faltare in terra &
uendicare tãta cruda morte & acto beftiale &inhumano / el Ca
pitano maggiore nõ uolle acõfentire / & fi reftaron fatij di tãta
ingiuria:& noi cipartimo da loro cõ mala uolõta & cõ molta uer
gogna noftra a caufa del noftro Capitano. Partimo di q̃fto luo
go / & comínciámo noftra nauicatione ifra leuãte & fcilocchoi &
cofi fi correua la terra:et facémo molte fchalev & mai trouãmo
gẽte chi cõ epfo noi uoleffin cõuerfare:et cofi nauicámo tãto / che
trouamo che la terra faceua la uolta p libecçio:come doblaftimo
un cauo / alquale ponémo nome elcauo di fcõ Auguftino / co/
minciamo a nauicare p libeccio / & difta q̃fto cauo dalla p̃decta
terra / che uedémo doue amazorono echriftiani.i 40. leghe uer
fo leuante:et fta q̃fto cauo 8.gradi fuori della linea equinoctiale
uerfo lauftro:et nauicãdo / hauémo un giorno uifta di molta gẽ
te / chi ftauano alla fpiaggia p uedere la marauiglia delle noftre
naui:et di che come nauicámo / fumo alla uolta loro / & furgé
mo i buon luogo / & fumo cõ li battelli a terra / & trouãmo la gẽ
te effere di migllor cõditione chi la paffata:et ancor chi cifuffe tra
uaglio dimefticarli / tuttauia celifacémo amici / & tractámo cõ
loro. In q̃fto luogo ftémo 5.giorni: & qui trouámo canna fiftola
molto groffa & uerde & fecca i cima delli arbori.Accordámo I
quefto luogho leuate un paio di huomini / per hauer chi noftraffino
la lingua:et uennono tre di loro uolunta per uenire a Porto/
gallo:& per quefto digia canfato di tanto fcriuere / fapra uoftra
Magnificentia / che partimo di quefto porto / fempre nauican
do per libeccio a uifta di terra / di continouo faccendo di molte
fcale / & parlando con infinita gente:et tanto fumo uerfo lau/
ftro / che gia ftauamo fuora del tropico di Capricorno:a donde
el polo del Meridione falzaua fopra lo Orizonte 32.gradi: et
di gia hauamo perduto del tucto lorfa minore / & la maggio/
re ci ftaua molto baffa / & quafi ci fimonftraua alfine dello Ori
zonte / & ci reggiauamo per le Stelle dellaltro polo del Meridio
ne:lequali fono molte / & molto maggiori / & piu lucenti che
le di q̃fto noftro poloset della maggior parte di epfe traffi le lor
figure / & maxime di q̃lle della prima / & maggior magnitudi/
ne / con la dichiaratione de lor circuli / che faceuano itorno alpo
lo del auftro / cõ la dichiaratione de lor diametri & femidiame/
tri / come fi potra uedere nelle mie 4.giornate:corrémo di q̃fta
cofta alpie di 7 40.leghe:et 140.dal cauo decto di fcõ Auguftino

c.ii.

uerſo elponête / &le 600.uerſo elllbecciozet uolendo ricõtare
le coſe che ĩ q̃ſta coſta uidi: & q̃llo che p̃aſſamo / non mibaſterebb
bealtretanti fogli: & in q̃ſta coſta nõ uedêmo coſa di pfituo / ſal
uo.ĩfinĩti arbori di uerzino & di caſſia / & di quelli cõ generano
la myrra / & altre marauiglie della narura / che nõ ſipoſſon rac/
cõtare:et di gia eſſendo ſtati nel uſaggio ben 4o. meſi / & uiſto
che in q̃ſta terra nó trouauamo coſa di minero alcuno / accordã
mo di diſpedirci di epſa /& andarci a cõmettere almare p altra
parte:et facto noſtro cõſiglio / fu deliberato cõ lıſeguiſſe q̃lla na
uigatione che mipareſſe bene: & tucto fu rimeſſo ĩ me elmando
della flocta: et allhora mandai che tucta la gente & flocta ſi pro/
uedeſſi dacqua & di legne p ſei meſi / che tãto giudicorono li uffı/
tiali delle naui ci potauamo nauicare cõ epſe. Facto noſtro pue
dimento di q̃ſta terra / comincıãmo noſtra nauicatione p eluen
to ſcilocchoz& fu adi 14.di Febraio / quando gia elſole ſandaua
cercando allo equinoctio / & tornaua uerſo q̃ſto noſtro emıſpe/
rıõdel ſeptentrione: & tanto nauicãmo p q̃ſto uento / che ci tro/
uãmo tanto alti / chel polo del meridione ciſtaua alto fuora del
noſtro orizonte ben 42. gradi / & piu nõ uedadamo le ſtelle ne
dellorſa minore / ne della maggiore orſa: & di gia ſtauamo di/
ſcoſto del porto di doue partimo ben 400. leghe p ſcilocchozet
queſto fu adi 3.daprile: & ĩ q̃ſto giorno comincio una tormenta
ın mare tãro forzola: che cifece amainare del tucto noſtre uele:
& corrauamo allarbero ſeco con molto uento / che era libeccio
cõ grandiſſimi mari / & laria molto tormentoſa:et tanta era la
tormêta / che tutta la flocta ſtaua con gran rimore: e nocte eron
molto grandi:che nocte renêmo adi ſepte daprile / che fu di 1⁄4.
hore:pch e elſole ſtaua uel fıne di Aries: et ın q̃ſta regione era lo
ĩuerno / come ben puo cõſiderare V. M. et andando ĩq̃ſta tor
menta adi ſepte daprile/ hauêmo uiſta di nuoua terra:dellaquale
cotrémo circha di 20. leghe / & la trouãmo tucta coſta braua: et
nõ uedêmo ĩ epſa porto alcuno / ne gente: credo pche era tãro el
freddo / che neſſuno della flocta ſi poteua rimediare / ne ſoppor
tarlo: di modo ch uiſtoci in tanto pericolo & ĩ tanta tormêta / che
apena potau: mo hauere uiſta luna naue dellaltra / p e gran mari
cõ faceuano / & p la gran ſerrazon del têpo / che accordãmo con
elcapitano maggiore fate ſegnale alla flocta che arriuaſſi / & la
ſciaſſimo la terra: et cene tornaſſimo alcãmino di Portogallo: et
fu molto buon cõſiglio:che certo erche ſe tardauamo quella no
cte / tutti ciperdauamo:pche come arriuàmo a poppa / & la no/

ete & laltro giorno fi circrebbe tanta tormenta / che dubitámo
perderci:et hauémo di fare peregrini & altre cerimonie / come
e/ufanza de marinai p tali tépi:corrémo 4.giorni / & turra via
ciuenauamo apffando alla linea eqnocciale / & in aria & i mari
piu téperati:et piacq a Dio fcamparci di táto pericolo: & noftra
nauicatione era p el uento intra el tramótano & greco; pche no
ftra ítentione era andare a riconofcere la cofta di ethiopia / che
ftauamo difcofto da epfa i 300.leghe p el golfo del mare atlanti
co; & có la gratia di dio a 10.g orni di Maggio fumo í epfa a una
terra uerfo lauftro/ch fidice La ferra liona:doue ftémo i4.giorni
pigliádo noftro rinfrefcaméto: & diqui partimo pigliádo noftra
nauicatione uerfo lifole delli azort/ch diftáno di ǫ̃to luogo della
Serra circa di 740.leghe:et fumo có lifole alfin di Luglio:doue
ftémo altri 16.giorni/pigliádo alcuna recreatione: & partimo di
epfe p lifbona:ch ftauamo piu allo occidéte 300.leghe:& entramo p ǫ̃to porto di Lifbona adí 7.di Septébre del 1402.a buon
faluaméto/Dio ringratiato fia có folo due naui; pche laltra ardémo nella Serra liona:pche nó poteua piu nauicare / che ftémo
in questo uiaggio circa di 16.mefi;& giorni 11.nauigámo fenza ueder la ftella tramótana / o lorfa maggiore & minore/che fi
dicono elcorno:et ci reggémo p le ftelle dello altro polo. Quefto
e/quáto uidi in ǫ̃to uiaggio / o giornata.

¶ Quarto Viaggio.

REstami di dire le cofe p me uifte nel quarto uiaggio / o g'or
nata: & perlo effere gia canfaro / & etiam pche q̃fto quarto
uiaggio nõ fiforni / fecõdo chi lo leuauo el ppofito / p una difgra
tia che ci acchadde nel golfo del mare atlantico: come nel pceffo
foito breuita intẽdera V .M . mingeguero deffere brieue . Parti
mo di q̃fto porto di Lifbona 6. naui di cõferua cõ ppofito di an
dare a fcoprire una ifola uerfo loriente / che fidice Melaccha: del
laquale fi ha nuoue effer molto riccha / & chi e / come elmagazino
di tucte fe naui che uẽgano del mare gangetico & del mare indi
co / come e / Calis camera di tutti enauili che paffano da leuante
a ponẽte / & da ponẽte a leuãte p la uia di Galigut : et q̃fta Me
laccha e / piu allocidẽte chi Caligut / & molto piu alta parte del
mezo di: pche fappiamo chi fta in paraggio di 33. gradi del polo
antartico . Partimo adi 10. di Maggio 1 4 0 3 et fumo diritti alle
ifole del cauo uerde / doue facẽmo noftro caragne / & pigliãmo
forte di rinfrefcamẽto / doue ftẽmo 1 5 giorni: et di qui partimo
a noftro uiaggio / nauicãdo p el uẽto fciloccho: et come elnoftro
Capitano maggiore fuffe huomo pfumptuofo & molto cauezu
to / uolle andare a riconofcere la Serra liona / terra dethiopia au
ftrale / fenza tenere neceffita alcuna / fe nó p farfi uedere / chi era
Capitano di fei naui / cõtro alla uolúta di tucti noi altri Capita
ni: et cofi nauicando / quãdo fumo cõ la decta terra / furon tãte
le turbonate che cidettono / & cõ epfe el tẽpo cõtrario / che ftan
do a uifta di epfa ben 4. giorni / mai nõ cilafciò elmal-tẽpo pi
gliar terra: di modo chi fumo forzati di tornare a noftra nauica
tione uera / & laffare la decta Serra: et nauicãdo di qui alfuduef
che e / uẽto ifra mezo di & libeccio: et quãdo fumo nauicati ben
300. leghe p el mõftro del mare / ftando di gia fuora della linea
equoctionale uerfo lauftro ben 5. grad. ci fidifcoperfe una terra
chi potauamo diftare di epfa 22. leghe: dellaq̃le cimarauigliãmo
et trouãmo chi era una ifola nelmezo del mare / & era molto al
ta cofa / ben marauigliofa della natura: pche nõ era piu che due
leghe di lungo / & una di largo: nellaquale ifola mai nõ fu habi
tato da gẽte alcuna: & fu la mala ifola p tutta la flocta: pche fa
pra V .M . che per el mal cõfiglio & reggimẽto del noftro Capita
no maggiore / perde qui fua naue: pche dette con epfa i uno fco
glio / & laperfe la nocte e di fcõ Lorenzo / che e / adi 10. dagofto / &
fi fu i fondo: & nõ fifaluo di epfa cofa alcuna / fe nõ la gente . Era
naue di 300. tonelli: nellaquale andaua tucta La importãza del
la flocta: & come la flocta tucta trauagliaffe i rimediarla / el Ca

pitano mi mando che io fuſſi con la mia naue alla decta iſola a
cerchare un buon ſurgidero / doue poteſſin ſurgere tutte le nauis
& come elmio battello ſtipato con 9.mia marinai fuſſi in ſei ui
gio & aiuto da ligare le naui / nō uolle chi lo leuaſſi / & chi mi fuſſi
ſine epſo:dicēdomi chi niileuerebbono alliſola:partimi della flo
cta come minando p liſola ſenza battello , & cō.meno la.mera
de mia marinai / & fui alla decta iſola / che diſtauo circha di 4.
leghe:nellaquale trouai un boniſſimo porto / doue ben ſicura /
mente poteuan ſurgere tucte le naui:doue aſpectai el mio Capi
tano & la flocta ben 8.giorni / & mai nō uennono:di modo cō
ſtauamo molto mal cōtenti , & le genti che meran reſtate nella
naue / ſtauano cō tāta paura / cō nō-li poteuo cōſolare:et ſtando
coſi /loctauo giōno uedēmo uentre una naue pel mare; & di pau
ra che non cipoteſſi uedere / ci leuāmo con noſtre naui / & fumo
ad'epſa / penſando cō mitraeua elmio battello & gente:et come
pareggiamo con epſa / dipoi di ſaltuata. ci dixe come la capita
na ſeta ita i fondo / & come la gente ſera ſaluata / & che elmio
battello & gente reſtaua con la flocta / laquale ſera ita per quel
mare auanti / che ci fu tāta graue tormenta / qual puo penſare
V.M.p trouarci 1000.leghe diſcoſto da Liſbona / & i g..lſo / &
con pocha gente:tuttauia facēmo roſtro alla fortuna , & anda,
mo tuttauia innanzi: tornāmo alla iſola / & fornimoci dacqua
& di legne con elbattello della mia conſerua:laquale iſola fro,
uāmo diſabitata / & teneua molte acque uiue & dolci / infini,
tiſſimi arbori / piena di tāti uccelli marini & terreſtri / che eron
ſenza numero:et eron tanto ſemplici / che ſi laſciauon piglia,
re con mano:et ranti nepigliāmo / che carichāmo un battello
di epſi animali: neſſuno non uedēmo / ſaluo Topi molto gran
di / & Ramarri con due code / & alchuna Serpe:et facta noſtra
prouiſione / ci dipartimo per eluento infra mezo di & libeccio
perche tenauamo un reggimento del Re / che ci mandaua / che
qualunche delle naui che ſiperdeſſe della flocta / o del ſuo Capi,
tano / fuſſi a tenere nella terra / che el uiaggio paſſato. Diſco,
primo in un porto / che li ponēmo nome la badia di tucti e ſan
cti:et piacque a Dio di darci tāto buon tempo / che in 17.giot
ni fumo a tenere terra in epſo / che diſtaua da liſola ben 300.
leghe:doue non trouāmo ne ilnoſtro Capitano / ne neſſuna al
tra naue della flocta:nelqual porto aſpectāmo ben dua meſi &
4.giorni:& uiſto che non ueniua ricapito alcuno / acchordēmo

la conserua / & io correr la costa:et nauigāmo piu inanzi 260.le
ghe / tráo chi giugnèmo i un porto:doue accordamo faf una for
teza / & la facèmo:& lasciámo i epsa 24.huomini christiani,che
ci haueua la mia cōserua / che haueua ricolti della naue capitana
che sera pduta:nelqual porto stēmo ben 4.mesi i fare la forteza
& carlcar nostre naul druerzino:pche nō potauamo andare piu
inanzi / a causa che non tenauamo genti / & mimancaua molti
apparecchi. Facto tucto q̄sto / accordámo di tornarcene a Portogallo / che cistaua p lluentro infra gréco & tramótano:& lassa-
mo li 24.huomini.che restoron nella forteza cō mantenimēto p
sei mesi / & iz.bòbarde / & molte altre armi / & pacificāmo tucta la gente di terra:dellaquale nōsse facto mentione i q̄sto ulag-
gio:nō pche nō uedessimo & pratificassimo cō infinita gente di
epsa:pche fumo i terra drento ben 30.huomini 40.leghe:doue
uidi tâte cose / chi le laselo di dire / riserbandole alle mie 4.gior
nate.Questa terra sta fuora della linea eqnoctiale alla parte del
lo austro 18.gradi / & fuora del mantenimento di Lisbona 37.
gradi / piu allocidēre secōdo ch mostrano enostri strumenti.Et
facto tucto q̄sto / ci dispedimo de christiani & della terra:et cominciámo nostra nauicatone al nornodeste / che e uentó infra
tramótana & greco / cō proposito dandare a dirittura cō nostra
nauicatione a questa citra di Lisbona:et in 77.giorni dipol tân
ti trauagli & pericoli entrámo i questo porto adi 18.di Giugno
1404.Dio laudato:doue fumo molto ben riceuuti / & fuora do
gni credere:pche tucta la citra cifaceua perduti:pche laltre naul
della flocta tucte seron perdute p la superbia & pazia del nostro
Capitano / che cōsi pagha Dio la superbia:et alpresente mitruo
tio qui in Lisbona / & non so quello uorra el R e fare di me / che
molto desidero riposarmi.El presente aportatore che e Benue-
nuro di Domenico Benuenuti / dira a V.M.di mio essere/ & di
alcune cose sisono lasciate di dire per prolixita:perche le ha ui-
ste & sentire / Dio sia ò c It   . Io sono ito stringēdo la let
tera quáto ho potuto:& hessi lasciato adire molte cose naturali /
acausa di scusare plixirā.V.M.miperdoni:laquale supplico ch
mirenga nel numero de sua seruidori:& uiraccomando ser An
tonio Vespucci mio fratello / & tucta la casa mia.Resto rogando
Dio/che ui accresca edi della uita:& ch salzi lo stato di cotesta ex
celsa Rep.& lhonore di V.M.& q̄ : Dara in Lisbona adi 4.di
Septembre 1604.

Seruitore Amerigo Vespucci in Lisbona.

Letter of Amerigo Vespucci

upon the isles newly
found in his
four Voyages.

[Letter of Amerigo Vespucci to Pier Soderini, Gonfalonier of the Republic of Florence.]

MAGNIFICENT Lord. After humble reverence and due commendations, etc. It may be that your Magnificence will be surprised by my rashness and the affront to your wisdom,[1] in that I should so absurdly bestir myself to write to your Magnificence the present so-prolix letter: knowing [as I do] that your Magnificence is continually employed in high councils and affairs concerning the good government of this sublime Republic. And will hold me not only presumptuous, but also idly-meddlesome in setting myself to write things, neither suitable to your station, nor entertaining, and written in barbarous style, and outside of every canon of literature:[2] but the confidence which I have in your virtues and in the truth of my writing, which are things [that] are not found written neither by the ancients nor by modern writers, as your Magnificence will in the sequel perceive, makes me bold.[3] The chief cause which moved [me] to write to you, was by the request of the present bearer, who is named Benvenuto Benvenuti our Florentine [fellow citizen], very much, as it is proven, your Magnificence's

---

[1] Literally "dared your wisdom" in a barbarous phrase which is meant for "your wisdom thus affronted."   [2] *Humanità.*

[3] Here *usato* is certainly the Spanish *osado*, or the Portuguese *ousado.*

servant, and my very good friend: who happening to be here
in this city of Lisbon, begged that I should make communication
to your Magnificence of the things seen by me in divers regions
of the world, by virtue of four voyages which I have made in
discovery of new lands: two by order of the King of Castile,[1]
King Don Ferrando VI., across the great gulph of the Ocean-sea
towards the west: and the other two by command of the puissant
King Don Manuel King of Portugal, towards the south: Telling
me that your Magnificence would take pleasure thereof, and that
herein he hoped to do you service: wherefore I set me to do it:
because I am assured that your Magnificence holds me in the
number of your servants, remembering that in the time of our
youth I was your friend, and now [*am your*] servant: and
[*remembering our*] going to hear the rudiments of grammar under
the fair example and instruction of the venerable monk friar of
Saint Mark Fra Giorgio Antonio Vespucci: whose counsels and
teaching would to God that I had followed: for as saith Petrarch,
I should be another man than what I am.   Howbeit soever,[2] I
grieve not: because I have ever taken delight in worthy matters:
and although these trifles of mine may not be suitable to your
virtues, I will say to you as said Pliny to Mæcenas, you were
sometime wont to take pleasure in my prattlings: even though
your Magnificence be continually busied in public affairs, you
will take some hour of relaxation to consume a little time in
laughable or amusing things: and as fennel is customarily given
atop of delicious viands to fit them for better digestion, so may
you, for a relief from your so heavy occupations, order this letter
of mine to be read: so that they[3] may withdraw you somewhat
from the continual anxiety and assiduous reflection upon public
affairs: and if I shall be prolix, I crave pardon,[4] my Magnificent
Lord.   Your Magnificence shall know that the motive of my
coming into this realm of Spain was to traffic in merchandise:

---

[1] This lack of precision with regard to Ferdinand's title may be compared
with similar carelessness on the early maps which refer to America.
[2] *Quomodo cunque sit.* Vespucci affected a little Latin. [3] "They" for "it.'
[4] *Veniam peto.*

and that I pursued this intent about four years : during which I saw and knew the inconstant shiftings of Fortune : and how she kept changing those frail and transitory benefits : and how at one time she holds man on the summit of the wheel, and at another time drives him back from her, and despoils him of what may be called his borrowed riches : so that, knowing the continuous toil which man undergoes to win them, submitting himself to so many discomforts and risks, I resolved to abandon trade, and to fix my aim upon something more praiseworthy and stable : whence it was that I made preparation for going to see part[1] of the world and its wonders : and herefor the time and place presented themselves most opportunely to me : which was that the King Don Ferrando of Castile being about to despatch four ships to discover new lands towards the west, I was chosen by his Highness to go in that fleet to aid in making discovery : and we set out from the port of Cadiz on the 10[2] day of May 1497, and took our route through the 'great gulph of the Ocean-sea : in which voyage we were 18 months [*engaged*] : and discovered much continental land and innumerable islands, and great part of them inhabited : of which there is no mention made by the ancient writers : I believe, because they had no knowledge thereof : for, if I remember well, I have read in some one [*of those writers*] that he considered that this Ocean-sea was an unpeopled sea : and of this opinion was Dante our poet in the xxvi. chapter of the Inferno, where he feigns the death of Ulysses : in which voyage I beheld things of great wondrousness, as your Magnificence shall understand. As I said above, we left the port of Cadiz four consort ships :[3] and began our voyage in a direct course to the Fortunate Isles, which are called to-day *la gran Canaria*, which are situated in the Ocean-sea at the extremity of the inhabited west, [*and*] set in the third climate : over which the North Pole has an elevation

---

[1] *Parte* is used by Vespucci as plural as well as singular, and consequently this means properly "parts" or "various parts," as it appears in the Latin version.

[2] The Latin version at the end of the *Cosmographiæ Introductio* has "20" instead of "10."

[3] *Navi di conserva.*

of 27 and a half degrees[1] beyond their horizon:[2] and they are 280 leagues distant from this city of Lisbon, by the wind between *mezzo di* and *libeccio:*[3] where we remained eight days, taking in provision of water, and wood, and other necessary things : and from here, having said our prayers, we weighed anchor, and gave the sails to the wind, beginning our course to westward, taking one quarter by south-west :[4] and so we sailed on till at the end of 37[5] days we reached a land which we deemed to be a continent: which is distant westwardly from the isles of Canary about a thousand leagues beyond the inhabited region[6] within the torrid zone : for we found the North Pole at an elevation of 16 degrees above its horizon,[7] and [*it was*] according to the shewing of our instruments, 75 degrees to the west of the isles of Canary: whereat we anchored with our ships a league and a half from land : and we put out our boats freighted with men and arms: we made towards the land, and before we reached it, had sight of a great number of people who were going along the shore: by which we were much rejoiced : and we observed that they were a naked race : they shewed themselves to stand in fear of us : I believe [*it was*] because they saw us clothed and of other appearance [*than their own*] : they all withdrew to a hill, and for whatsoever signals we made to them of peace and of friendliness, they would not come to parley with us : so that, as the night was now coming on, and as the ships were anchored in a dangerous place, being on a rough and shelterless coast, we decided to remove from there the next day, and to go in search of some harbour or bay, where we might place our ships in safety : and we sailed with the maestrale wind,[8] thus running along the coast with the

[1] The Latin has "27¾."

[2] That is, *which are situate at 27½ degrees north latitude.*

[3] South-south-west. It is to be remarked that Vespucci always uses the word *wind* to signify the course in which it blows, not the quarter from which it rises.

[4] West and a quarter by south-west.   [5] Latin has 27.

[6] This phrase is merely equivalent to a repetition of *from the Canaries,* these islands having been already designated *the extreme western limit of inhabited land.*

[7] That is, 16 degrees north latitude. If his computations be correct, we might say that the landfall was on the northern coast of Honduras.

[8] North-west. Latin has *vento secundum collem.*

land ever in sight, continually in our course observing people along the shore: till after having navigated for two days, we found a place sufficiently secure for the ships, and anchored half a league from land, on which we saw a very great number of people : and this same day we put to land with the boats, and sprang on shore full 40 men in good trim : and still the land's people appeared shy of converse with us, and we were unable to encourage them so much as to make them come to speak with us : and this day we laboured so greatly in giving them of our wares, such as rattles and mirrors, beads,[1] balls, and other trifles, that some of them took confidence and came to discourse with us : and after having made good friends with them, the night coming on, we took our leave of them and returned to the ships : and the next day when the dawn appeared we saw that there were infinite numbers of people upon the beach, and they had their women and children with them : we went ashore, and found that they were all laden with their worldly goods[2] which are suchlike as, in its [*proper*] place, shall be related : and before we reached the land, many of them jumped into the sea and came swimming to receive us at a bowshot's length [*from the shore*], for they are very great swimmers, with as much confidence as if they had for a long time been acquainted with us : and we were pleased with this their confidence. For so much as we learned of their manner of life and customs, it was that they go entirely naked, as well the men as the women, without covering any shameful part, not otherwise than as they issued from their mother's womb. They are of medium stature, very well proportioned : their flesh is of a colour that verges into red like a lion's mane : and I believe that if they went clothed, they would be as white as we : they have not any hair upon the body, except the hair of the head which is long and black, and especially in the women, whom it renders handsome :

---

[1] The word is *cente*, supposed to be a misprint for *conte*, an Italianised form of the Spanish *cuentas*. *Spalline* (palline, diminutive of palle) is a word not given in the dictionaries. The Latin translator seems to have read the original as *certe cristalline.*

[2] *Mantenimenti.* The word "all" (*tucte*) is feminine, and probably refers only to the women.

in aspect they are not very good-looking, because they have broad faces, so that they would seem Tartar-like : they let no hair grow on their eyebrows, nor on their eyelids nor elsewhere, except the hair of the head : for they hold hairiness to be a filthy thing : they are very light-footed in walking and in running, as well the men as the women : so that a woman recks nothing of running a league or two, as many times we saw them do : and herein they have à very great advantage over us Christians : they swim [*with an expertness*] beyond all belief, and the women better than the men : for we have many times found and seen them swimming two leagues out at sea without any thing to rest upon.   Their arms are bows and arrows very well made, save that they have no iron nor any other kind of hard metal [*wherewith to tip the arrows*] : and instead of iron they put animals' or fishes' teeth, or a spike of tough wood, with the point hardened by fire : they are sure marksmen, for they hit whatever they aim at : and in some places the women use these bows : they have other weapons, such as fire-hardened spears, and also clubs with knobs, beautifully carved. Warfare is used amongst them, [which they carry on] against people not of their own language, very cruelly, without granting life to any one, except [*to reserve him*] for greater suffering. When they go to war, they take their women with them not that these may fight, but because they carry behind them their worldly goods : for a woman carries on her back for thirty or forty leagues a load which no man could bear : as we have many times seen them do.   They are not accustomed to have any Captain, nor do they go in any ordered array, for every one is lord of himself : and the cause of their wars is not for lust of dominion, nor of extending their frontiers, nor for inordinate covetousness, but for some ancient enmity which in by-gone times arose[1] amongst them : and when asked why they made war, they knew not any other reason to give us than that they did so to avenge the death of their ancestors, or of their parents : these people have neither King, nor Lord, nor do they yield obedience to any one, for they live in their own liberty : and how

---

[1] The expression in the original is *e suta*, an error for *è surta*.

they be stirred up to go to war is [*this*] that when the enemies
have slain or captured any of them, his oldest kinsman rises up
and goes about the highways haranguing them to go with him
and avenge the death of such his kinsman : and so are they
stirred up by fellow-feeling : they have no judicial system, nor do
they punish the ill-doer : nor does the father, nor the mother
chastise the children : and marvellously [*seldom*] or never did we
see any dispute among them : in their conversation they appear
simple, and [*yet*] are very cunning and acute in that which
concerns them :[1] they speak little and in a low tone : they use
the same articulations as we, since they form their utterances
either with the palate, or with the teeth, or on the lips :[2] except
that they give different names to things. Many are the varieties
of tongues : for in every 100 leagues we found a change of
language, so that they are not understandable each to the other.
The manner of their living is very barbarous, for they eat at no
certain hours, and as oftentimes as they will : and it does not
matter much to them that the will may come rather at midnight
than by day, for they eat at all hours :[3] and their repast is [made]
upon the ground without a table-cloth or any other cover, for
they have their meats either in earthen basins which they make
therefor, or in the halves of pumpkins : they sleep in certain
very large nettings made of cotton,[4] suspended in the air : and
although this their [*fashion of*] sleeping may seem uncomfortable,
I say that it is sweet to sleep in those [*nettings*]: and we slept
better in them than in quilts. They are a people of neat exterior,
and clean of body, because of so continually washing themselves as they do : when, saving your reverence, they evacuate the
stomach they do their utmost not to be observed : and as much
as in this they are cleanly and bashful, so much the more are

---

[1] *Che loro cuple.* The Spanish word *cumplir*, with the sense of being
important or suitable.

[2] He means that they have no sounds in their language unknown to
European organs of speech, all being either palatals or dentals or labials.

[3] The words from "and it does not matter" down to "at all hours" omitted
in the Latin.

Bambacia.

they filthy and shameless in making water : since, while standing speaking to us, without turning round or shewing any shame, they let go their nastiness, for in this they have no shame : there is no custom of marriages amongst them : each man takes as many women as he lists : and when he desires to repudiate them, he repudiates them without any imputation of wrong-doing to him, or of disgrace to the woman : for in this the woman has as much liberty as the man : they are not very jealous and are immoderately libidinous, and the women much more so than the men, so that for decency I omit to tell you the artifice they practice to gratify[1] their inordinate lust : they are very prolific women, and do not shirk any work during their pregnancies : and their travails in childbed are so light that, a single day after parturition, they go abroad everywhere, and especially to wash themselves in the rivers, and are [*then*] as sound as fishes : they are so void of affection and cruel, that if they be angry with their husbands they immediately adopt an artificial method by which the embryo is destroyed in the womb, and procure abortion, and they slay an infinite number of creatures by that means : they are women of elegant persons very well proportioned, so that in their bodies there appears no ill-shapen part or limb : and although they go entirely naked, they are fleshy women, and, of their sexual organ, that portion which he who has never seen it may imagine, is not visible, for they conceal with their thighs everything except that part for which nature did not provide, which is, speaking modestly, the pectignone.[2]   In fine, they have no shame of their shameful parts, any more than we have in displaying the nose and the mouth : it is marvellously [*rare*] that you shall see a woman's paps hang low, or her belly fallen in by too much childbearing, or other wrinkles, for they all appear as though they had never brought forth children : they shewed themselves very desirous of having connexion with us Christians.   Amongst those people we did not learn that they had any law, nor can they be called Moors nor Jews, and [*they are*] worse than pagans : because we never

---

[1] In the original, *contar* for *contentare*.   [2] Bigger bosom, *mons Veneris.*

saw them offer any sacrifice: nor even had they a house of prayer: their manner of living I judge to be Epicurean: their dwellings are in common: and their houses [*are*] made in the style of huts,[1] but strongly made, and constructed with very large trees, and covered over with palm-leaves, secure against storms and winds: and in some places [*they are*] of so great breadth and length, that in one single house we found there were 600 souls: and we saw a village of only thirtéen[2] houses where there were four thousand[3] souls: every eight or ten years[4] they change their place of habitation: and when asked why they did so: [*they said it was*] because of the soil[5] which, from its filthiness, was already unhealthy and corrupted, and that it bred aches in their bodies, which seemed to us a good reason: their riches consist of birds' plumes of many colours, or of rosaries[6] which they make from fishbones, or of white or green stones which they put in their cheeks and in their lips and ears, and of many other things which we in no wise value: they use no trade, they neither buy nor sell. In fine, they live and are contented with that which nature gives them. The wealth that we enjoy in this our Europe and elsewhere, such as gold, jewels, pearls, and other riches, they hold as nothing: and although they have them in their own lands, they do not labour to obtain them, nor do they value them. They are liberal in giving, for it is rarely they deny you anything: and on the other hand, free in asking, when they shew themselves your friends: the greatest sign of friendship which they shew you is that they give you their wives and their daughters, and a father or a mother deems himself [*or herself*] highly honored, when they bring you a daughter, even though she be a young virgin, if you sleep with her: and hereunto they use every expression of friendship. When they die,

---

[1] Waldseemüller has "bell-towers," having misread *campane* for *capanne*, huts or cabins.

[2] Latin has *eight*.   [3] Latin, *ten thousand*.

[4] Latin has *seven* for *ten*.

[5] *Suolo*, the ground or flooring, which Waldseemüller absurdly misread *sole*, the sun. Varnhagen, no less strangely, translates it "the atmosphere."

[6] *Paternostrini*, rosaries or chaplets of beads used by illiterate Catholics.

they use divers manners of obsequies, and some they bury with
water and victuals at their heads : thinking that they shall have
[*whereof*] to eat : they have not nor do they use ceremonies of
torches [1] nor of lamentation. In some other places they use the
most barbarous and inhuman burial,[2] which is that when a
suffering or infirm [*person*] is as it were at the last pass of death,
his kinsmen carry him into a large forest, and attach one of those
nets of theirs, in which they sleep, to two trees, and then put him
in it, and dance around him for a whole day : and when the
night comes on they place at his bolster, water with other
victuals, so that he may be able to subsist for four or six days :
and then they leave him alone and return to the village : and if
the sick man helps himself, and eats, and drinks, and survives,
he returns to the village, and his [*friends*] receive him with
ceremony : but few are they who escape : without receiving any
further visit they die, and that is their sepulture : and they have
many other customs which for prolixity are not related. They
use in their sicknesses various forms of medicines,[3] so different
from ours that we marvelled how any one escaped : for many
times I saw that with a man sick of fever, when it heightened
upon him, they bathed him from head to foot with a large
quantity of cold water : then they lit a great fire around him,
making him turn and turn again every two hours, until they
tired him and left him to sleep, and many were [*thus*] cured :
with this they make much use of dieting, for they remain three
days without eating, and also of blood-letting, but not from the
arm, only from the thighs and the loins and the calf of the leg :
also they provoke vomiting with their herbs which are put into
the mouth : and they use many other remedies which it would be
long to relate : they are much vitiated in the phlegm and in the
blood because of their food which consists chiefly of roots of
herbs, and fruits and fish : they have no seed of wheat nor other
grain : and for their ordinary use and feeding, they have a root

---

[1] *Lumi*, lights, tapers, candles, as in Catholic ceremonies.
[2] *Interramento* is the word, but he means only " funeral rite."
[3] That is, " medical treatment."

of a tree, from which they make flour, tolerably good, and they
call it Iuca, and [*there are*] others who call it Cazabi, and others
Ignami:[1] they eat little flesh except human flesh: for your
Magnificence must know that herein they are so inhuman that
they outdo every custom [*even*] of beasts: for they eat all their
enemies whom they kill or capture, as well females as males, with
so much savagery, that [*merely*] to relate it appears a horrible
thing: how much more so to see it, as, infinite times and in
many places, it was my hap to see it: and they wondered to
hear us say that we did not eat our enemies: and this your
Magnificence may take for certain, that their other barbarous
customs are such that expression is too weak for the reality: and
as in these four voyages I have seen so many things diverse from
our customs, I prepared to write a common-place-book [2] which I
name LE QUATTRO GIORNATE: in which I have set down the
greater part of the things which I saw, sufficiently in detail, so
far as my feeble wit has allowed me: which I have not yet
published, because I have so ill a taste for my own things that I
do not relish those which I have written, notwithstanding that
many encourage me to publish it: therein everything will be seen
in detail: so that I shall not enlarge further in this chapter: as
in the course of the letter we shall come to many other things
which are particular: let this suffice for the general. At this
beginning, we saw nothing in the land of much profit, except
some show of gold: I believe the cause of it was that we did not
know the language: but in so far as concerns the situation and
condition of the land, it could not be better: we decided to leave
that place, and to go further on, continuously coasting the shore:
upon which we made frequent descents, and held converse with
a great number of people: and after some days we went into a
harbour where we underwent very great danger: and it pleased
the Holy Ghost to save us: and it was in this wise. We
landed in a harbour, where we found a village built like Venice
upon the water: there were about 44 large dwellings in the form

---

[1] *Ignami* is the Portuguese *inhame*, African *yam*.

[2] *Zibaldone*, miscellany, *omnium-gatherum*.

of huts erected upon very thick piles,[1] and they had their doors or entrances in the style of drawbridges : and from each house one could pass through all, by means of the drawbridges which stretched from house to house : and when the people thereof had seen us, they appeared to be afraid of us, and immediately drew up all the bridges : and while we were looking at this strange action, we saw coming across the sea about 22 canoes, which are a kind of boats of theirs, constructed from a single tree : which came towards our boats, as if they had been surprised by our appearance and clothes, and kept wide of us: and thus remaining, we made signals to them that they should approach us, encouraging them with every token of friendliness : and seeing that they did not come, we went to them, and they did not stay for us, but made to the land, and, by signs, told us to wait, and that they would soon return : and they went to a hill in the back-ground,[2] and did not delay long : when they returned, they led with them 16 of their girls, and entered with these into their canoes, and came to the boats : and in each boat they put 4 of the girls. How greatly we marvelled at this behaviour your Magnificence can imagine, and they placed themselves with their canoes among our boats, coming to speak with us: insomuch that we deemed it a mark of friendliness: and while thus engaged, we beheld a great number of people advance swimming towards us across the sea, who came from the houses: and as if they were approaching us without any apprehension: just then there appeared at the doors of the houses certain old women, uttering very loud cries and tearing their hair to exhibit grief: whereby they made us suspicious, and we each betook ourselves to arms : and instantly the girls whom we had in the boats, threw themselves into the sea, and the men of the canoes drew away from us, and began with their bows to shoot arrows at us : and those who were swimming each carried a lance held, as covertly as they could, beneath the water: so that, recognizing

[1] Waldseemüller has 20 instead of 44, and repeats his error of "bell-towers" for "huts."

[2] Varnhagen says "went straight to land," evidently mistaking *drieto* (*dietro*) for *dricto*, and ignoring *monte*.

the treachery, we engaged with them, not merely to defend ourselves, but to attack them vigorously, and we overturned with our
boats many of their skiffs or canoes, for so they call them, we
made a slaughter [*of them*], and they all flung themselves into the
water to swim, leaving their canoes abandoned, with considerable
loss on their side, they went swimming away to the shore : there
were killed of them about 15 or 20, and many were left wounded :
of ours 5 were wounded, and all, by the grace of God, escaped
[*death*]: we captured two of the girls and two men: and we
proceeded to their houses, and entered therein, and in them all
we found nothing but two old women and a sick man: we
took away from them many things, but of small value : and we
would not burn their houses, because it seemed to us [*as though
that would be*] a burden upon our conscience: and we returned to
our boats with five prisoners : and betook ourselves to the ships,
and put a pair of irons on the feet of each of the captives, except
the girls: and when the night came on, the two girls and
one of the men escaped in the most subtle manner possible: and
next day we decided to quit that harbour and go further onwards:
we proceeded continuously skirting the coast, [*until*] we had
sight of another tribe distant perhaps some 80 leagues from the
former tribe : and we found them very different in speech and
customs: we resolved to cast anchor, and went ashore with the
boats, and we saw on the beach a great number of people
amounting probably to 4000 souls: and when we had reached the
shore, they did not stay for us, and betook themselves to flight
through the forests, abandoning their things: we jumped on land,
and took a pathway that led to the forest : and at the distance of
a bow-shot we found their tents, where they had made very large
fires, and two [*of them*] were cooking their victuals, and roasting
several animals, and fish of many kinds : where we saw that they
were roasting a certain animal which seemed to be a serpent,
save that it had no wings,[1] and was in its appearance so foul

---

[1] *Alia*—wings or fins. Vespucci must have been thinking of the fabulous
dragon.

that we marvelled much at its loathsomeness : Thus went we
on through their houses, or rather tents, and found many of those
serpents alive, and they were tied by the feet and had a cord
around their snouts, so that they could not open their mouths, as
is done [*in Europe*] with mastiff-dogs so that they may not bite :
they were of such savage aspect that none of us dared to take one
away, thinking that they were poisonous : they are of the bigness
of a kid, and in length an ell and a half :[1] their feet are long and
thick, and armed with big claws : they have a hard skin, and are
of various colours : they have the muzzle and aspect of a serpent :
and from their snouts there rises a crest like a saw which extends
along the middle of the back as far as the tip of the tail : in fine
we deemed them to be serpents and venomous, and [*yet*] they
were used as food : we found that [*those people*] made bread out of
little fishes which they took from the sea, first boiling them, [*then*]
pounding them, and making thereof a paste, or bread, and they
baked them on the glowing embers : thus did they eat them : we
tried it, and found that it was good : they had so many other kinds
of eatables, and especially of fruits and roots, that it would be a
large matter to describe them in detail : and seeing that the
people did not return, we decided not to touch nor take away
anything of theirs, so as better to reassure them : and we left in
the tents for them many of our things, placed where they should
see them, and returned by night to our ships : and the next day,
when it was light, we saw on the beach an infinite number of
people : and we landed : and although they appeared timorous
towards us, they took courage nevertheless to hold converse with
us, giving us whatever we asked of them : and shewing themselves
very friendly towards us, they told us that those were their
dwellings, and that they had come hither for the purpose of
fishing : and they begged that we would visit their dwellings and
villages, because they desired to receive us as friends : and they
engaged in such friendship because of the two captured men
whom we had with us, as these were their enemies : insomuch

---

[1] *Braccio uno e mezo.* This animal was the iguana.

that, in view of such importunity on their part, holding a council, we determined that 28 of us Christians in good array should go with them, and in the firm resolve to die if it should be necessary: and after we had been here some three days, we went with them inland : and at three leagues from the coast we came to a village of many people and few houses, for there were no more than nine [*of these*]: where we were received with such and so many barbarous ceremonies that the pen suffices not to write them down : for there were dances, and songs, and lamentations mingled with rejoicing, and great quantities of food : and here we remained the night : where they offered us their women, so that we were unable to withstand them : and after having been here that night and half the next day, so great was the number of people who came wondering to behold us that they were beyond counting : and the most aged begged us to go with them to other villages which were further inland, making display of doing us the greatest honour : wherefore we decided to go : and it would be impossible to tell you how much honour they did us: and we went to several villages, so that we were nine days journeying, so that our Christians[1] who had remained with the ships were already apprehensive concerning us : and when we were about 18 leagues in the interior of the land, we resolved to return to the ships : and on our way back, such was the number of people, as well men as women, that came with us as far as the sea, that it was a wondrous thing : and if any of us became weary of the march, they carried us in their nets very refreshingly : and in crossing the rivers, which are many and very large, they passed us over by skilful means so securely that we ran no danger whatever, and many of them came laden with the things which they had given us, which consisted of their sleeping-nets, and very rich feathers, many bows and arrows, innumerable popinjays[2] of divers colours : and others brought with them loads of their household goods, and of animals : but a greater marvel will I tell you, that, when we had to cross a river, he deemed himself lucky who was able to carry us on his back : and when we reached the

[1] *I.e.*, comrades.   [2] *Pappagalli*, perroquets.

sea, our boats having arrived, we entered into them : and so great
was the struggle which they made to get into our boats, and to
come to see our ships, that we marvelled [*thereat*] : and in our
boats we took as many of them as we could, and made our way
to the ships, and so many [*others*] came swimming that we found
ourselves embarrassed in seeing so many people in the ships, for
there were over a thousand persons all naked and unarmed : they
were amazed by our [*nautical*] gear and contrivances, and the
size of the ships : and with them there occurred to us a very
laughable affair, which was that we decided to fire off some of our
great guns,[1] and when the explosion took place, most of them
through fear cast themselves [*into the sea*] to swim, not otherwise
than frogs on the margins of a pond, when they see something
that frightens them, will jump into the water, just so did those
people : and those who remained in the ships were so terrified
that we regretted our action : however we reassured them by
telling them that with those arms we slew our enemies : and
when they had amused themselves in the ships the whole day, we
told them to go away because we desired to depart that night,
and so separating from us with much friendship and love, they
went away to land.   Amongst that people and in their land, I
knew and beheld so many of their customs and ways of living,
that I do not care to enlarge upon them : for Your Magnificence
must know that in each of my voyages I have noted the most
wonderful things, and I have indited it all in a volume after the
manner of a geography : and I intitle it LE QUATTRO GIORNATE :
in which work the things are comprised in detail, and as yet there
is no copy of it given out, as it is necessary for me to revise it.[2]
This land is very populous, and full of inhabitants, and of
numberless rivers, [*and*] animals : few [*of which*] resemble ours,
excepting lions, panthers, stags, pigs, goats, and deer :[3] and even
these have some dissimilarities of form : they have no horses nor

---

[1] *Artiglierie.*   [2] *Conferirla.*

[3] In the text the colon follows " few," which alters the sense considerably,
and makes the statement run thus, " Numberless rivers and few animals : they
resemble ours," &c.; but the real intention is evidently better conveyed by
adding the words in brackets, and displacing the colon in question.

mules, nor, saving your reverence, asses nor dogs, nor any kind
of sheep or oxen : but so numerous are the other animals which
they have—and all are savage, and of none do they make use for
their service—that they could not be counted. What shall we
say of their different birds ? which are so numerous, and of so
many kinds, and of such various-coloured plumages, that it is a
marvel to behold them. The land is very pleasant and fruitful,
full of immense woods and forests : and it is always green, for
the foliage never drops off. The fruits are so many that they are
numberless and entirely different from ours. This land is within
the torrid zone, close to or just under the parallel which marks
the Tropic of Cancer : where the pole of the horizon has an
elevation of 23 degrees, at the extremity of the second climate.[1]
Many tribes came to see us, and wondered at our faces and our
whiteness : and they asked us whence we came : and we gave
them to understand that we had come from heaven, and that we
were going to see the world, and they believed it. In this land
we placed baptismal fonts, and an infinite [*number of*] people
were baptized, and they called us in their language Carabi, which
means men of great wisdom. We took our departure from that
port : and the province is called Lariab : and we navigated along
the coast, always in sight of land, until we had run 870 leagues of
it, still going in the direction of the maestrale [*north-west*] making
in our course many halts, and holding intercourse with many
peoples : and in several places we obtained gold by barter but not
much in quantity, for we had done enough in discovering the
land and learning that they had gold. We had now been thirteen
months on the voyage : and the vessels and the tackling were
already much damaged, and the men worn out by fatigue : we
decided by general council to haul our ships on land and examine
them for the purpose of stanching leaks,[2] as they made much
water, and of caulking and tarring them afresh, and [*then*] returning towards Spain : and when we came to this determination,
we were close to a harbour the best in the world : into which

[1] That is, 23 degrees north latitude ; possibly referring to the coast near
Tampico (Mexico).　　　　[2] *Stancharle* (? *stagnarle*).

we entered with our vessels: where we found an immense number of people: who received us with much friendliness: and on the shore we made a bastion[1] with our boats and with barrels and casks, and our artillery, which commanded every point:[2] and our ships having been unloaded and lightened,[3] we drew them upon land, and repaired them in everything that was needful: and the land's people gave us very great assistance: and continually furnished us with their victuals: so that in this port we tasted little of our own, which suited our game well:[4] for the stock of provisions which we had for our return-passage was little and of sorry kind: where [*i.e., there*] we remained 37 days: and went many times to their villages, where they paid us the greatest honour: and [*now*] desiring to depart upon our voyage, they made complaint to us how at certain times of the year there came from over the sea to this their land, a race of people very cruel, and enemies of theirs: and by means of treachery or of violence slew many of them, and ate them: and some they made captives, and carried them away to their houses, or country: and how they could scarcely contrive to defend themselves from them, making signs to us that [*those*] were an island-people and lived out in the sea about a hundred leagues away: and so piteously did they tell us this that we believed them: and we promised to avenge them of so much wrong: and they remained overjoyed herewith: and many of them offered to come along with us, but we did not wish to take them for many reasons, save that we took seven of them, on condition that they should come [*i.e., return home*] afterwards in canoes because we did not desire to be obliged to take them back to their country: and they were contented: and so we departed from those people, leaving them very friendly towards us: and having repaired our ships, and

---

[1] Fort or barricade. The Latin misreads it "a new boat."

[2] *Che giocavano per tucto.*

[3] *Allogiate* is slurred over by the Latin and Varnhagen. I take it to be intended for *allegiate*, and this to be an old form, corresponding to the French *alléger*, of *allegerite* or *alleviate:* lightened, eased.

[4] *Che ci feciono buon giuoco.*

sailing for seven days out to sea between north-east and east: and at the end of the seven days we came upon the islands, which were many, some [*of them*] inhabited, and others deserted: and we anchored at one of them : where we saw a numerous people who called it Iti : and having manned our boats with strong crews, and [*taken*] three guns in each, we made for land : where we found [*assembled*] about 400 men, and many women, and all naked like the former [*peoples*]. They were of good bodily presence, and seemed right warlike men : for they were armed with their weapons, which are bows, arrows, and lances: and most of them had square wooden targets : and bore them in such wise that they did not impede the drawing of the bow : and when we had come with our boats to about a bowshot of the land, they all sprang into the water to shoot their arrows at us and to prevent us from leaping upon shore : and they all had their bodies painted of various colours, and [*were*] plumed with feathers : and the interpreters[1] who were with us told us that when [*those*] displayed themselves so painted and plumed, it was to betoken that they wanted to fight : and so much did they persist in preventing us from landing, that we were compelled to play with our artillery : and when they heard the explosion, and saw some of their number fall dead, they all drew back to the land : wherefore, forming our Council, we resolved that 42 of our men should spring on shore, and, if they waited for us, fight them : thus having leaped to land with our weapons, they advanced towards us, and we fought for about an hour, but we had little advantage of them, except that our arbalasters and gunners killed some of them, and they wounded certain of our men : and this was because they did not stand to receive us within reach of lance-thrust or sword-blow : and so much vigour did we put forth at last, that we came to sword-play, and when they tasted our weapons, they betook themselves to flight through the mountains and the forests, and left us conquerors of the field with many of them dead and a good number wounded : and for

---

[1] *Le lingue*, a Portuguese idiom.

that day we took no other pains to pursue them, because we were very weary, and we returned to our ships, with so much gladness on the part of the seven men who had come with us that they could not contain themselves [*for joy*] : and when the next day arrived, we beheld coming across the land a great number of people, with signals of battle, continually sounding horns, and various other instruments which they use in their wars : and all [*of them*] painted and feathered, so that it was a very strange sight to behold them : wherefore all the ships held council, and it was resolved that since this people desired hostility with us, we should proceed to encounter them and try by every means to make them friends : in case they would not have our friendship, that we should treat them as foes, and so many of them as we might be able to capture should all be our slaves : and having armed ourselves as best we could, we advanced towards the shore, and they sought not to hinder us from landing, I believe from fear of the cannons : and we jumped on land, 57 men in four squadrons, each one [*consisting of*] a captain and his company : and we came to blows with them : and after a long battle [*in which*] many of them [*were*] slain, we put them to flight, and pursued them to a village, having made about 250 of them captives, and we burnt the village, and returned to our ships with victory and 250 prisoners[1] leaving many of them dead and wounded, and of ours there were no more than one killed, and 22 wounded, who all escaped [*i.e., recovered*], God be thanked. We arranged our departure, and the seven men, of whom five were wounded, took an island-canoe, and, with seven prisoners that we gave them,

---

[1] Varnhagen thought we ought to read "25" (not 250), like the Latin version, and to correct the figures "222" lower down into "22," in both the text and the Latin. But he was in error, having omitted to observe that the figures "250" occur *twice*. He evidently looked more on the Latin than the text. Besides, a capture of only 25 savages would be very little indeed for the European force to make, whether we reckon it at 57 men or 228 men, as he and the Latinizer read it (four squadrons, each of 57 men, with its captain), especially when they had entered into hostilities with the express intention of making captives. [He afterwards corrected himself.]

four women and three men, returned to their [*own*] country full of gladness, wondering at our strength : and we thereupon made sail for Spain with 222 captive slaves : and reached the port of Cadiz on the 15 day of October 1498, where we were well received and sold our slaves. Such is what befel me, most noteworthy, in this my first voyage.

ENDS THE FIRST VOYAGE.

BEGINS THE SECOND.

Second Voyage.

[*Woodcut of two Ships at Sea.*]

———◆———

AS for the second voyage, and what I saw in it most worthy of record, it is as follows here. We started from the port of Cadiz, three ships in company, on the 16 day of May 1499[1] and began our voyage in a direct course to the islands of Cape Verde, passing in sight of the island of Great Canary: and sailed on until we dropped anchor at an island which is called the Island of Fire:[2] and having here taken in our provision of water and firewood, we resumed our voyage towards the south-west:[3] and in 44 days[4] we touched upon a new land: and we deemed that it was [*part of*] a continent, and continuous with that [*land*] of which mention is made above:[5] the which [*new land*] is situated within the Torrid Zone, and southward of the equinoctial line: above which the southern pole rises to the elevation of 5 degrees, beyond every climate:[6] and it is 500 leagues distant south-westwardly[7] from the said islands:[8] and we found that the days were equal with the nights: for we reached it on the 27 day of June, when

---

[1] 1499. Latin has 1489, by error.   [2] *Lisola del fuoco.*   [3] *Per illibeccio.*
[4] The Latin has " 19 days," and so has Varnhagen, notwithstanding that his *text* is correct.
[5] *I.e.,* in the preceding relation of the first voyage. The Latin makes a blunder here, and says, "opposite to," instead of "continuous with." The translator must have read " *contraria* " for " *continua.*"
[6] This means, simply, at 5 degrees south latitude.
[7] *Per el vento libeccio.*   [8] *I.e.,* the Canaries.

the sun is nigh the Tropic of Cancer : which land we found to be all overflowed with water and full of very large rivers.[1] As yet[2] we saw no people : we brought our ships to anchor and put out our boats : in them we pulled to the land, and as I have said, we found it full of the largest rivers and inundated by very great floods which we met with : and we attempted it in many places to see if we could enter therein : and because of the great floods poured by the rivers, however strenuously we strove, we could find no spot that was not inundated : we observed on the waters many tokens that the land was inhabited : and seeing that in this quarter we could not enter it, we decided to return to the ships and to attempt landing in another place : and we weighed our anchors, and · sailed east-south-east,[3] always coasting the shore which trended in that direction, and in a space of 40 leagues we made attempts to land in several places : and it was all lost time : we found on that coast the sea-currents so strong that they did not allow us to navigate, and they all ran from south-east to north-west : consequently, seeing so many impediments to our navigation, we held a council, and decided to turn our course to the north-west : and we sailed along the land till we arrived at a very fine port : which was formed by a large island that was situated at the mouth, inside of which there was a bay, very deeply indented : and while sailing by the side of the island to enter into the harbour, we beheld many people : and rejoicing thereat, we directed our vessels thither, so as to drop anchor where we saw the people, being probably [*then*] about four leagues away to seaward from them :[4] and proceeding thus we had sight of a canoe that was coming from the high sea : in which there were coming many persons : and we resolved to seize it :[5] and we turned our vessels round to meet it, navigating

---

[1] Varnhagen inserts here (from the Latin) a statement about the greenness of the land, and that it was full of large trees ; which does not at all appear in the text.

[2] *In questo principio.*   [3] *Infra levante e sciloccho.*

[4] There is some confusion here ; they could hardly have been able to see a crowd of people at four leagues' distance.   [5] *Haverla alla mano.*

in such order that we should not lose it : and sailing towards it with a brisk breeze,[1] we observed that they were at a stand-still, with their oars lifted, I believe in wonder at our ships : and when they perceived that we were advancing to approach them, they dipped their oars in the water and began to row towards the land : and as in our company there was a caravel of 45 tons, a very quick sailor, she took station to windward[2] of the canoe : and when it seemed to be time to bear down upon it, [*the caravel*] shook out[3] full sail and made for [*the canoe*] and we likewise : and when the caravel came abreast of it and did not seek to board [*the canoe*], she passed by, and then stood still against the wind : and when they saw themselves at a vantage, they began to struggle hard with their oars to escape : and we, who had our boats already astern manned with good crews, thinking that they would take it [*the canoe*], and they laboured for more than two hours, and at last, if the little caravel had not tacked again upon them, we should have lost it [*the canoe*] : and when they found themselves hemmed in by the caravel and the boats, they all flung themselves into the sea, probably some 70 men [*in number*] :[4] and they were at a distance of about two leagues from land : and following them with our boats, the whole day, we were unable to take more than two of them, for, certain it was, all the others reached the land in safety : and in the canoe there remained four boys : who were not of their tribe : for they brought them as captives from another land : and they had castrated them, for they were all without the virile member, and had the wound still fresh : whereat we marvelled much : and being taken into the ships they told us by signs that [*the men of the canoe*] had castrated them in order to eat them: and we learned that those were a people who are called Camballi, very savage, who ate human flesh. Towing the canoe astern, we made in our ships for the land and anchored at the [*distance of*] half a league : and as we saw great numbers of people on the shore, we rowed to the land in our boats, taking with us the two men we had captured : and having landed, all

---

[1] *Fresco tempo.*
[2] *Barlovento.*
[3] *Allargho li apparechi.*
[4] Latin has " 20 men."

the people fled away, and betook themselves to the forests: and we let go one of the [*two*] men, giving him several little bells,[1] and [*indicating*] that we desired to be their friends: which he [*whom*] we sent to them effected very well, and brought with him all the tribe, who were about 400 men and many women: who came without any weapons to where we were with our boats: and having made good friendship with them, we restored to them the second captive, and sent to the ships for their canoe and gave it back to them. This canoe was 26 paces long, and two ells[2] broad, and entirely hollowed out of a single tree, and very elaborately made; and when they had docked it in a river and put it in a safe place, they all fled away, and would no further hold intercourse with us, which seemed to us a quite barbarous action, so that we deemed them a people of little faith and ill condition. With them we saw some little gold which they had in their ears. We departed thence, and made our way to the inner part of the bay:[3] where we found such a multitude of people, that it was marvellous: with whom on landing we made a friendship: and many of us went with them to their villages, very safely, and well-received. In this place we obtained[4] 150 pearls which they gave us in exchange for a little bell, and some little gold which they gave us for nothing:[5] and in this land we found that they drank a wine made of their fruits and grain, in the manner of beer, both white and red: and the best was made of *myrobalans*,[6] and was very good: and they ate infinite numbers of these, it being then the season for them. It is a very good fruit, pleasant to the taste, and healthful to the body. The soil abounds greatly with everything they need for subsistence, and the people [*were*] of polite behaviour and the most pacific we had

---

[1] *Sonagli*, little bells or rattles.

[2] *Braccia.*

[3] Instead of the simple statement, "and made our way," &c., the Latin inserts " having voyaged along that coast for about eighty leagues we came to a safe harbour," which is absurd, but has apparently influenced Varnhagen, who evidently made the mistake of incautiously referring sometimes to the Latin only and sometimes to the Italian text, thus failing to see all the discrepancies.

[4] *Rischattammo.* The Latin has 500, instead of 150.

[5] *Di gratia.*   [6] *Mirabolani.*

as yet met with. We remained in this harbour for seventeen days with much pleasure : and every day fresh people, from the interior of the country, came to see us, wondering at our appearance and whiteness, and our clothing and arms, and at the shape and great size of the ships. From those people we had information of a tribe that lived further to the west of them, who were their enemies, who had an infinite quantity of pearls : and that those [*pearls*] which they [*our friends*] had were what they had taken from them [*the enemies*] in their wars : and they told us how they fished for them, and in what manner they [*the pearls*] were produced, and we found that they spoke with truth, as Your Magnificence shall hear. We departed from this harbour and navigated along the coast : on which we continually saw clouds of smoke [1] arising, with people on the beach : and at the end of several days we came to anchor in a harbour, for the purpose of repairing one of our ships, which had sprung a great leak : [2] where we found that there was a large population : with whom we were not able, neither by force nor for love, to obtain any conversation whatever : and when we went on land, they struggled fiercely to prevent us from doing so : and when they could hold out no longer, they fled through the forests and did not await us. Finding them so barbarous, we went away from hence : and proceeding on our voyage we had sight of an island distant 15 leagues out to sea from the [*main-*] land : and we decided on going to see if it were inhabited. We found therein the most brutish and loathsome people that were ever seen, and they were on this wise. In behaviour and looks, they were very repulsive : and they all had their cheeks swollen out with a green herb inside, which they were constantly chewing like beasts, so that they could scarcely utter speech : and each one had [*suspended*] upon his neck, two dried gourds, one of which was full of that herb which they kept in their mouths, and the other [*full*] of a white flour, which looked like powdered chalk, and from time to time, with a small stick which they kept moistening in their mouths, they dipped it into the flour and then put it into

---

[1] *Fumalte*, by error for *fumate*. Varnhagen has transcribed *fumatte*.
[2] *Faceva molta acqua.*

their mouths inside both cheeks, thus mixing with flour the herb which they had in their mouths: and this they did very frequently: and marvelling at such a thing, we were unable to comprehend this secret, nor with what object they acted thus. These people when they saw us, came to us as familiarly as if we had been united with them in friendship: going with them along the beach, talking, and desirous of drinking fresh water, they made signs to us that they had none, and offered us some of that herb and flour of theirs, so that we concluded by inference that this island was poor in water, and that it was to preserve themselves against thirst they kept that herb in their mouths, and the flour for the same [*reason*]. We went through the island for a day and a half without ever finding any flowing water: and we observed that the water which they drank was of a dew which fell by night on certain leaves that looked like asses' ears, and [*which*] became full of water, and hereof they drank: it was most excellent water: and [*i.e., but*] they had not those leaves in many places. They had no form of victuals, nor roots, as on the mainland: and they subsisted on fish which they took in the sea; and of these they had very great abundance, and they were most expert fishermen: and they presented to us many turtles, and many very excellent fish of great size: their women did not use to keep the herb in their mouths like the men, but all [*the women*] carried a gourd with water and drank thereof. They had no villages, neither of houses nor huts, save that they dwelt underneath arbours, which protected them from the sun, and not from the water; for I believe it rained very seldom in that island: when they were at sea fishing, they all had a leaf of great size and so broad, that they were quite in shadow beneath it, and they used to fix it in the ground: and as the sun revolved so did they turn the leaf: and in this manner they protected themselves from the sun. The island contains many animals of various kinds: and they drink marsh-water: and seeing that they had nothing profitable [*for us*] we departed, and took our course to another island: and we found [*afterwards*] that a race of very great stature dwelt therein: we then landed to see if we found [*could find*] fresh water: and imagining that the island was

not inhabited because we saw no people, going along the shore
we beheld very large footprints of men on the sand : and we
judged, if their other members were of corresponding size, that
they must be very big men : and proceeding onwards, we came
upon a pathway which led to the interior of the land : and nine of
us agreed : and concluded that the island being small could not
contain within itself many people : and thereupon we went
onward through it, to see what manner of people they were : and
after we had gone for about a league, we beheld in a valley five of
their huts, which appeared uninhabited : and we made our way to
them and found only five women, two old ones and three girls,
so lofty in stature that we gazed at them in astonishment : and
when they saw us, so much terror overcame them that they had
not even spirit to flee away : and the two old women began to
invite us with words, bringing us many things to eat, and they
put us in a hut : and they were in stature taller than a tall man,
so that they would be quite as big of body as was Francesco
degli Albizi, but better proportioned : insomuch that we were all
of a mind to take away the three girls from them by force : and to
carry them to Castile as a prodigy : and while thus discoursing,
there began to enter through the door of the hut full 36 men
much bigger than the women : men so well built that it was a
famous sight to see them : who put us in such uneasiness that we
would much rather have been in our ships than in the company of
such people. They carried very large bows and arrows, with large
knobbed clubs : and they spoke among themselves in such a tone
as though they meant to lay hands upon us : seeing that we were
in such danger, we debated of various plans among ourselves :
some [*of us*] said that we ought to attack immediately in the
house : and others that it were better on the open ground
[*outside*] : and others who said that we ought not to begin the
quarrel until we should see what they meant to do : and we
agreed to go forth from the hut and to make our way slily
towards the ships : and so we did : and having taken our way we
returned to the ships : those [*savages*] however came following
behind us, always at the distance of a stone's throw, speaking
amongst themselves : I believe that they were no less afraid of

us, than we were of them: because we halted sometimes, and
they did the same without approaching nearer, until we reached
the shore where the boats were awaiting us: and we entered into
them: and when we were at some distance, they danced about
and shot many arrows at us: but we had little dread of them
now: we fired two gunshots at them, more to terrify them than
to do any hurt: and at the explosion they all fled inwards:[1]
and so we departed from them, having as it seemed to us escaped
from a perilous day's work. They went entirely naked like the
others. I call that island, the Isle of Giants, because of their
great size: and we proceeded onward still skirting the coast on
which it befel us many times to have to fight them, as they
sought not to allow us to take anything from the land: and since
it was our desire to return now to Castile, as we had been
about a year at sea, and had [*but*] a small stock of provisions
[*remaining*], and that little damaged by reason of the great heats
that we endured: because from the time when we started for the
isles of Cape Verde till now, we had continually navigated in the
torrid zone, and twice crossed the equinoctial line: for as I have
said above we had gone to 5 degrees below it southwardly:[2] and
here we were at 15 degrees north of it.[3] Being in this mind, it
pleased the Holy Ghost to give us some relief for so much travail:
which was, that while we were seeking a harbour wherein to
repair our vessels, we met with a nation which received us with
great friendliness: and we found that they had a great abundance
of very fine oriental pearls: with whom we stayed for 47 days:
and we bought from them 119 marks[4] of pearls for very little
merchandize: for I believe they did not cost us the value of forty
ducats: since that which we gave them was nothing but little
bells and looking-glasses and beads, *dieci-palle*,[5] and sheets of
tin, indeed, for a single little bell a man gave as many pearls as

---

[1] *Al monte.* Upwards, or to the further end.   [2] Cape St. Roque.

[3] A little north of Caracas, probably 12 degrees (not 15).

[4] *Marchi, marco*—a weight of eight ounces.

[5] *Conte, dieci palle et foglie di octone. Dieci palle* must be some sort of
balls or playing-marbles, perhaps the same as the *spalline* of the first voyage.

he had. From them [*the natives*] we learned how and where they
fished for them [*the pearls*] : and they gave us many [*of the*]
oysters in which they grew : we bought [*also*] an oyster in which
130 pearls were growing, and others with less : The Queen took[1]
from me that with the 130 : and others I took care she should
not see. And Your Magnificence must know that unless the
pearls are matured, and drop out of themselves, they do not last :
because they perish quickly : and of this I have had actual
experience : when they are mature, they lie within the shell
detached and set in the flesh :[2] and these ones are good :
whatsoever bad ones they had, though the most of them were
rough and ill-formed, still they were worth good money : because
the mark sold for   [3] : and at the end of 47 days we quitted
the people, leaving them very friendly towards us.   We departed,
and through the necessity of our victualling we made for the
island of Antiglia[4] which is the same that Christophal Colombo
discovered several years ago : where we took in much store of
provision : and remained two months and 17 days :[5] where we
underwent many perils and troubles with the very Christians who
were in this island along with Colombo :[6] I believe through envy :
but, in order not to be prolix, I refrain from narrating them.
We departed from the said island on the 22 day of July : and we
navigated during a month and a half : and entered into the port
of Cadiz, which was on the 8 day of September, by daylight,
my second voyage : God [*be*] praised.

ENDED THE SECOND VOYAGE.

BEGINS THE THIRD.

[1] From "the Queen took " down to "she should not see" omitted in Latin.
[2] The text is obscure ; the Latin is explicatory, and I presume correct, in
its account of the nature of pearls.
[3] A blank in the text. From " good " to "sold for " omitted in Latin.
[4] Hispaniola.
[5] The Latin " 2 months and 2 days."
[6] " Along with Columbus," omitted in Latin and not noted by Varnhagen.

Third Voyage.

[*Woodcut of a Ship at Sea.*]

BEING afterwards in Seville, resting myself from so many travails that I had in those two voyages undergone, and purposing to return to the land of the pearls: when Fortune not contented with my labours, for I know not how it came into the mind of this most serene King Don Manuel of Portugal, to wish to employ me: and being in Seville without any thought of coming to Portugal, there comes to me a messenger with a letter of his royal crown,[1] which desired me to come to Lisbon to speak with his Highness, promising to give me recompense. I was not of opinion that I should come: I sent away the messenger, saying that I was ill in health, and that when I should be well and his Highness still desired to employ me, that I would do whatever he should command me. And seeing that he could not have me, he decided to send for me [*i.e., to fetch me*] Giuliano di Bartholomeo del Giocondo, residing here in Lisbon, with a commission to bring me by whatever means. The said Giuliano came to Seville: through whose coming and entreaty I was compelled to come:[2] but my coming was regarded with ill-favour by so many as knew me: because I quitted Castile where honour had been done me, and the King kept me in good

---

[1] *I.e.*, an official letter from the Crown.

[2] He means "go," and in the next line "going," but was led to say "come" and "coming" from the consciousness that he was writing his letter in Lisbon.

ownership:[1] the worst was that I went *insalutato hospite :*[2] and having presented myself before this King [*of Portugal*], he shewed himself pleased with my coming: and prayed me to join the company of three of his ships which were ready to go in discovery of new lands.: and as a King's request is a command, I had to consent to whatever he desired of me: and we sailed from this port of Lisbon, three ships in company, on the 10 day of May 1501, and took our route directly for the Island of Great Canary: and we passed in sight of it without halting: and from hence we went skirting along the coast of Africa on the west side: on which coast we exercised our fishing-skill on a kind of fish which are called Parchi;[3] where we stopped three days: and from hence we made for the coast of Ethiopia, to a port which is called Besechicce,[4] which is within the Torrid Zone: over which the North Pole is at an elevation of 14½ degrees, situated in the first climate:[5] where we remained 11 days, taking in water and firewood: because my intention was to make our seaway southwardly through the Atlantic gulf.[6] We quitted this Ethiopian port, and navigated south-westwardly,[7] taking one quarter by south, until after a course of 67 days we anchored at a land which was 700 leagues to the south-west of the said port: and in those 67 days we had the worst weather that ever any seafarer had, through numerous storm-showers,[8] whirlwinds, and tempests which struck us: because we were in a very adverse season since the greater part of our navigation was continually close to the equinoctial line, for in the month of June it is winter: and we found that the day was equal with the night: and we found that the shadow was always towards the south: it pleased God to shew us new land, and [*this*] was on the 17 day of August: when we anchored at half a league [*from the shore*]: and put out our boats: and went to inspect the land, whether it was inhabited by people, and who these people were: and we found

---

[1] *In buona possessione* (? "in high consideration," as Latin has it).
[2] "Without bidding adieu to my host."   [3] Portuguese *Pargos*.
[4] Latin has *Besilicca*.   [5] That is, 14½ degrees north latitude.
[6] Ocean.   [7] *Libeccio*.   [8] *Aguazeri* (waterspouts ?).

that it was inhabited by a people who were worse than animals: however Your Magnificence must understand that as yet [1] we saw no people, but we perceived well that it was inhabited from many signs that we observed therein: we took possession of it for this most serene King [*Don Manuel*] : [2] which land we found to be very pleasant and green, and of goodly appearance : it was 5 degrees towards the south beyond the equinoctial line : and for that day [3] we returned to the ships : and because we were in great want of water and firewood, we determined the next day to return to the shore to provide ourselves with what was needful : and, when on land, we beheld some people on the top of a hill, who stood gazing and did not venture to come down : they were naked, and of the same colour and fashion as were the other former [*savages we had met with elsewhere*] : and although we strove to induce them [1] to come and speak with us, we were totally unable to reassure them, for they had no trust in us : and seeing their obstinacy, and [*as*] it was already late, we returned to the ships, leaving on the ground for them several little bells and looking-glasses, and other things within their ken : and when we were at a distance on sea, they descended from the hill and came for the things we had left them, displaying great wonderment at these : and for that day we provided ourselves only with water : the next morning we saw from the ships that the land's people were making many clouds of smoke : and thinking that they were calling us [*to them*] wè went on shore where we found that great numbers of them had come, and yet they remained aloof from us : and they made signs to us that we should go with them into the interior of the land : wherefore two of our Christians were moved to ask the Captain that he would give them leave as they wished to undertake the risk of going with those [*savages*] into the land, to see what [*manner of*] people they were, and whether they had any riches, or spices, or druggeries ; and so much did they beseech that the captain was pleased [*to*

---

[1] *In questo principio.*   The Latin says, by mistake, " King of Castile."
[3] *Per questo ci di*, by mistake for *per questo di ci.* It is *ita* in Latin.
   By signals, of course.

allow it] : and they prepared themselves with many things for barter [*and*] quitted us with the order that they should not be more than 5 days before returning : because we would wait for them just so long : and they took their way through the country : and we [*remained*] by the ships awaiting them : and almost every day people came to the beach and would never hold speech with us : and the seventh day we went on land, and found that they had brought their women with them : and when we leaped to shore, the land's men sent many of their women to speak with us : and seeing they did not become confident, we decided to send one of our men to them, who was a young fellow given to feats of strength ;[1] and, to reassure them,[2] we entered into our boats : and he went among the women : and when he reached them, they made a great circle around him, touching him and gazing at him in wonderment : and while he was thus [*encircled*] we saw a woman come from the hill, and she carried a great stake in her hand : and when she reached to where our Christian stood, she came behind him : and, lifting the club, gave him such a tremendous blow that she stretched him dead on the ground, in an instant the other women took hold of him by the feet and dragged him along by his feet towards the hill : and the men bounded towards the beach, and with their bows and arrows [*began*] to shoot at us : and they put our people into such terror, the boats being held fast by the small anchors which were sunk in the ground, that, because of the numerous arrows [*the natives*] shot into the boats, no one had courage to snatch up his arms : however we fired 4 gunshots at them, and they took no effect, save that on hearing the explosion, they all fled towards the hill and to where the women were already [*cutting*] the Christian into bits : and at a great fire which they had made, they were roasting him before our eyes, holding up several pieces towards us and [*then*] eating them : and the men [*were*] making signs to us by their gestures how they had killed the other two Christians and eaten them : which grieved us greatly, seeing with our eyes

---

[1] *Che molto faceva lo sforzo.*

[2] Text has "him," by a typographical error of " *lo* " for " *le*."

the cruelty they were exercising on the dead man, to all of us it
was an intolerable offence : and more than 40 of us being determined to jump on land and revenge such a cruel death, and an
action [*so*] bestial and inhuman, the Admiral would not give
his consent, and so they [*the natives*] remained glutted with
so great a villainy:[2] and we departed from them ill-willingly,
and with much shamefulness because of our Captain. We
quitted that place, and began our navigation east-south-east,
and thus the land trended : and we made many descents on land,
and never did we meet a tribe that was willing to hold parley
with us : and thus we navigated onward till we found that [*the
line of*] the land was turning to south-westward:[3] when we
doubled a cape, to which we gave the name of Cape St. Augustine,[4] we began to sail south-west, and this cape is 150 leagues
distant to the east of the aforesaid land which we saw, where they
slew the Christians : and this cape is 8 degrees south of the
equinoctial line : and while [*thus*] sailing we had sight one day of
many people who were standing on the beach to behold the
wondrous sight of our ships and the manner of our navigation, we directed our course towards them, and anchored in a
good place, and made in our boats for land, and found them a
better-conditioned people than the last : and although it was a
toil to us to tame them, yet we made them our friends and held
intercourse with them. We stayed 5 days in this place : and
here we found *canna fistola* very thick and green, and dry on the
tops of the trees. We decided to take in this place a couple of
[*native*] men, so that they should explain for us the language :
and there came three of their own free will to come to Portugal :
and for the present, tired [*as I am*] already of so much writing,
Your Magnificence shall know, that we departed from that port,
navigating always within sight of land in a south-west direction,
frequently making descents upon shore, and speaking with an
infinite number of peoples : and so far did we proceed southwards

---

[1] *Capitano maggiore.*   [2] *Di tanta ingiuria,* wrong-doing.
[3] *Libeccio.*   [4] The Latin has St. Vincent.

that we were now beyond the Tropic of Capricorn, where the
South Pole was at an elevation of 32 degrees above the horizon :
and we had already quite lost [*sight of*] Ursa Minor, and [*Ursa*]
Major was very low, and appeared to us to be almost on the line
of the horizon, and we guided ourselves by the stars of the other
pole [*that*] of the South : which are numerous, and much larger
and more brilliant than those of our pole : and I drew diagrams
of most of them, and especially of those of the first and greatest
magnitude, with an exposition of the orbits which they describe
around the southern pole, and a declaration of their diameters
and semidiameters, as may be seen in my 4 Giornate :[1] we
ran along this coast to the length of 750 leagues, 150 leagues
west of the cape called [*Cape*] St. Augustine, and 600[2] leagues
to the south-west : and if I wished to narrate the things
which I saw on this coast, and what we underwent, twice the
number of leaves [*of paper*] would not suffice me : and on this
coast we saw nothing of value,[3] except an infinite number of
dye-wood and cassia-trees, and those which beget myrrh, and
other wonders of nature which cannot be recounted : and having
already been fully 10 months voyaging, and seeing that in this
land we found nothing of mineral [*wealth*] we decided to hasten
away from there, and to put to sea for some other quarter : and
having held our council, it was resolved that the course should be
followed which I should think fitting : and the command of the
fleet was entirely handed over to me : and I then ordered that all
the crews and the fleet should provide themselves with water and
wood for six months, as the masters of the ships judged that we
might navigate in them for so much time.   Having taken in our
stores from this land, we began our voyage towards the south-east :
and it was on the 15[4] day of February when the sun was already
nearing the Equinox, and turning towards this our northern
hemisphere : and so long did we sail by that wind, that we

---

[1] "*Le Quattro Giornate,*" the projected book to which he has already
made more than one reference.

[2] Latin has 700.   [3] *Profecto.*   [4] Latin has 13.

found ourselves [*at*] so high[1] [*a latitude*] that the southern pole stood quite 52 degrees above our horizon, and we no longer beheld the stars either of Ursa Minor or Ursa Major: and we were already at a distance of full 500 leagues south-east from the harbour whence we had set out: and this was on the 3 day of April, and on that day there arose a tempest of so much violence upon the sea that we were compelled to haul down all our sails, and we scudded under bare poles before the great wind, which was south-west with enormous waves and a very stormy sky: and so fierce was the tempest that all the fleet was in great dread: the nights were very long: so that on the seventh day of April we had a night which was 15 hours long: for the sun was at the end of Aries: and in that region it was winter [*then*] as Your Magnificence may well consider, and while in this tempest on the seventh[2] day of April, we had sight of a new land, along which we ran for about 20 leagues, and found that it was wholly a rough coast:[3] and we beheld therein neither any harbour nor any people, because, as I believe, of the cold which was so intense that no one in our fleet could fortify himself against it or endure it: insomuch that, finding ourselves in so great a danger and in such a tempest that one ship could hardly see another for the great billows that were running and for the deep gloominess[4] of the weather, we agreed with the Admiral[5] to signal to [*the rest of*] the fleet to approach and that we should abandon [*this*] land: and turn round in the direction of Portugal: and it was a very good resolve: for it is certain that if we had delayed that night, we had all been lost: because when we turned a-stern,[6] both that night and the next day, the tempest grew to such a height that we were in fear of being lost: and we had to make [*vows of*] pilgrimage and other ceremonies, as is the custom of sailors at such times: we scudded for 5 days,[7] and kept

---

[1] So high—that is, so far south.
[2] 2nd April, Latin.   [3] *Costa brava* in the Spanish sense.
[4] *Serrazon*, from the Portuguese *cerração*.   [5] *Capitano maggiore.*
[6] *Come arrivammo a poppa*, from Spanish *arribar.*
[7] In Latin there is added here "in which five days we made 250 leagues of sea-passage."

4

still drawing nearer to the equinoctial line, with the weather and the sea [*becoming*] more temperate: and it pleased God that we should escape from so great a peril: and our course was with the wind between north and north-east :[1] because our intention was to go and reconnoitre the coast of Ethiopia,[2] as we were distant therefrom [*only*] 300[3] leagues across the gulf of the Atlantic Sea: and by the grace of God on the 10 day of May we came to a land therein, [*lying*] southward, which is called La serra liona :[4] where we stayed 15 days, taking our refreshment: and from here we departed taking our course towards the islands of the Azores, which are distant about 750 leagues from this place of the Serra: and we reached the islands at the end of July: where we stayed 15 days more, taking some recreation: and we quitted them for Lisbon: being [*then*] 300 leagues to the west [*of it*] : and we entered into this port of Lisbon on the 7 day of September 1502, in good condition, God be thanked, with two ships only: because we [*had*] burnt the other in Serra liona: as it was disabled from further navigation, for we were about 15[5] months on this voyage: and for 11 days we navigated without seeing the Polar Star, or the Greater and Lesser Bear, which are called the Corno:[6] and we steered by the stars of the other hemisphere.   This is what I saw in this voyage or giornata.

[1] *Tramontano* and *greco*.   [2] Africa.

[3] Like Varnhagen, I read this distance as 300 leagues, but the text may mean either "1300," or "in 300," and is more like the former.

[4] Sierra Leone.   [5] Latin has 16.

[6] *Corno*—evidently a typographical error for *carro*, the Wain.

ƒourtß Qoyage.

[Woodcut of a Ship at Anchor, two figures in it, and one on land; towers in the background.]

IT remains for me to tell the things seen by me in the fourth voyage, or giornata: and as I am already wearied, and also because this fourth voyage was not carried out in accordance with the purpose I [had] formed, through a mishap which befel us in the gulf of the Atlantic Sea, as Your Magnificence shall learn briefly in the sequel: I will endeavour to be brief. We departed from this port of Lisbon 6 ships in company, with the intention of going to discover an island towards the east, which is called Melaccha: of which there are news that it is very rich, and that it is as it were the storehouse of all the ships which come from the Gangetic sea and from the Indian Sea, (just as Cadiz is the waiting-room[1] of all the vessels which pass from east to west, and from west to east) by the route of Galigut,[2] and this Melaccha is more westerly than Caligut, and much more to the southward:[3] for we know that it lies at the level[4] of 33[5] degrees of the antarctic hemisphere. We departed on the 10 day of May 1503 and made directly for the isles of Cape Verde, were we careened, and took some manner of

---

[1] *Camera.*

[2] This puzzling sentence leads us to infer that the object was a South-west passage to India. When he says that Malacca was west of Calicut, he means probably that it was nearer to his New World. The brackets inserted here are not in the original.

[3] Mistranslated in the Latin. *Alta* is an error for *alla.*   [4] *Paraggio.*

[5] As Varnhagen justly corrects, this must have been meant for " 3."

refreshment, where we stayed 13[1] days : and from here we departed on our voyage, sailing by the south-east wind : and as our
Admiral was a presumptuous and very obstinate man, he would
go to examine Serra liona, a land of Southern Ethiopia, without
having any need except to make it be seen that he was Captain of
six ships, against the wish of all the rest of us Captains : and thus
navigating, when we reached the said land, so great were the
whirlwinds that struck us, and with them the weather so adverse,
that [*although*] we were in sight of it [*the shore*] quite four days,
the foul weather never allowed us to land : so that we were
compelled to return to our proper course, and to quit the said
Serra : and navigating hence to the *suduest* which is the wind
between south and south-west :[2] and when we had sailed full 300
leagues through the immensity[3] of the sea, being then quite
3 degrees south of the equinoctial line, we became aware of a
land from which we were probably 22[4] leagues distant : whereat
we marvelled : and we found that it was an island in the middle
of the sea and was very lofty, a very marvellous work of nature :
since it was no more than two leagues in length and one in
breadth : in which island, never had there been inhabitation by
any people : and it was Bad Island[5] for all the fleet : for Your
Magnificence must know that by the ill-counsel and management
of our Admiral he lost his ship here : since he struck with it upon
a rock, and it split open on St. Laurence's night, which was on
the 10 day of August, and went to the bottom : and there was
nothing saved thereof except the crew. It was a ship of 300 tons :
in which went all the importance of the fleet : and when all the
fleet were labouring to save it, the Chief commanded me to
make with my ship for the said island to seek a good anchorage,
where all the ships might anchor : and as my boat manned with
9 of my sailors was engaged and aiding to belay the ships, he

---

[1] Latin has " 12," and misunderstands the *careenage*.

[2] *Infra mezzo di e libeccio.* *Suduest* is a typographical blunder for
sudsudueste.

[3] *Mostro* (?).   [4] Latin has " *duodecim.*"

[5] *La mala isola,* Fernando Noronha.   [6] *Ligare* (? bind together).

willed that I should not take it, and that I should proceed without
it : telling me that they should take it to me at the island : I
quitted the fleet for the island as he ordered me, without a boat,
and with the deficiency of half my crew, and I went to the said
island, which was about 4 leagues distant : in which I found an
excellent harbour, where all the ships could anchor very safely :
where I awaited my Chief and the fleet fully 8 days, and they
never came : so that we were very discontented, and the men that
had remained with me in the ship were in such dread, that I was
unable to console them : and being thus, the eighth day we
beheld a ship coming upon the sea, and from fear that it might
not see us, we weighed with our ship,[1] and made for it, thinking
that it brought me my boat and crew : and when we came along-
side of it, after having saluted, they told us how the admiral's ship
had gone to the bottom, and how the crew had been saved, and
that my boat and crew had remained with the fleet, which had
gone further on that sea, which was to us so great an annoyance
as Your Magnificence may conceive, finding ourselves 1000 leagues
away from Lisbon, and on the ocean,[2] and with a little crew :
however we set our prow[3] at Fortune, and went still onward : we
returned to the island, and provided ourselves with water and
timber by means of my companion's boat : which island we found
uninhabited, and it contained many fresh and sweet waters,[4]
innumerable trees, [*and was*] full of so many sea and land birds
that they were beyond count : and they were so tame, that they
allowed themselves to be taken with the hand : and so
many of them did we take that we loaded a boat with
those animals : we saw none [*other*] except very large rats and
lizards with double tails, and some snakes : and having made our
provision, we departed by the wind betwixt south and south-west,
for we had an ordinance of the King which commanded us that
whichever of the ships should lose sight of the fleet or of its
Chief, should make for the land that we discovered in the
previous voyage, at a harbour to which we had given the name of

---

[1] *Nostre navi* for *nostra nave.* He had only one (see *supra*).
[2] *Golfo.*   [3] *Facemmo rostro.*   [4] That is, streams or springs.

Badia di tucti e sancti:[1] and it pleased God to give us such good weather, that in 17 days we reached land therein, which was distant from the island full 300 leagues: where we found neither our Admiral nor any other ship of the fleet: in which harbour we waited quite two months and 4 days: and seeing that there was no arrival, we agreed, my partner and I, to run the coast: and we sailed 260 leagues further on, till[2] we arrived in a harbour: where we decided to construct a fort, and we did so: and left therein 24 Christian men whom my partner had for us, whom she had collected from the flagship[3] that had been lost: in which port we stayed quite 5 months making the fortress and loading our ships with verzino:[4] as we were unable to proceed further, because we had not men [*enough*] and I was deficient of many pieces of ship-tackle. All this done, we determined to turn our course towards Portugal, which lay in the direction of the wind between north-east and north:[5] and we left the 24 men who remained in the fort with provision for six months, and [*with*] 12 big guns[6] and many other arms, and we pacified all the land's people: of whom no mention has been made in this voyage: not because we did not see and traffic with an infinite number of them: for we went, quite 30 men of us, 40 leagues inland: where I saw so many things that I omit to tell them, reserving them for my 4 Giornate. This land lies 18 degrees south of the equinoctial line, and 37 degrees to the west of the longitude of Lisbon, as is demonstrated by our instruments. And all this being done, we took leave of the Christians and the land: and began our navigation to *nornordeste,*[7] which is the wind between north and north-east, with the intention of making our navigation in a direct course to this city of Lisbon: and in 77 days, after so many travails and perils, we entered into this port on the 18 day of June 1504, God [*be*] praised: where we were received very well and beyond all belief:

---

[1] Mistake for *Bahia de todos os Santos.* This confusion of *d* and *h* in Vespucci's handwriting led to a long-continued error in the maps.

[2] *Tlão,* for *tāto,* so far that, until.   [3] *Nave capitana.*

[4] Brazil-wood, or dye-wood.   [5] *Greco* and *tramontano.*   [6] *Bombarde.*

[7] It is printed *nornodeste.*

because all the city believed us lost: since the other ships of the fleet had all been lost through the arrogance and folly of our Admiral, for so does God reward pride: and at present I find myself here in Lisbon, and I know not what the King will want to do with me, for I desire much to take repose.[1] The present bearer, who is Benvenuto di Domenico Benvenuti, will tell your Magnificence of my condition, and of some things which, for prolixity, have been left unsaid: for he has seen and felt them, God be......[2] I have gone on compressing the letter as much as I could, and there have been omitted to be told many natural things,[3] because of avoiding prolixity. May Your Magnificence pardon me: whom I beseech to hold me in the number of your servants: and I recommend to you Ser Antonio Vespucci, my brother, and all my family. I remain, praying of God that he may increase the days of your life, and that the state of this sublime Republic and the honour of Your Magnificence may be exalted, etc. Given in Lisbon on the 4 day of September 1504.

[*Your*] servant AMERIGO VESPUCCI in Lisbon.

---

[1] The Latin substitutes "this messenger in the meantime commending much to your Majesty. Americus Vesputius. In Lisbon," for all the text which follows the word "repose."

[2] *Dio sia ō cli*, followed by a blank. This is incomprehensible, and may be "God be . . . ." (something not understood by the printer), or *di sui occhi* . . . . ("with his own eyes . . . ."), which would imply that Benvenuto had accompanied Vespucci in this voyage.

[3] Things relating to natural history.

G. NORMAN AND SON, PRINTERS, HART STREET, COVENT GARDEN, LONDON.

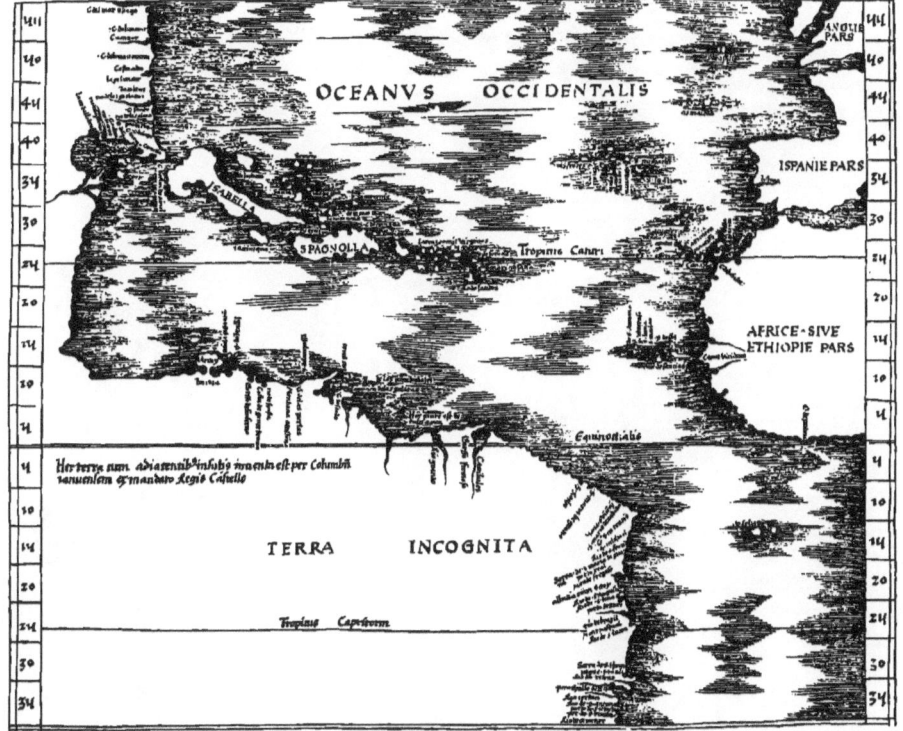

THE ADMIRAL'S MAP, FROM THE STRASSBURG PTOLEMY OF 1513 (reduced).

NARRATIVE

ENGLISH PLANTATION

OF

VIRGINIA

By THOMAS HARIOT

First printed at London in 1588
now reproduced after De Bry's illustrated edition
printed at Frankfort in 1590

the illustrations having
been designed in Virginia in 1585
by
JOHN WHITE

London
BERNARD QUARITCH, 15 Piccadilly, W.
MDCCCXCIII.

London:
G. Norman and Son, Printers, Hart Street,
Covent Garden.

Preface.

THE history of the first English settlement in the United States, and of its failure, is well known. But the text of the actual narrative from which all the writers upon the subject have, either directly or at second-hand, derived their facts, is not familiar to any save professed students. It is rare in any form, and the present reproduction will serve a useful purpose in making known to thousands who would otherwise never have a chance of learning it, the story as told by a prominent man among the original colonists.

When it entered into the ingenious and adventurous head of Sir Walter Ralegh to seek for lands in the New World lying sufficiently northward of the Spanish possessions to render a settlement feasible and legitimate, sufficiently southward of Cabot's British explorations on the Labrador coast to be useful and profitable, Queen Elizabeth granted him a patent, in virtue of which he sent out two barques on a preliminary expedition in 1584, in which possession was formally taken of the island of Wokokan, off the coast of Florida. The second and more substantial expedition to the same regions was made in 1585. Sir Richard Grenville, acting as General in the name of Ralegh, started from Plymouth on April 9th in that year, in the command of seven ships, manned with soldiers, sailors, and a number of adventurous Englishmen who were to make their homes in Virginia—a name bestowed on the country north of Florida in

honour of the Virgin Queen of England. Their course was not
directly to the shore they aimed at ; it bore them first to Puerto
Rico, and then to Hispaniola, in which Spanish settlements the
English ships succeeded in obtaining stores, although their
welcome from King Philip's officers and colonists was naturally
not too cordial. Thence making their way northwards, they
reached the island of Roanoke and founded a settlement.
Grenville and his officers remained for a couple of months to
see things satisfactorily arranged ; he appointed Ralph Lane
governor of the new colony, and left with him a hundred and
seven men whose names are recorded by Hakluyt as the first
settlers in Virginia. Thomas Hariot was one of these ; and to
him we owe the narrative which is now reprinted. Another was
John White, the draughtsman whose designs illustrating the
manners and ways of the natives, and the Fauna and Flora of the
new land, were carried to Europe a year later and, by Richard
Hakluyt's interposition, entrusted for engraving to the hands of
the famous artist Theodore de Bry, of Frankfort. Hakluyt's list
does not give the name of John White exactly as we know it—it
appears in manuscript on the original leaves of the drawings (now
preserved in the British Museum) as " John White " and " John
With." There are, however, two names amongst those detailed
by Hakluyt either of which may be taken to represent the man—
" John Wright " and " John Twyt." There is a " John White "
mentioned several times by Hakluyt, but he was apparently a
seaman of higher rank than any of those settlers who remained
with Lane. He made several voyages and held nautical command in 1587 and 1590—that of 1590 being his fifth expedition.
Whoever the draughtsman was, his pictures shew that he was an
artist of considerable merit, and the original drawings in the
British Museum prove that De Bry was not, as he is frequently
supposed to have been, an inventive illustrator of the books in
his compilation, but a faithful engraver of authentic designs.

The non-arrival of supplies from England began to daunt the
colonists, while the relations between them and the Indians grew
so embarrassing that, under the existing conditions, the colony
was doomed to failure, and its abandonment for the time was

resolved upon. Sir Francis Drake visited Roanoke on June 10th, 1586, and Lane asked him to convey them back to England. He agreed to do so, and desired the settlers to make ready for sailing in August with Abraham Kendall and Griffith Herne, whom he appointed to the command of two vessels for that purpose; but he soon changed his mind. With characteristic rapidity of decision, Drake distributed the hundred and four men among his various ships and set out with them on June 19th. They reached Portsmouth on July 27th, and so ended the first English attempt to colonize the New World. The attempt was, however, renewed the following year successfully, as will be found recorded in divers histories.

Hariot wrote his book for the information of Ralegh, and was perhaps himself not the real transmitter of the story to the press. It was printed in London in 1588 without any illustrations. That first edition is now so rare that only four copies are known to be extant. If one turned up for sale at the present time, or at any time within the next twenty years, it would probably bring a price of not less than two thousand five hundred dollars. The second edition (which is here reproduced) is more valuable because it was illustrated by De Bry, who in the meanwhile had visited London and obtained the privilege of engraving John White's beautiful designs. The statement, on the title-page of the plates, that Hakluyt had translated the letterpress accompanying those designs from Latin into English, may simply mean that he had De Bry's work in manuscript before him; or it may be taken to show that the Latin edition of De Bry's first part was already in type. It matters little either way. The descriptions annexed to the plates were perhaps taken down by De Bry in Latin from John White's oral explanations, and were therefore the only original which Hakluyt could follow. The illustrations are of distinct anthropological importance and exactness, and convey a clearer notion of the ways and manners of the Red Indians at the time of the English plantation than any narrative could express. De Bry's edition was first printed in English as soon as the engravings were ready; and then translated into Latin and German in order to serve as the first fasciculus of his great

Collection of Voyages. The English volume, printed at Frankfort, is excessively rare, although not so rare as the little quarto printed at London two years before. A copy, if it were sold to-day, would probably bring a thousand dollars at the least.

A few slight obvious misprints are corrected in this re-impression.

AMORE ET VIRTVTE

TO THE RIGHT
WORTHIE AND HONOV-
RABLE, SIR VVALTER RALEGH,
KNIGHT, SENESCHAL OF THE DVCHIES OF
Cornewall and Exeter, and L. Warden of the
stannaries in Deuon and Cornewall.
T.B. wisheth true felictie.

*S*IR, *seeing that the parte of the* Worlde, *which is betwene the*
FLORIDA and the Cap BRETON nowe nammed VIRGINIA,
to the honneur of yours most souueraine Ladye and Queene
ELIZABETH, hath ben descouuerd by yours meanes and great
chardges. And that your Collonye hath heen theer established to
your great honnor and prayse, and noe lesser proffit vnto the common
welth: Yt ys good raison that euery man euertwe him selfe for to
showe the benefit which they haue receue of yt. Theerfore, for
my parte I haue been allwayes Defirous for to make yow knowe the
good will that J haue to remayne still your most humble seruant.
I haue thincke that J cold faynde noe better occasion to declare yt,
then takinge the paines to cott in copper (the most diligentlye and
well that wear in my possible to doe) the Figures which doe leuelye
represent the forme and maner of the Jnhabitants of the same

8

countrye with theirs ceremonies, sollemne feastes, and the manner and situation of their Townes, or Villages. Addinge vnto euery figure a brief declaration of the same, to that ende that euerye man cold the better vnderstand that which is in [it] liuelye represented. Moreouer J haue thincke that the aforesaid figures wear of greater commendation, Jf somme Histoire which traitinge of the commodites and fertillitye of the said countreye weare Ioyned with the same, therfor haue I serue miselfe of the rapport which Thomas Hariot hath lattely sett foorth, and haue causse them booth togither to be printed for to dedicate vnto you, as a thinge which by reigtte dooth allreadye apparteyne vnto you. Therfore doe I creaue that you will accept this little Booke, and take yt In goode partte. And desiringe that fauor that you will receue me in the nomber of one of y?ur most humble seruantz, besechinge the lord to blese and further you in all yours good doinges and actions, and allso to preserue, and keepe you allwayes in good helthe. And soe J comitt you vnto the almyhttie, from Franckfort the first of Apprill 1590.

Your most humble seruant,

THEODORVS de BRY.

TO THE ADVEN-
TVRERS, FAVORERS, AND
VVELVVILLERS OF THE EN-
TERPRISE FOR THE INHABITTING
and planting in VIRGINIA.

SINCE the first vndertaking by Sir Walter Ralegh to deale in the action of discouering of that Countrey which is now called and known by the name of VIRGINIA; many voyages hauing bin thither made at sundrie times to his great charge, as first in the yeere 1584, and afterwardes in the yeeres 1585, 1586, and now of late this last yeare of 1587. There haue bin diuers and variable reportes with some slaunderous and shamefull speeches bruited abroade by many that returned from thence. Especially of that discouery which was made by the Colony transported by Sir Richard Greinuile in the yeare 1585, being of all the others the most principal and as yet of most effect, the time of their abode in the countrey beeing a whole yeare, when as in the other voyage before they staied but sixe weekes; and the others after were onelie for supply and transportation, nothing more being discouered then had been before. Which reports haue not done a litle wrong to many that otherwise would haue also fauoured & aduentured in the action, to the honour and benefite of our nation, besides the particular profite and credite

which would redound to them selues the dealers therein ; as I
hope by the sequele of euents to the shame of those that haue
auouched the contrary shalbe manifest : if you the aduenturers,
fauourers, and welwillers do but either encrease in number, or in
opinion continue, or hauing bin doubtfull renewe your good liking
and furtherance to deale therein according to the worthinesse
thereof alreadye found and as you shall vnderstand hereafter to be
requisite.   Touching which woorthines through cause of the
diuersitie of relations and reportes, manye of your opinions coulde
not bee firme, nor the mindes of some that are well disposed, bee
setled in any certaintie.

I haue therefore thought it good beeing one that haue beene
in the discouerie and in dealing with the naturall inhabitantes
specially imploied ; and hauing therefore seene and knowne more
then the ordinarie : to imparte so much vnto you of the fruites of
our labours, as that you may knowe howe iniuriously the enterprise
is slaundered.   And that in publike manner at this present
chiefelie for two respectes.

First that some of you which are yet ignorant or doubtfull of
the state thereof, may see that there is sufficient cause why the
cheefe enterpriser with the fauour of her Maiestie, notwithstanding
suche reportes ; hath not onelie since continued the action by
sending into the countrey againe, and replanting this last yeere a
new Colony ; but is also readie, according as the times and meanes
will affoorde, to follow and prosecute the same.

Secondly, that you seeing and knowing the continuance of the
action by the view hereof you may generally know & learne what
the countrey is, & thervpon consider how your dealing therein if it
proceede, may returne you profit and gaine ; bee it either by
inhabitting & planting or otherwise in furthering thereof.

And least that the substance of my relation should be doubtful
vnto you as of others by reason of their diuersitie : I will first open
the cause in a few wordes wherefore they are so different ; referring
my selue to your fauourable constructions, and to be adiudged of
as by good consideration you shall finde cause.

Of our companie that returned, some for their misdemenour
and ill dealing in the countrey, haue beene there worthily punished ;

who by reason of their badde natures, haue maliciously not onelie
spoken ill of their Gouernours ; but for their sakes flaundered the
countrie it selfe.   The like also haue those done which were of
their consort.

Some beeing ignorant of the state thereof, notwithstanding
since their returne amongest their friendes and acquaintance and
also others, especially if they were in companie where they might
not be gainesaide ; woulde seeme to knowe so much as no men
more ; and make no men so great trauailers as themselues.   They
stood so much as it maie seeme vppon their credite and reputation
that hauing been a twelue moneth in the countrey, it woulde haue
beene a great disgrace vnto them as they thought, if they coulde
not haue saide much whether it were true or false.   Of which some
haue spoken of more then euer they saw or otherwise knew to bee
there ; othersome haue not bin ashamed to make absolute deniall
of that which although not by them, yet by others is most certainely
and there plentifully knowne.   And othersome make difficulties of
those things they haue no skill of.

The cause of their ignorance was, in that they were of that
many that were neuer out of the Iland where wee were seated, or
not farre, or at the leastwise in few places els, during the time of
our aboade in the countrey ; or of that many that after golde and
siluer was not so soone found, as it was by them looked for, had
little or no care of any other thing but to pamper their bellies ; or
of that many which had little vnderstanding, lesse discretion, and
more tongue then was needfull or requisite.

Some also were of a nice bringing vp, only in cities or townes,
or such as neuer (as I may say) had seene the worlde before.
Because there were not to bee found any English cities, nor such
faire houses, nor at their owne wish any of their olde accustomed
daintie food, nor any soft beds of downe or fethers : the countrey
was to them miserable, & their reports thereof according.

Because my purpose was but in briefe to open the cause of
the varietie of such speeches ; the particularities of them, and of
many enuious, malicious, and slaunderous reports and deuises els,
by our owne countrey men besides ; as trifles that are not worthy
of wise men to bee thought vpon, I meane not to trouble you

withall : but will passe to the commodities, the substance of that which I haue to make relation of vnto you.

The treatise whereof for your more readie view & easier vnderstanding I will diuide into three speciall parts. In the first I will make declaration of such commodities there alreadie found or to be raised, which will not onely serue the ordinary turnes of you which are and shall bee the planters and inhabitants, but such an ouerplus sufficiently to bee yelded, or by men of skill to bee prouided, as by way of trafficke and exchaunge with our owne nation of England, will enrich your selues the prouiders ; those that shal deal with you ; the enterprisers in general ; and greatly profit our owne countrey men, to supply them with most things which heretofore they haue bene faine to prouide either of strangers or of our enemies : which commodities for distinction sake, I call *Merchantable.*

In the second, I will set downe all the comodities which wee know the countrey by our experience doeth yeld of it selfe for victuall, and sustenance of mans life ; such as is vsually fed vpon by the inhabitants of the countrey, as also by vs during the time we were there.

In the last part I will make mention generally of such other commodities besides, as I am able to remember, and as I shall thinke behooffull for those that shall inhabite, and plant there to knowe of ; which specially concerne building, as also some other necessary vses : with a briefe description of the nature and maners of the people of the countrey.

THE FIRST PART,
OF MARCHAN-
TABLE COMMO-
DITIES.

Silke of graſſe or graſſe Silke.

THERE is a kind of grasse in the countrey vppon the blades where of there groweth very good silke in forme of a thin glittering skin to bee stript of. It groweth two foote and a halfe high or better: the blades are about two foot in length, and half inch broad. The like groweth in Persia, which is in the selfe same climate as Virginia, of which very many of the silke workes that come from thence into Europe are made. Here of if it be planted and ordered as in Persia, it cannot in reason be otherwise, but that there will rise in shorte time great profite to the dealers therein ; seeing there is so great vse and vent thereof as well in our countrey as els where. And by the meanes of sowing & planting in good ground, it will be farre greater, better, and more plentifull then it is. Although notwithstanding there is great store thereof in many places of the countrey growing naturally and wilde.

Which also by proof here in England, in making a piece of silke Grogran, we found to be excellent good.

*W*orme Silke.

In manie of our iourneyes we found silke wormes fayre and great ; as bigge as our ordinary walnuttes. Although it hath not beene our happe to haue found such plentie as elsewhere to be in the coutrey we haue heard of; yet seeing that the countrey doth naturally breede and nourish them, there is no doubt but if art be added in planting of mulbery trees and others fitte for them in commodious places, for their feeding and nourishing ; and some of them carefully gathered and husbanded in that fort as by men of skill is knowne to be necessarie : there will rise as great profite in time to the Virginians, as thereof doth now to the Persians, Turkes, Italians and Spaniards.

Flaxe and Hempe.

The trueth is that of Hempe and Flaxe there is no great store in any one place together, by reason it is not planted but as the soile doth yeeld it of it selfe ; and howsoeuer the leafe, and stemme or stalke doe differ from ours; the stuffe by the iudgement of men of skill is altogether as good as ours. And if not, as further proofe should finde otherwise ; we haue that experience of the soile, as that there cannot bee shewed anie reason to the contrary, but that it will grow there excellent well; and by planting will be yeelded plentifully : seeing there is so much ground whereof some may well be applyed to such purposes. What benefite heereof may growe in cordage and linnens who can not easily understand ?

Allum.

There is a veine of earth along the sea coast for the space of fourtie or fiftie miles, whereof by the iudgement of some that haue made triall heere in England, is made good Allum, of that kinde which is called Roche Allum.   The richnesse of such a commoditie is so well knowne that I neede not to saye any thing thereof. The same earth doth also yeelde White Copresse, Nitrum, and Alumen Plumeum, but nothing so plentifully as the common Allum ; which be also of price and profitable.

Wapeih.

Wapeih, a kinde of earth so called by the naturall inhabitants ; very like to terra sigillata : and hauing beene refined, it hath beene found by some of our Phisitions and Chirurgeons to bee of the same kinde of vertue and more effectuall.   The inhabitants vse it very much for the cure of sores and woundes : there is in diuers places great plentie, and in some places of a blewe sort.

Pitch, Tarre, Rozen, and Turpentine.

There are those kindes of trees which yeelde them abundantly and great store.   In the very same Iland where wee were seated, being fifteene miles of length, and fiue or sixe miles in breadth, there are fewe trees els but of the same kind ; the whole Iland being full.

Saffafras.

Sassafras, called by the inhabitantes *Winauk,* a kinde of wood of most pleasand and sweete smel, and of most rare vertues in phisick for the cure of many diseases.   It is found by experience to bee farre better and of more vses then the wood which is called *Guaiacum,* or *Lignum vitæ.*   For the description, the manner of vsing and the manifolde vertues thereof, I referre you to the booke of *Monardus,* translated and entituled in English, *The ioyfull newes from the West Indies.*

Cedar.

Cedar, a very sweet wood and fine timber; wherof if nests of chests be there made, or timber therof fitted for sweet & fine bedsteads, tables, deskes, lutes, virginalles & many things else, (of which there hath beene proofe made already) to make vp fraite with other principal commodities will yield profite.

Wine.

There are two kinds of grapes that the soile doth yeeld naturally: the one is small and sowre of the ordinarie bignesse as ours in England: the other farre greater & of himselfe lushious sweet. When they are planted and husbanded as they ought, a principall commoditie of wines by them may be raised.

Oyle.

There are two sortes of *Walnuttes* both holding oyle, but the one farre more plentifull then the other. When there are milles & other deuises for the purpose, a commodity of them may be raised because there are infinite store. There are also three scuerall kindes of *Berries* in the forme of Oke akornes, which also by the experience and vse of the inhabitantes, wee finde to yeelde very good and sweete oyle. Furthermore the *Beares* of the countrey are commonly very fatte, and in some places there are many: their fatnesse because it is so liquid, may well be termed oyle, and hath many speciall vses.

Furres.

All along the Sea coast there are great store of *Otters*, which beeyng taken by weares and other engines made for the purpose, will yeelde good profite. Wee hope also of *Marterne furres*, and make no doubt by the relation of the people but that in some

places of the countrey there are store: although there were but
two skinnes that came to our handes. *Luzarnes* also we haue
vnderstading of, although for the time we saw none.

Deare skinnes.

Deare skinnes dressed after the manner of *Chamoes* or vndressed
are to be had of the naturall inhabitants thousands yeerely by way
of trafficke for trifles: and no more wast or spoile of Deare then
is and hath beene ordinarily in time before.

Ciuet cattes.

In our trauailes, there was founde one to haue beene killed by
a saluage or inhabitant: and in an other place the smell where
one or more had lately beene before: whereby we gather besides
then by the relation of the people that there are some in the
countrey: good profite will rise by them.

Iron.

In two places of the countrey specially, one about fourescore
and the other six score miles from the Fort or place where wee
dwelt: wee founde neere the water side the ground to be rockie,
which by the triall of a minerall man, was founde to holde Iron
richly.   It is founde in manie places of the countrey else.   I knowe
nothing to the contrarie, but that it maie bee allowed for a good
marchantable commoditie, considering there the small charge for
the labour and feeding of men: the infinite store of wood: the
want of wood and deerenesse thereof in England: & the necessity
of ballasting of shippes.

Copper.

A hundred and fiftie miles into the maine in two townes wee
founde with the inhabitaunts diuerse small plates of copper, that
had beene made as wee vnderstood, by the inhabitantes that dwell

B

farther into the countrey : where as they say are mountaines and Riuers that yeelde also whyte graynes of Mettall, which is to bee deemed *Siluer*. For confirmation whereof at the time of our first arriuall in the Countrey, I sawe with some others with mee, two small peeces of siluer grosly beaten about the weight of a Testrone, hangyng in the eares of a *Wiroans* or *chiefe Lorde* that dwelt about fourescore myles from vs; of whom thorowe enquiry, by the number of dayes and the way, I learned that it had come to his handes from the same place or neere, where I after vnderstood the copper was made and the white graynes of mettall founde. The aforesaide copper wee also founde by triall to holde siluer.

Pearle.

Sometimes in feeding on muscles wee founde some pearle; but it was our hap to meete with ragges, or of a pide colour; not hauing yet discouered those places where wee hearde of better and more plentie. One of our companie; a man of skill in such matters, had gathered together from among the sauage people aboute fiue thousande: of which number he chose so many as made a fayre chaine, which for their likenesse and vniformitie in roundnesse, orientnesse, and pidenesse of many excellent colours, with equalitie in greatnesse, were verie fayre and rare; and had therefore beene presented to her Maiestie, had wee not by casualtie and through extremity of a storme, lost them with many things els in comming away from the countrey.

Sweete Gummes.

Sweete Gummes of diuers kindes and many other Apothecary drugges of which wee will make speciall mention, when wee shall recciue it from such men of skill in that kynd, that in taking reasonable paines shall discouer them more particularly then wee haue done; and than now I can make relation of, for want of the examples I had prouided and gathered, and are nowe lost, with other thinges by causualtie before mentioned.

Dyes of diuers kindes.

There is Shoemake well knowen, and vsed in England for blacke; the feede of an hearbe called Wasewówr: little small rootes called Cháppacor ; and the barke of the tree called by the inhabitaunts Tangomóckonomindge : which Dies are for diuers sortes of red : their goodnesse for our English clothes remaynes yet to be proued. The inhabitants vse them onely for the dying of hayre ; and colouring of their faces, and Mantles made of Deare skinnes; and also for the dying of Rushes to make artificiall workes withall in their Mattes and Baskettes; hauing no other thing besides that they account of, apt to vse them for. If they will not proue merchantable there is no doubt but the Planters there shall finde apte vses for them, as also for other colours which wee knowe to be there.

Oade.

A thing of so great vent and vse amongst English Diers, which cannot bee yeelded sufficiently in our owne countrey for spare of ground ; may bee planted in Virginia, there being ground enough, The grouth therof need not to be doubted when as in the Ilandes of the Asores it groweth plentifully, which is in the same climate. So likewise of Madder.

Suger canes.

Whe carried thither Suger canes to plant which beeing not so well preserued as was requisit, & besides the time of the yere being past for their setting when we arriued, wee could not make that proofe of them as wee desired. Notwithstanding seeing that they grow in the same climate, in the South part of Spaine and in Barbary, our hope in reason may yet continue. So likewise for *Orenges*, and *Lemmons*, there may be planted also *Quinses*. Wherbi may grow in reasonable time if the action be diligently prosecuted no small commodities in *Sugers*, *Suckets*, and *Marmalades*.

Many other commodities by planting may there also bee

raised, which I leaue to your discret and gentle considerations:
and many also may bee there which yet we haue not discouered.
Two more commodities of great value one of certaintie, and the
other in hope, not to be planted, but there to be raised & in short
time to be prouided and prepared, I might haue specified. So
likewise of those commodities already set downe I might haue
said more; as of the particular places where they are founde and
best to be planted and prepared: by what meanes and in what
reasonable space of time they might be raised to profit and in
what proportion; but because others then welwillers might bee
therewithall acquainted, not to the good of the action, I haue
wittingly omitted them: knowing that to those that are well
disposed I haue vttered, according to my promise and purpose,
for this part sufficient.

THE SECOND PART,

OF SVCHE COMMO-

DITIES AS VIRGINIA IS

knowne to yeelde for victuall and fuſtenãce
of mans life, vſually fed vpon by the
naturall inhabitants : as alſo by vs
during the time of our aboad.
And firſt of ſuch as are
ſowed and husbanded.

PAGATOWR, a kinde of graine so called by the inhabitants ;
the same in the West Indies is called MAYZE : English men
call it Guinney wheate or Turkie wheate, according to the
names of the countreys from whence the like hath beene brought.
The graine is about the bignesse of our ordinary English peaze
and not much different in forme and shape : but of diuers colours :
some white, some red, some yellow, and some blew. All of them
yeelde a very white and sweete flowre : beeing vsed according to
his kinde it maketh a very good bread. Wee made of the same
in the countrey some mault, whereof was brued as good ale as

was to be desired. So likewise by the help of hops therof may
bee made as good Beere. It is a graine of marueilous great
increase; of a thousand, fifteene hundred and some two thousand
fold. There are three sortes, of which two are ripe in an eleuen
and twelue weekes at the most : sometimes in ten, after the time
they are set, and are then of height in stalke about sixe or seuen
foote. The other sort is ripe in fourteene, and is about ten foote
high, of the stalkes some beare foure heads, some three, some
one, and two : euery head containing fiue, sixe, or seuen hundred
graines within a fewe more or lesse. Of these graines besides
bread, the inhabitants make victuall eyther by parching them ; or
seething them whole vntill they be broken ; or boyling the floure
with water into a pappe.

Okindgier, called by vs *Beanes*, because in greatnesse & partly
in shape they are like to the Beanes in England ; sauing that
they are flatter, of more diuers colours, and some pide. The
leafe also of the stemme is much different. In taste they are
altogether as good as our English peaze.

Wickonzówr, called by vs *Peaze*, in respect of the beanes for
distinction sake, because they are much lesse ; although in forme
they little differ ; but in goodnesse of tast much, & are far better
then our English peaze. Both the beanes and peaze are ripe in
tenne weekes after they are set. They make them victuall either
by boyling them all to pieces into a broth ; or boiling them whole
vntill they bee soft and beginne to breake as is vsed in England,
eyther by themselues or mixtly together : Sometime they mingle
of the wheate with them. Sometime also beeing whole sodden,
they bruse or pound them in a morter, & thereof make loaues
or lumps of dowishe bread, which they vse to eat for varietie.

Macócqwer, according to their seuerall formes called by vs,
Pompions, Mellions, and *Gourdes*, because they are of the like
formes as those kindes in England. In *Virginia* such of seuerall
formes are of one taste and very good, and do also spring from
one seed. There are of two sorts ; one is ripe in the space of a
moneth, and the other in two moneths.

There is an hearbe which in Dutch is called *Melden*. Some of
those that I describe it vnto, take it to be a kinde of Orage ; it

groweth about foure or fiue foote high: of the seede thereof they
make a thicke broth, and pottage of a very good taste: of the
stalke by burning into ashes they make a kinde of salt earth,
wherewithall many vse sometimes to season their brothes; other
salte they knowe not. Wee our selues, vsed the leaues also for
pothearbes.

There is also another great hearbe in forme of a Marigolde,
about sixe foote in height; the head with the floure is a spanne
in breadth. Some take it to bee *Planta Solis:* of the seedes
heereof they make both a kinde of bread and broth.

All the aforesaide commodities for victuall are set or sowed,
sometimes in groundes apart and seuerally by themselues; but
for the most part together in one ground mixtly: the manner
thereof with the dressing and preparing of the ground, because I
will note vnto you the fertilitie of the soile; I thinke good briefly
to describe.

The ground they neuer fatten with mucke, dounge or any
other thing; neither plow nor digge it as we in England, but
onely prepare it in sort as followeth. A fewe daies before they
sowe or set, the men with wooden instruments, made almost in
forme of mattockes or hoes with long handles; the women with
short peckers or parers, because they vse them sitting, of a foote
long and about fiue inches in breadth: doe onely breake the
vpper part of the ground to rayse vp the weedes, grasse, & old
stubbes of corne stalkes with their rootes. The which after a
day or twoes drying in the Sunne, being scrapte vp into many
small heapes, to saue them labour for carrying them away; they
burne into ashes. (And whereas some may thinke that they vse
the ashes for to better the grounde; I say that then they woulde
eyther disperse the ashes abroade; which wee obserued they doe
not, except the heapes bee too great: or els would take speciall
care to set their corne where the ashes lie, which also wee finde
they are carelesse of.) And this is all the husbanding of their
ground that they vse.

Then their setting or sowing is after this maner. First for
their corne, beginning in one corner of the plot, with a pecker they
make a hole, wherein they put foure graines with that care they

touch not one another, (about an inch asunder) and couer them with the moulde againe : and so through out the whole plot, making such holes and vsing them after such maner : but with this regard that they bee made in rankes, euery ranke differing from other halfe a fadome or a yarde, and the holes also in euery ranke, as much.   By this meanes there is a yarde spare ground betwene euery hole : where according to discretion here and there, they set as many Beanes and Peaze : in diuers places also among the seedes of *Macocqwer*, *Melden* and *Planta Solis*.

The ground being thus set according to the rate by vs experimented, an English Acre conteining fourtie pearches in length, and foure in breadth, doeth there yeeld in croppe or of-come of corne, beanes, and peaze, at the least two hundred London bushelles : besides the *Macocqwer*, *Melden,* and *Planta Solis* : When as in England fourtie bushelles of our wheate yeelded out of such an acre is thought to be much.

I thought also good to note this vnto you, if you which shall inhabite and plant there, maie know how specially that countrey corne is there to be preferred before ours : Besides the manifold waies in applying it to victuall, the increase is so much that small labour and paines is needful in respect that must be vsed for ours. For this I can assure you that according to the rate we haue made proofe of, one man may preparè and husbande so much grounde (hauing once borne corne before) with lesse then foure and twentie houres labour, as shall yeelde him victuall in a large proportion for a twelue moneth if hee haue nothing clse, but that which the same ground will yeelde, and of that kinde onelie which I haue before spoken of : the saide ground being also but of fiue and twentie yards square.   And if neede require, but that there is ground enough, there might be raised out of one and the selfsame ground two haruestes or of-comes ; for they sowe or set and may at anie time when they thinke good from the middest of March vntill the ende of Iune : so that they also set when they haue eaten of their first croppe.   In some places of the countrey notwithstanding they haue two haruests, as we haue heard, out of one and the same ground.

For English corne neuertheles whether to vse or not to vse it, you that inhabite maie do as you shall haue farther cause to thinke best. Of the grouth you need not to doubt; for barlie, oates and peaze, we haue seene proof of, not beeing purposely sowen but fallen casually in the worst sort of ground, and yet to be as faire as any we haue euer seene here in England. But of wheat because it was musty and hat taken salt water wee could make no triall : and of rye we had none. Thus much haue I digressed and I hope not vnnecessarily : nowe will I returne againe to my course and intreate of that which yet remaineth appertaining to this Chapter.

There is an herbe which is sowed a part by it selfe & is called by the inhabitants Vppówoc : In the West Indies it hath diuers names, according to the seuerall places & countries where it groweth and is vsed : The Spaniardes generally call it Tobacco. The leaues thereof being dried and brought into powder : they vse to take the fume or smoke thereof by sucking it through pipes made of claie into their stomacke and heade ; from whence it purgeth superfluous fleame & other grosse humors, openeth all the pores & passages of the body : by which meanes the vse thereof not only preserueth the body from obstructions ; but also if any be, so that they haue not beene of too long continuance, in short time breaketh them : wherby their bodies are notably preserued in health, & know not many greeuous diseases wherewithall wee in England are oftentimes afflicted.

This Vppówoc is of so precious estimation amongest them, that they thinke their gods are maruelously delighted therwith : Wherupon sometime they make hallowed fires & cast·some of the pouder therein for a sacrifice : being in a storme vppon the waters, to pacifie their gods, they cast some vp into the aire and into the water : so a weare for fish being newly set vp, they cast some therein and into the aire : also after an escape of danger, they cast some into the aire likewise : but all done with strange gestures, stamping, somtime dauncing, clapping of hands, holding vp of hands, & staring vp into the heauens, vttering therewithal and chattering strange words & noises.

We our selues during the time we were there vsed to suck it after their maner, as also since our returne, & haue found manie rare and wonderful experiments of the vertues thereof ; of which the relation woulde require a volume by it selfe : the vse of it by so manie of late, men & women of great calling as else, and some learned Phisitions also, is sufficient witnes.

And these are all the commodities for sustenance of life that I know and can remember they vse to husband : all else that followe are founde growing naturally or wilde.

Of Rootes.

OPENAVK are a kind of roots of round forme, some of the bignes of walnuts, some far greater, which are found in moist & marish grounds growing many together one by another in ropes, or as thogh they were fastened with a string. Being boiled or sodden they are very good meate.

OKEEPENAVK are also of round shape, found in dry grounds : some are of the bignes of a mans head. They are to be eaten as they are taken out of the ground, for by reason of their drinesse they will neither roste nor seeth. Their tast is not so good as of the former rootes, notwithstanding for want of bread & somtimes for varietie the inhabitants vse to eate them with fish or flesh, and in my iudgement they doe as well as the houshold bread made of rie heere in England.

Kaishcúpenauk a white kind of roots about the bignes of hen egs & nere of that forme : their tast was not so good to our seeming as of the other, and therfore their place and manner of growing not so much cared for by vs : the inhabitants notwithstanding vsed to boile & eate many.

Tsinaw a kind of roote much like vnto the which in England is called the *China root* brought from the East Indies. And we know not anie thing to the cotrary but that it maie be of the same kind. These roots grow manie together in great clusters and doe bring foorth a brier stalke, but the leafe in shape far vnlike ; which beeing supported by the trees it groweth neerest vnto, wil reach or climbe to the top of the highest. From these roots while they be new or fresh beeing chopt into small pieces & stampt, is strained with water a iuice that maketh bread, & also being boiled, a very good spoonemeate in maner of a gelly, and is much better in tast if it bee tempered with oyle.   This *Tsinaw* is not of that sort which by some was caused to be brought into England or the *China roote*, for it was discouered since, and is in vse as is afore saide: but that which was brought hither is not yet knowne neither by vs nor by the inhabitants to serue for any vse or purpose ; although the rootes in shape are very like.

Coscúshaw, some of our company tooke to bee that kinde of roote which the Spaniards in the West Indies call *Cassauy*, whereupon also many called it by that name: it groweth in very muddie pooles and moist groundes.   Being dressed according to the countrey maner, it maketh a good bread, and also a good sponemeate, and is vsed very much by the inhabitants : The iuice of this root is poison, and therefore heede must be taken before any thing be made therewithal : Either the rootes must bee first sliced and dried in the Sunne, or by the fire, and then being pounded into floure wil make good bread : or els while they are greene they are to bee pared, cut into pieces and stampt ; loues of the same to be laid neere or ouer the fire vntill it be floure, and then being well pounded againe, bread, or spone meate very good in taste, and holsome may be made thereof.

Habascon is a roote of hoat taste almost of the forme and bignesse of a Parseneepe, of it selfe it is no victuall, but onely a helpe beeing boiled together with other meates.

There are also *Leekes* differing little from ours in England that grow in many places of the countrey, of which, when we came in places where, wee gathered and eate many, but the naturall inhabitants neuer.

Of Fruites.

CHESTNVTS, there are in diuers places great store : some they vse to eate rawe, some they stampe and boile to make spoone-meate, and with some being sodden they make such a manner of dowe bread as they vse of their beanes before mentioned.

WALNVTS : There are two kindes of Walnuts, and of then infinit store : In many places where very great woods for many miles together the third part of trees are walnuttrees.   The one kind is of the same taste and forme or litle differing from ours of England, but that they are harder and thicker shelled: the other is greater and hath a verie ragged and harde shell: but the kernell great, verie oylie and sweete. Besides their eating of them after our ordinarie maner, they breake them with stones and pound them in morters with water to make a milk which they vse to put into some sorts of their spoonmeate; also among their sodde wheat, peaze, beanes and pompions which maketh them haue a farre more pleasant taste.

MEDLARS a kind of verie good fruit, so called by vs chieflie for these respectes: first in that they are not good vntill they be rotten: then in that they open at the head as our medlars, and are about the same bignesse: otherwise in taste and colour they are farre different: for they are as red as cheries and very sweet: but whereas the cherie is sharpe sweet, they are lushious sweet.

METAQVESVNNAVK, a kinde of pleasaunt fruite almost of the shape & bignes of English peares, but that they are of a perfect red colour as well within as without. They grow on a plant whose leaues are verie thicke and full of prickles as sharpe as needles. Some that haue bin in the Indies, where they haue seen that kind of red die of great price which is called Cochinile to grow, doe describe his plant right like vnto this of Metaque-sunnauk but whether it be the true Cochinile or a bastard or wilde kind, it cannot yet be certified; seeing that also as I heard, Cochinile is not of the fruite but founde on the leaues of the plant; which leaues for such matter we haue not so specially obserued.

GRAPES there are of two sorts which I mentioned in the marchantable cõmodities.

STRABERIES there are as good & as great as those which we haue in our English gardens.

MVLBERIES, Applecrabs, Hurts or Hurtleberies, such as wee haue in England.

SACQVENVMMENER a kinde of berries almost like vnto capres but somewhat greater which grow together in clusters vpon a plant or herb that is found in shalow waters: being boiled eight or nine hours according to their kind are very good meate and holesome, otherwise if they be eaten they will make a man for the time franticke or extremely sicke.

There is a kind of reed which beareth a seed almost like vnto our rie or wheat, & being boiled is good meate.

In our trauailes in some places wee founde *wilde peaze* like vnto ours in England but that they were lesse, which are also good meate.

Of a kinde of fruite or berrie in forme of Acornes.

There is a kind of berrie or acorne, of which there are fiue sorts that grow on seuerall kinds of trees; the one is called *Sagatémener*, the second *Osámener*, the third *Pummuckóner*. These kind of acorns they vse to drie vpon hurdles made of reeds with fire vnderneath almost after the maner as we dry malt in England. When they are to be vsed they first water them vntil they be soft & then being sod they make a good victuall, either to eate so simply, or els being also pounded, to make loaues or lumpes of bread. These be also the three kinds of which, I said before, the inhabitants vsed to make sweet oyle.

An other sort is called *Sapúmmener* which being boiled or parched doth eate and taste like vnto chestnuts. They sometime also make bread of this sort.

The fifth sort is called *Mangúmmenauk*, and is the acorne of their kind of oake, the which beeing dried after the maner of the first sortes, and afterward watered they boile them, & their seruants or sometime the chiefe themselues, either for variety or for want of bread, doe eate them with their fish or flesh.

Of Beaſtes.

Deare, in some places there are great store : neere vnto the sea coast they are of the ordinarie bignes as ours in England, & some lesse : but further vp into the countrey where there is better seed they are greater : they differ from ours onely in this, their tailes are longer and the snags of their hornes looke backward.

Conies, Those that we haue seen & al that we can heare of are of a grey colour like vnto hares: in some places there are such plentie that all the people of some townes make them mantles of the furre or flue of the skinnes of those they vsually take.

Saquenúckot & *Maquówoc* ; two kindes of small beastes greater then conies which are very good meat. We neuer tooke any of them our selues, but sometime eate of such as the inhabitants had taken & brought vnto vs.

Squirels which are of a grey colour, we haue taken & eaten.

Beares which are all of black colour. The beares of this countrey are good meat; the inhabitants in time of winter do vse to take & eate manie, so also somtime did wee. They are taken commonlie in this sort. In some Ilands or places where they are, being hunted for, as soone as they haue spiall of a man they presently run awaie, & then being chased they clime and get vp the next tree they can, from whence with arrowes they are shot downe starke dead, or with those wounds that they may after easily be killed ; we sometime shotte them downe with our caleeuers.

I haue the names of eight & twenty seuerall sortes of beasts which I haue heard of to be here and there dispersed in the countrie, especially in the maine : of which there are only twelue kinds that we haue yet discouered, & of these that be good meat we know only them before mentioned. The inhabi-tãnts somtime kil the *Lyon* & eat him : & we somtime as they came to our hands of their *Wolues* or *woluish Dogges,* which I haue not set downe for good meat, least that some woulde vnder-stand my iudgement therin to be more simple than needeth, although I could alleage the difference in taste of those kindes from ours, which by some of our company haue beene experi-mented in both.

Of Foule.

Turkie cockes and *Turkie hennes: Stockdoues: Partridges: Cranes: Hernes :* & in winter great store of *Swannes* & *Geese.* Of al sortes of foule I haue the names in the countrie language of foure-score and six of which number besides those that be named, we haue taken, eaten, & haue the pictures as they were there drawne with the names of the inhabitaunts of seuerall strange sortes of water foule eight, and seuenteene kinds more of land foul, although wee haue seen and eaten of many more, which for want of leasure there for the purpose coulde not bee pictured: and after wee are better furnished and stored vpon further discouery, with their strange beastes, fishe, trees, plants, and hearbes, they shall bee also published.

There are also *Parats, Faulcons, & Marlin haukes*, which although with vs they bee not vsed for meate, yet for other causes I thought good to mention.

Of Fishe.

For foure monethes of the yeere, February, March, Aprill and May, there are plentie of *Sturgeons:* And also in the same monethes of *Herrings*, some of the ordinary bignesse as ours in England, but the most part farre greater, of eighteene, twentie inches, and some two foote in length and better; both these kindes of fishe in those monethes are most plentifull, and in best season which wee founde to bee most delicate and pleasaunt meate.

There are also *Troutes, Porpoises, Rayes, Oldwiues, Mullets, Plaice*, and very many other sortes of excellent good fish, which we haue taken & eaten, whose names I know not but in the countrey language; wee haue of twelue sorts more the pictures as they were drawn in the countrey with their names.

The inhabitants vse to take then two maner of wayes, the one is by a kind of wear made of reedes which in that countrey are very strong. The other way which is more strange, is with poles made sharpe at one ende, by shooting them into the fish after the maner as Irishmen cast dartes; either as they are rowing in their boates or els as they are wading in the shallowes for the purpose.

There are also in many places plentie of these kindes which follow.

Sea crabbes, such as we haue in England.

Oystres, some very great, and some small; some rounde and some of a long shape: They are founde both in salt water and brackish, and those that we had out of salt water are far better than the other as in our owne countrey.

Also *Muscles, Scalopes, Periwinkles,* and *Creuises.*

Seekanauk, a kinde of crustie shell fishe which is good meate, about a foote in breadth, hauing a crustie tayle, many legges like a crab ; and her eyes in her backe.   They are founde in shallowes of salt waters ; and sometime on the shoare.

There are many *Tortoyses* both of lande and sea kinde, their backes & bellies are shelled very thicke ; their head, feete, and taile, which are in appearance, seeme ougly as though they were membres of a serpent or venemous : but notwithstanding they are very good meate, as also their egges.   Some haue bene founde of a yard in bredth and better.

And thus haue I made relation of all sortes of victuall that we fed vpon for the time we were in *Virginia,* as also the inhabitants themselues, as farre foorth as I knowe and can remember or that are specially worthy to bee remembred.

THE THIRD AND
LAST PART,
OF SVCH OTHER
THINGES AS IS BEHOOF-
full for thofe which shall plant and inhabit
to know of; with a defcription of
the nature and manners of
the people of the
countrey.

Of commodities for building and other necefsary vfes.

THOSE other things which I am more to make rehearsall of, are such as concerne building, and other mechanicall necessarie vses; as diuers sortes of trees for house & ship timber, and other vses els: Also lime, stone, and brick, least that being not mentioned some might haue bene doubted of, or by some that are malicious reported the contrary.

Okes, there are as faire, straight, tall, and as good timber as any can be, and also great store, and in some places very great.

Walnut trees, as I haue saide before very many, some haue

c

bene seen excellent faire timber of foure & fiue fadome, & aboue fourescore foot streight without bough.

Firre trees fit for masts of ships, some very tall & great.

Rakiock, a kind of trees so called that are sweet wood of which the inhabitans that were neere vnto vs doe commonly make their boats or Canoes of the form of trowes ; only with the helpe of fire, hatchets of stones, and shels ; we haue known some so great being made in that sort of one tree that they haue carried well xx. men at once, besides much baggage: the timber being great, tal, streight, soft, light, & yet tough enough I thinke (besides other vses) to be fit also for masts of ships.

Cedar, a sweet wood good for seelings, Chests, Boxes, Bedsteedes, Lutes, Virginals, and many things els, as I haue also said before. Some of our company which haue wandered in some places where I haue not bene, haue made certaine affirmation of *Cyprus* which for such and other excellent vses, is also a wood of price and no small estimation.

Maple, and also *Wich-hazle*, wherof the inhabitants vse to make their bowes.

Holly a necessary thing for the making of birdlime.

Willowes good for the making of weares and weeles to take fish after the English manner, although the inhabitants vse only reedes, which because they are so strong as also flexible, do serue for that turne very well and sufficiently.

Beech and *Ashe*, good for caske hoopes : and if neede require, plow worke, as also for many things els.

Elme.

Sassafras trees.

Ascopo a kinde of tree very like vnto Lawrell, the barke is hoat in tast and spicie, it is very like to that tree which Monardus describeth to bee *Cassia Lignea* of the West Indies.

There are many other strange trees whose names I knowe not but in the *Virginian* language, of which I am not nowe able, neither is it so conuenient for the present to trouble you with particular relation : seeing that for timber and other necessary vses I haue named sufficient: And of many of the rest but that they may be applied to good vse, I know no cause to doubt.

Now for Stone, Bricke and Lime, thus it is. Neere vnto the Sea coast where wee dwelt, there are no kinde of stones to bee found (except a fewe small pebbles about foure miles off) but such as haue bene brought from farther out of the maine. In some of our voiages wee haue seene diuers hard raggie stones, great pebbles, and a kinde of grey stone like vnto marble, of which the inhabitants make their hatchets to cleeue wood. Vpon inquirie wee heard that a little further vp into the Countrey were of all sortes verie many, although of Quarries they are ignorant, neither haue they vse of any store whereupon they should haue occasion to seeke any. For if euerie housholde haue one or two to cracke Nuttes, grinde shelles, whet copper, and sometimes other stones for hatchets, they haue enough : neither vse they any digging, but onely for graues about three foote deepe : and therefore no maruaile that they know neither Quarries, nor lime stones, which both may bee in places neerer than they wot of.

In the meane time vntill there bee discouerie of sufficient store in some place or other conuenient, the want of you which are and shalbe the planters therein may be as well supplied by Bricke : for the making whereof in diuers places of the countrey there is clay both excellent good, and plentie ; and also by lime made of Oister shels, and of others burnt, after the maner as they vse in the Iles of Tenet and Shepy, and also in diuers other places of England : Which kinde of lime is well knowne to bee as good as any other. And of Oister shels there is plentie enough : for besides diuers other particular places where are abundance, there is one shallowe sounde along the coast, where for the space of many miles together in length, and two or three miles in breadth, the grounde is nothing els beeing but halfe a foote or a foote vnder water for the most part.

This much can I say further more of stones, that about 120 miles from our fort neere the water in the side of a hill was founde by a Gentleman of our company, a great veine of hard ragge stones, which I thought good to remember vnto you.

Of the nature and manners of the people.

It resteth I speake a word or two of the naturall inhabitants,

their natures and maners, leauing large discourse thereof vntill
time more conuenient hereafter : nowe onely so farre foorth, as that
you may know, how that they in respect of troubling our inhabit-
ing and planting, are not to be feared ; but that they shall haue
ause both to feare and loue vs that shall inhabite with them.

They are a people clothed with loose mantles made of Deere
skins, & aprons of the same rounde about their middles ; all els
naked ; of such a difference of statures only as wee in England ;
hauing no edge tooles or weapons of yron or steele to offend vs
withall, neither know they how to make any : those weapons that
they haue, are onlie bowes made of Witch hazle, & arrowes of
reeds ; flat edged truncheons also of wood about a yard long,
neither haue they any thing to defend themselues but targets
made of barcks ; and some armours made of stickes wickered
together with thread.

Their townes are but small, & neere the sea coast but few,
some containing but 10 or 12 houses : some 20. the greatest that
we haue seene haue bene but of 30 houses : if they be walled it is
only done with barks of trees made fast to stakes, or els with
poles onely fixed vpright and close one by another.

Their houses are made of small poles made fast at the tops in
rounde forme after the maner as is vsed in many arbories in our
gardens of England, in most townes couered with barkes, and in
some with artificiall mattes made of long rushes ; from the tops of
the houses downe to the ground.   The length of them is commonly
double to the breadth, in some places they are but 12 and 16
yardes long, and in other some wee haue seene of foure and
twentie.

In some places of the countrey one onely towne belongeth to
the gouernment of a *Wiróans* or chiefe Lorde ; in other some two
or three, in some sixe, eight, & more ; the greatest *Wiróans* that
yet we had dealing with had but eighteene townes in his gouernmēt,
and able to make not aboue seuen or eight hundred fighting men
at the most : The language of euery gouernment is different from
any other, and the farther they are distant the greater is the
difference.

Their maner of warres amongst themselues is either by sudden surprising one an other most commonly about the dawning of the day, or moone light; or els by ambushes, or some suttle deuiscs: Set battels are very rare, except it fall out where there are many trees, where eyther part may haue some hope of defence, after the deliueric of euery arrow, in leaping behind some or other.

If there fall out any warres between vs & them, what their fight is likely to bee, we hauing aduantages against them so many maner of waies, as by our discipline, our strange weapons and deuiscs els; especially by ordinance great and small, it may be easily imagined; by the experience we haue had in some places, the turning vp of their heeles against vs in running away was their best defence.

In respect of vs they are a people poore, and for want of skill and iudgement in the knowledge and vse of our things, doe esteeme our trifles before thinges of greater value: Notwithstanding in their proper manner considering the want of such meanes as we haue, they seeme very ingenious; For although they haue no such tooles, nor any such craftes, sciences and artes as wee; yet in those thinges they doe, they shewe excellencie of wit. And by howe much they vpon due consideration shall finde our manner of knowledges and craftes to exceede theirs in perfection, and speed for doing or execution, by so much the more is it probable that they shoulde desire our friendships & loue, and haue the greater respect for pleasing and obeying vs. Whereby may bee hoped if meanes of good gouernment bee vsed, that they may in short time be brought to ciuilitie, and the imbracing of true religion.

Some religion they haue alreadie, which although it be farre from the truth, yet beyng as it is, there is hope it may bee the easier and sooner reformed.

They beleeue that there are many Gods which they call *Montóac*, but of different sortes and degrees; one onely chiefe and great God, which hath bene from all eternitie. Who as they affirme when hee purposed to make the worlde, made first other goddes of a principall order to bee as meanes and instruments to bee vsed in the creation and gouernment to follow; and after the Sunne, Moone, and Starres, as pettie goddes and the instruments of the other order more principall. First they say were made waters, out of which by the gods was made all diuersitie of creatures that are visible or inuisible.

For mankind they say a woman was made first, which by the woorking of one of the goddes, conceiued and brought foorth children : And in such sort they say they had their beginning.

But how manie yeeres or ages haue passed since, they say they can make no relation, hauing no letters nor other such meanes as we to keepe recordes of the particularities of times past, but onelie tradition from father to sonne.

They thinke that all the gods are of human shape, & therfore they represent them by images in the formes of men, which they call *Kewasowok*, one alone is called *Kewás;* Them they place in houses appropriate or temples which they call *Mathicómuck;* Where they woorship, praie, sing, and make manie times offerings vnto them.   In some *Machicomuck* we haue seene but one *Kewas*, in some two, and in other some three ; The common sort thinke them to be also gods.

They beleeue also the immortalitie of the soule, that after this life as soone as the soule is departed from the bodie according to the workes it hath done, it is eyther carried to heauen the habitacle of gods, there to enioy perpetuall blisse and happinesse, or els to a great pitte or hole, which they thinke to bee in the furthest partes of their part of the worlde towarde the sunne set, there to burne continually : the place they call *Popogusso*.

For the confirmation of this opinion, they tolde mee two stories of two men that had been lately dead and reuiued againe, the one happened but few yeres before our comming in the countrey of a wicked man which hauing beene dead and buried, the next day the earth of the graue beeing seene to moue, was taken vp againe ; Who made declaration where his soule had beene, that is to saie very neere entring into *Popogusso*, had not one of the gods saued him & gaue him leaue to returne againe, and teach his friends what they should doe to auoid that terrible place of torment.

The other happened in the same yeere wee were there, but in a towne that was threescore miles from vs, and it was tolde mee for straunge newes that one beeing dead, buried and taken vp

THE TRVE PICTVRES
AND FASHIONS OF
THE PEOPLE IN THAT PAR-
TE OF AMERICA NOVV CAL-
LED VIRGINIA, DISCOVVRED BY ENGLISHMEN

sent thither in the years of our Lorde 1585. att the speciall charge
and direction of the Honourable SIR WALTER RALEGH Knight
Lord Warden of the stannaries in the duchies of
Corenwal and Oxford who therin hath bynne
fauored and auctorifed by her MAAIESTIE
and her letters patents

Translated out of Latin into English by
RICHARD HACKLVIT.

DILIGENTLYE COLLECTED AND DRAW-
ne by IHON WHITE who was sent thither speciallye and for the
same purpose by the said SIR WALTER RALEGH the
year abouesaid 1585. and also the year 1588.
now cutt in copper and first published
by THEODORE de BRY att his
owne chardges.

THE TABLE
OF ALL THE PICTV-
RES CONTAINED IN
this Booke of Virginia.

D

To the gentle Reader.

ALTHOUGH (frendlye Reader) man by his disobedience, weare depriued of those good Gifts wher with he was indued in his creation, yet he was not berefte of wit to prouyde for hym selfe, nor discretion to deuise things necessarie for his vse, except suche as appartayne to his soules healthe, as may be gathered by this sauage nations, of whome this present worke intreateth. For although they haue noe true knoledge of God nor of his holye worde and are destituted of all lerninge, Yet they passe vs in many thinges, as in Sober feedinge and Dexteritye of witte, in makinge without any instrument of mettall thinges so neate and so fine, as a man would scarselye beleue the same, Vnless the Englishemen Had made proofe Therof by their trauailes into the contrye. Consideringe, Therfore that yt was a thinge worthie of admiration, I was verye willinge to offer vnto you the true Pictures of those people wich by the helpe of Maister Richard Hakluyt of Oxford Minister of Gods Word, who first Incouraged me to publish the Worke, I creaued out of the verye original of Maister Ihon White an Englisch paynter who was sent into the contrye by the queenes Maiestye, onlye to draw the description of the place, lyuely to describe the shapes of the Inhabitants their apparell, manners of Liuinge, and fashions, att the speciall Charges of the worthy knighte, Sir W A L T E R R A L E G H, who bestowed noe Small Sume of monnye in the serche and Discouerye of that countrye, From the yeere, 1584, to the ende of The yeare 1588. Morouer this booke which intreateth of that parte of the new World which the Englishemen call by the name of Virginia I heer sett out in the first place, beinge therunto requested of my Frends, by Reason of the memorye of the fresh and late performance therof, albeyt I haue in hand the Historye of Florida wich should bee first sett foorthe because yt was discouured by the Frencheman longe befor the discouerye of Virginia, yet I hope shortlye also to publish the same, A Victorye, doubtless so Rare, as I thinke the like hath not ben heard nor seene. I craeued both of them at London, and brought Them hither to Franckfurt, wher I and my sonnes hauen taken ernest paynes in grauinge the pictures ther of in Copper, seeing yt is a matter of noe small importance. Touchinge the stile of both the Discourses, I haue caused yt to bee Reduced into verye Good Frenche and Latin by the aide of verye worshipfull frend of myne. Finallye I hartlye Request thee, that yf any seeke to Contrefaict thes my bookx, (for in this dayes many are so malicious that they seeke to gayne by other men labours) thow wouldest giue noe credit vnto suche conterfaited Drawghte. For dyuers secret marks lye hiddin in my pictures, which wil breede Confusion vnless they bee well obserued.

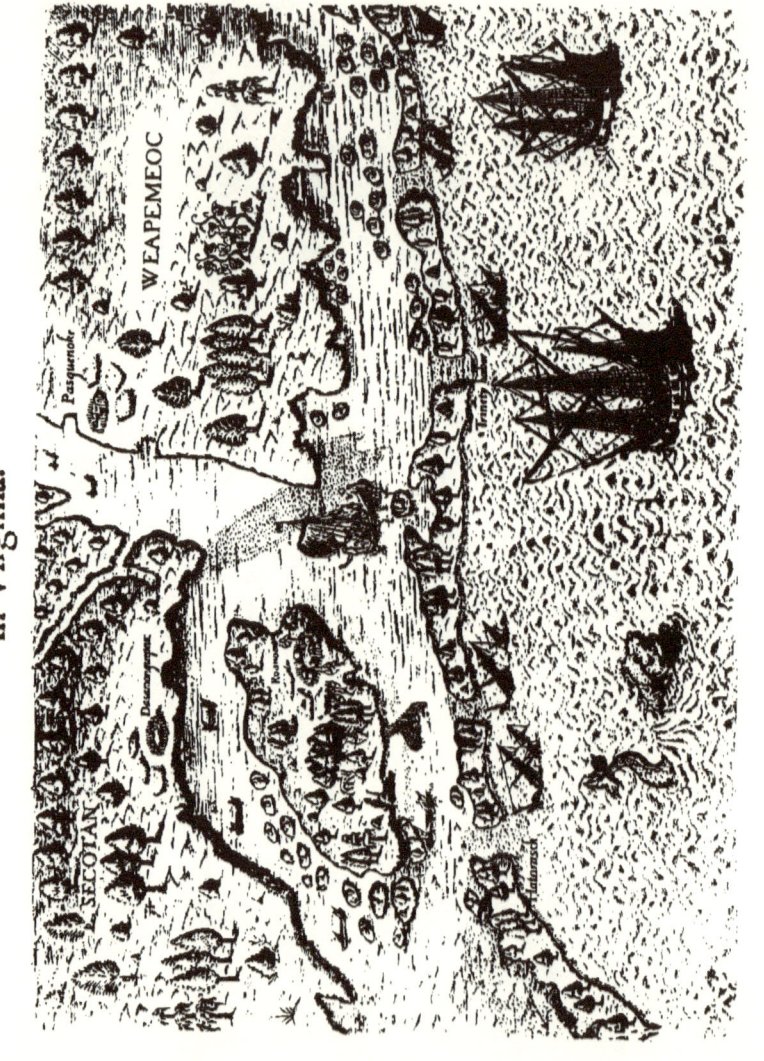

The arriual of the Englifhemen   II.

in Virginia.

II.

The arriual of the Englifhemen
in Virginia.

THE sea coasts of Virginia arre full of Ilands, wher by the entrance into the mayne lãd is hard to finde. For although they bee separated with diuers and sundrie large Diuision, which seeme to yeeld conuenient entrance, yet to our great perill we proued that they wear shallowe, and full of dangerous flatts, and could neuer perce opp into the mayne land, vntill wee made trialls in many places with or small pinness. At lengthe wee fownd an entrance vppon our mens diligent serche therof. Affter that wee had passed opp, and sayled ther in for a short space we discouered a mightye riuer fallinge downe in to the sownde ouer against those Ilands, which neuertheless wee could not saile opp any thinge far by Reason of the shallewnes, the mouth ther of beinge annoyed with sands driuen in with the tyde therfore saylinge further, wee came vnto a Good bigg yland, the Inhabitants therof as soone as they saw vs began to make a great and horrible crye, as people which neuer befoer had seene men apparelled like vs, and camme a way makinge out crys like wild beasts or men out of their wyts. But beenge gentlye called backe, wee offred them of our wares, as glasses, kniues, babies,* and other trifles, which wee thougt they deligted in. Soe they stood still, and perceuinge our Good will and courtesie came fawninge vppon vs, and bade us welcome. Then they brougt vs to their village in the iland called, Roanoac, and vnto their Weroans or Prince, which entertained vs with Reasonable curtesie, althoug they wear amased at the first sight of vs. Suche was our arriuall into the parte of the world, which we call Virginia, the stature of bodye of wich people, theyr attire, and maneer of lyuinge, their feasts, and banketts, I will particullerlye declare vnto yow.

---

* Babies or babes, *i.e.* dolls.

A weroan or great Lorde of Virginia. III.

III.

A weroan or great Lorde of Virginia.

THE Princes of Virginia are attyred in suche manner as is expressed in this figure. They weare the haire of their heades long and bynde opp the ende of the same in a knot vnder their eares. Yet they cutt the topp of their heades from the forehead to the nape of the necke in manner of a cokscombe, stickinge a faier longe fether of some berd att the Begininge of the creste vppon their foreheads, and another short one on bothe seides about their eares. They hange at their eares ether thicke pearles, or somwhat els, as the clawe of some great birde, as cometh in to their fansye. Moreouer They ether pownes, or paynt their forehead, cheeks, chynne, bodye, armes, and leggs, yet in another sorte then the inhabitants of Florida. They weare a chaine about their necks of pearles or beades of copper, wich they muche esteeme, and ther of wear they also braselets on their armes. Vnder their brests about their bellyes appeir certayne spotts, whear they vse to lett them selues bloode, when they are sicke. They hange before them the skinne of some beaste verye feinelye dresset in suche sorte, that the tayle hangeth downe behynde. They carye a quiuer made of small rushes holding their bowe readie bent in one hand, and an arrowe in the other, redie to defend themselues. In this manner they goe to warr, or to their solemne feasts and banquetts. They take muche pleasure in huntinge of deer wher of ther is great store in the contrye, for yt is fruitfull, pleasant, and full of Goodly woods. Yt hathe also store of riuers full of diuers sorts of fishe. When they go to battel they paynt their bodyes in the most terible manner that thei can deuise.

One of the chieff Ladyes of Secota.

THE woemen of Secotam are of Reasonable good proportion. In their goinge they carrye their hands danglinge downe, and air dadil in a deer skinne verye excellëtlye wel dressed, hanginge downe fro their nauell vnto the mydds of their thighes, which also couereth their hynder parts. The reste of their bodies are all bare. The forr parte of their haire is cutt shorte, the rest is not ouer Longe, thinne, and softe, and falling downe about their shoulders: They weare a Wreath about their heads. Their foreheads, cheeks, chynne, armes and leggs are pownced. About their necks they wear a chaine, ether pricked or paynted. They haue small eyes, plaine and flatt noses, narrow foreheads, and broade mowths. For the most parte they hange at their eares chaynes of longe Pearles, and of some smootht bones. Yet their nayles are not longe, as the woemen of Florida. They are also delighted with walkinge in to the fields, and beside the riuers, to see the huntinge of deers and catchinge of fische.

On of the Religeous men in the towne of Secota.   V.

V.

One of the Religeous men in the
towne of Secota.

THE Priests of the aforesaid Towne of Secota are well stricken in yeers, and as yt seemeth of more experience then the comon sorte. They weare their heare cutt like a creste, on the topps of thier heades as other doe, but the rest are cutt shorte, sauinge those which growe aboue their foreheads in manner of a perriwigge. They also haue somwhat hanginge in their ears. They weare a shorte clocke made of fine hares skinnes quilted with the hayre outwarde. The rest of their bodie is naked. They are notable enchaunters, and for their pleasure they frequent the riuers, to kill with their bowes, and catche wilde ducks, swannes, and other fowles.

A younge gentill Woeman doughter VI.
of Secota

VI.

A younge gentill woeman doughter
of Secota.

VIRGINS of good parentage are apparelled altogether like
the woemen of Secota aboue mentionned, sauing that they
weare hanginge abowt their necks in steede of a chaine
certaine thicke, and rownde pearles, with little beades of copper,
or polished bones betweene them. They pounce their foreheads,
cheeckes, armes and legs. Their haire is cutt with two ridges
aboue their foreheads, the rest is trussed opp on a knott behinde,
they haue broade mowthes, reasonable fair black eyes: they lay
their hands often vppon their Shoulders, and couer their brests in
token of maydenlike modestye. The rest of their bodyes are
naked, as in the picture is to bee seene. They deligt also in
seeinge fishe taken in the riuers.

A cheiff Lorde of Roanoac.   VII.

VII.

A cheiff Lorde of Roanoac.

THE cheefe men of the yland and towne of Roanoac weare the haire of their crounes of theyr heades cutt like a cokes combe, as the others doe. The rest they wear longe as woemen and truss them opp in a knott in the nape of their necks. They hange pearles stringe vppon a threed att their eares, and weare bracelets on their armes of pearles, or small beades of copper or of smoothe bone called minsal, nether paintinge nor powncinge of them selues, but in token of authoritye, and honor, they wear a chaine of great pearles, or copper beades or smoothe bones abowt their necks, and a plate of copper hinge vppon a stringe, from the nauel vnto the midds of their thighes. They couer themselues before and behynde as the woemen doe with a deers skynne handsomley dressed, and fringed. More ouer they fold their armes together as they walke, or as they talke one with another in signe of wisdome. The yle of Roanoac is verye pleisant, and hath plaintie of fishe by reason of the Water that enuironeth the same.

A cheiff Ladye of Pomeiooc.   VIII.

VIII.

A cheiff Ladye of Pomeiooc.

ABOUT 20. milles from that Iland, neere the lake of
Paquippe, ther is another towne called Pomeioock hard
by the sea. The apparell of the cheefe ladyes of that
towne differeth but litle from the attyre of those which lyue in
Roanoac. For they weare their haire trussed opp in a knott, as
the maiden doe which we spake of before, and haue their skinnes
pownced in the same manner, yet they wear a chaine of great
pearles, or beades of copper, or smoothe bones 5. or 6. fold about
their necks, bearinge one arme in the same, in the other hand
they carye a gourde full of some kinde of pleasant liquor. They
tye deers skinne doubled about them crochinge hygher about
their breasts, which hange downe before almost to their knees,
and are almost altogither naked behinde. Commonlye their
yonge daugters of 7. or 8. yeares olde do wait vpon them
wearinge abowt them a girdle of skinne, which hangeth
downe behinde, and is drawen vnder neath betwene their thighes,
and bownde aboue their nauel with mosse of trees betwene that
and their skinnes to couer their priuities withall. After they be
once past 10. yeares of age, they wear deer skinnes as the older
sorte do. They are greatlye Diligted with puppetts, and babes
which wear brought oute of England.

An aged manne in his winter IX.
garment.

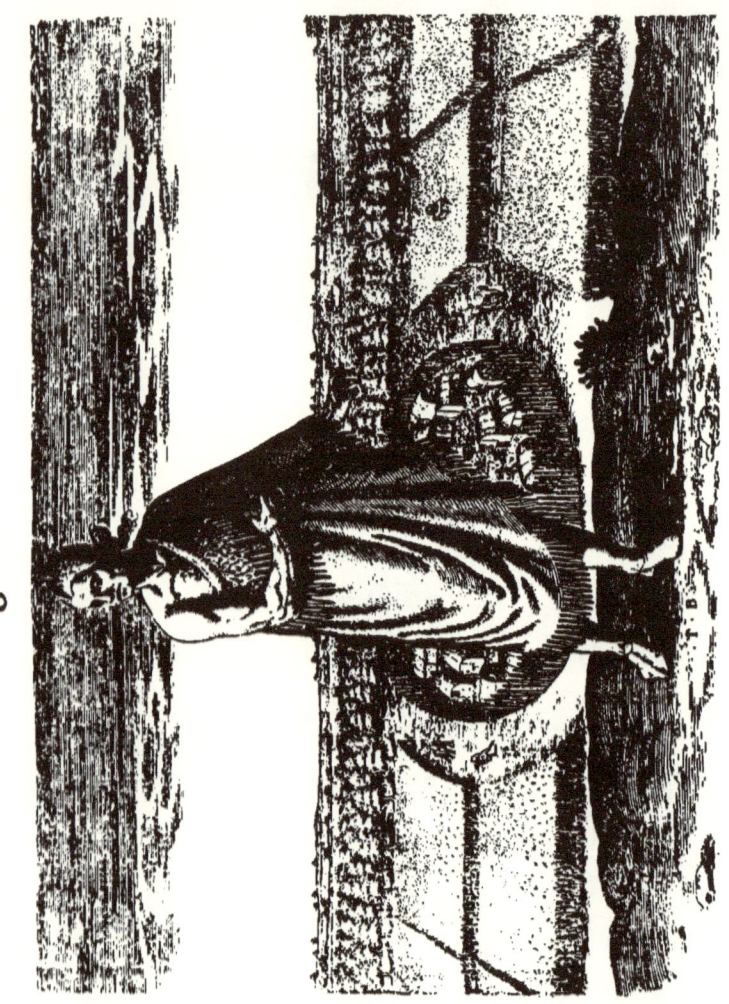

IX.

An aged manne in his winter garment.

THE aged men of Pommeioocke are couered with a large skinne which is tyed vppon their shoulders on one side and hangeth downe beneath their knees wearinge their other arme naked out of the skinne, that they maye bee at more libertie. Those skynnes are Dressed with the hair on, and lyned with other furred skinnes. The yonnge men suffer noe hairr at all to growe vppon their faces but assoone as they growe they put them away, but when they are come to yeeres they suffer them to growe although to say truthe they come opp very thinne. They also weare their haire bownde op behynde, and, haue a creste on their heads like the others. The contrye abowt this plase is soe fruit full and good, that England is not to bee compared to yt.

Their manner of careynge ther Chil-   X.
dern and a tyere of the cheiffe Ladyes of the
towne of Dasamonquepeuc.

X.

Their manner of careynge ther Childern
and atyere of the cheiffe Ladyes of the
towne of Dafamonquepeuc.

IN the towne of Dasemonquepeuc distant from Roanoac 4. or
5. milles, the woemen are attired, and pownced, in suche
sorte as the woemen of Roanoac are, yet they weare noe
wreathes vppon their heads, nether haue they their thighes
painted with small pricks. They haue a strange manner of
bearing their children, and quite contrarie to ours. For our
woemen carrie their children in their armes before their brests,
but they taking their sonne by the right hand, bear him on their
backs, holdinge the left thighe in their lefte arme after a strange,
and conuesnall* fashion, as in the picture is to bee seene.

XI.

The Coniuerer.

againe as the first, shewed that although his bodie had lien dead in the graue, yet his soule was aliue, and had trauailed farre in a long broade waie, on both sides whereof grewe most delicate and pleasaunt trees, bearing more rare and excellent fruites then euer hee had seene before or was able to expresse, and at length came to most braue and faire houses, neere which hee met his father, that had beene dead before, who gaue him great charge to goe backe againe and shew his friendes what good they were to doe to enioy the pleasures of that place, which when he had done he should after come againe.

What subtilty soeuer be in the *Wiroances* and Priestes, this opinion worketh so much in manie of the common and simple sort of people that it maketh them haue great respect to their Gouernours, and also great care what they do, to auoid torment after death, and to enioy blisse ; althought notwithstanding there is punishment ordained for malefactours, as stealers, whore-moongers, and other sortes of wicked doers ; some punished with death, some with forfeitures, some with beating, according to the greatnes of the factes.

And this is the summe of their religion, which I learned by hauing special familiarity with some of their priestes. Wherein they were not so sure grounded, nor gaue such credite to their traditions and stories but through conuersing with vs they were brought into great doubts of their owne, and no small admiration of ours, with earnest desire in many, to learne more than we had meanes for want of perfect vtterance in their language to expresse.

Most thinges they sawe with vs, as Mathematicall instruments, sea compasses, the vertue of the loadstone in drawing yron, a perspectiue glasse whereby was shewed manie strange sightes, burning glasses, wildefire woorkes, gunnes, bookes, writing and reading, spring clocks that seeme to goe of themselues, and manie other thinges that wee had, were so straunge vnto them, and so farre exceeded their capacities to comprehend the reason and meanes how they should be made and done, that they thought they were rather the works of gods then of men, or at the leastwise they had bin giuen and taught vs of the gods. Which made manie of them to haue such opinion of vs, as that if they knew not the trueth of god and religion already, it was rather to be had from vs, whom God so specially loued then from a people that were so simple, as they found themselues to be in comparison of vs. Whereupon greater credite was giuen vnto that we spake of concerning such matters.

Manie times and in euery towne where I came, according as I was able, I made declaration of the contentes of the Bible; that therein was set foorth the true and onelie GOD, and his mightie woorkes, that therein was contayned the true doctrine of saluation through Christ, with manie particularities of Miracles and chiefe poyntes of religion, as I was able then to vtter, and thought fitte for the time. And although I told them the booke materially & of it self was not of anie such vertue, as I thought they did conceiue, but onely the doctrine therein contained ; yet would many be glad to touch it, to embrace it, to kisse it, to hold it to their brests and heades, and stroke ouer all their bodie with it; to shewe their hungrie desire of that knowledge which was spoken of.

The *Wiroans* with whom we dwelt called *Wingina*, and many of his people would be glad many times to be with vs at our praiers, and many times call vpon vs both in his owne towne, as also in others whither he sometimes accompanied vs, to pray and sing Psalmes; hoping thereby to bee partaker of the same effectes which wee by that meanes also expected.

Twise this *Wiroans* was so grieuously sicke that he was like to die, and as hee laie languishing, doubting of anie helpe by his owne priestes, and thinking he was in such daunger for offending vs and thereby our god, sent for some of vs to praie and bee a meanes to our God that it would please him either that he might liue or after death dwell with him in blisse, so likewise were the requestes of manie others in the like case.

On a time also when their corne began to wither by reason of a drouth which happened extraordinarily, fearing that it had come to passe by reason that in some thing they had displeased vs, many woulde come to vs & desire vs to praie to our God of England, that he would preserue their corne, promising that when it was ripe we also should be partakers of the fruite.

There could at no time happen any strange sicknesse, losses, hurtes, or any other crosse vnto them, but that they would impute to vs the cause or meanes therof for offending or not pleasing vs.

One other rare and strange accident, leauing others, will I mention before I ende, which mooued the whole countrey that either knew or hearde of vs, to haue vs in wonderfull admiration.

There was no towne where we had any subtile deuise practised against vs, we leauing it vnpunished or not reuenged (because wee sought by all meanes possible to win them by gentlenesse) but that within a few dayes after our departure from euerie such towne, the people began to die very fast, and many in short space ; in some townes about twentie, in some fourtie, in some sixtie, & in one sixe score, which in trueth was very manie in respect of their numbers.   This happened in no place that wee coulde learne but where wee had bene, where they vsed some practise against vs, and after such time ; The disease also so strange, that they neither knew what it was, nor how to cure it ; the like by report of the oldest men in the countrey neuer happened before, time out of minde.   A thing specially obserued by vs as also by the naturall inhabitants themselues.

Insomuch that when some of the inhabitants which were our friends & especially the *Wiroans Wingina* had obserued such effects in foure or fiue towns to follow their wicked practises, they were perswaded that it was the worke of our God through our meanes, and that wee by him might kil and slai whom wee would without weapons and not come neere them.

And thereupon when it had happened that they had vnderstanding that any of their enemies had abused vs in our iourneyes, hearing that wee had wrought no reuenge with our weapons, & fearing vpon some cause the matter should so rest : did come and intreate vs that we woulde bee a meanes to our God that they as others that had dealt ill with vs might in like sort die ; alleaging howe much it would be for our credite and profite, as also theirs ; and hoping furthermore that we would do so much at their requests in respect of the friendship we professe them.

Whose entreaties although wee shewed that they were

vngodlie, affirming that our God would not subiect him selfe to anie such praiers and requestes of men : that in deede all thinges haue beene and were to be done according to his good pleasure as he had ordained : and that we to shew our selues his true seruants ought rather to make petition for the contrarie, that they with them might liue together with vs, bee made partakers of his truth & serue him in righteousnes ; but notwithstanding in such sort, that wee referre that as all other thinges, to bee done according to his diuine will & pleasure, and as by his wisedome he had ordained to be best.

Yet because the effect fell out so sodainly and shortly after according to their desires, they thought neuerthelesse it came to passe by our meanes, and that we in vsing such speeches vnto them did but dissemble the matter, and therefore came vnto vs to giue vs thankes in their manner that although wee satisfied them not in promise, yet in deedes and effect we had fulfilled their desires.

This maruelous accident in all the countrie wrought so strange opinions of vs, that some people could not tel whether to think vs gods or men, and the rather because that all the space of their sicknesse, there was no man of ours knowne to die, or that was specially sicke : they noted also that we had no women amongst vs, neither that we did care for any of theirs.

Some therefore were of opinion that wee were not borne of women, and therefore not mortall, but that wee were men of an old generation many yeeres past then risen againe to immortalitie.

Some woulde likewise seeme to prophesie that there were more of our generation yet to come, to kill theirs and take their places, as some thought the purpose was by that which was already done.

Those that were immediately to come after vs they imagined to be in the aire, yet inuisible & without bodies, & that they by our intreaty & for the loue of vs did make the people to die in that sort as they did by shooting inuisible bullets into them.

To confirme this opinion their phisitions to excuse their ignorance in curing the disease, would not be ashamed to say, but earnestly make the simple people beleue, that the strings of blood that they sucked out of the sicke bodies, were the strings where-withal the inuisible bullets were tied and cast.

Some also thought that we shot them our selues out of our pieces from the place where we dwelt, and killed the people in any such towne that had offended vs as we listed, how farre distant from vs soeuer it were.

And other some saide that it was the speciall woorke of God for our sakes, as wee our selues haue cause in some sorte to thinke no lesse, whatsoeuer some doe or maie imagine to the contrarie, specially some Astrologers knowing of the Eclipse of the Sunne which wee saw the same yeere before in our voyage thytherward, which vnto them appeared very terrible. And also of a Comet which beganne to appeare but a few daies before the beginning of the said sicknesse. But to exclude them from being the speciall an accident, there are farther reasons then I thinke fit at this present to bee alleadged.

These their opinions I haue set downe the more at large that it may appeare vnto you that there is good hope they may be brought through discreet dealing and gouernement to the imbracing of the trueth, and consequently to honour, obey, feare and loue vs.

And although some of our companie towardes the ende of the yeare, shewed themselues too fierce, in slaying some of the people, in some towns, vpon causes that on our part, might easily enough haue been borne withall: yet notwithstanding because it was on their part iustly deserued, the alteration of their opinions generally & for the most part concerning vs is the lesse to bee doubted. And whatsoeuer els they may be, by carefulnesse of our selues neede nothing at all to be feared.

The best neuerthelesse in this as in all actions besides is to be endeuoured and hoped, & of the worst that may happen notice to bee taken with consideration, and as much as may be eschewed.

The Conclusion.

Now I haue as I hope made relation not of so fewe and smal things but that the countrey of men that are indifferent & wel disposed maie be sufficiently liked. If there were no more knowen then I haue mentioned, which doubtlesse and in great reason is nothing to that which remaineth to bee discouered, neither the soile, nor commodities. As we haue reason so to gather by the difference we found in our trauails : for although all which I haue before spoken of, haue bin discouered & experimented not far from the sea coast where was our abode & most of our trauailing : yet somtimes as we made our iourneies farther into the maine and countrey; we found the soyle to bee fatter ; the trees greater and to growe thinner ; the grounde more firme and deeper mould ; more and larger champions ; finer grasse and as good as euer we saw any in England ; in some places rockie and farre more high and hillie ground ; more plentie of their fruites ; more abondance of beastes ; the more inhabited with people, and of greater pollicie & larger dominions, with greater townes and houses.

Why may wee not then looke for in good hope from the inner parts of more and greater plentie, as well of other things, as of those which wee haue alreadie discouered ? Vnto the Spaniardes happened the like in discouering the maine of the West Indies. The maine also of this countrey of *Virginia*, extending some wayes so many hundreds of leagues, as otherwise then by the relation of the inhabitants wee haue most certaine knowledge of, where yet no Christian Prince hath any possession or dealing, cannot but yeeld many kinds of excellent commodities, which we in our discouerie haue not yet seene.

What hope there is els to be gathered of the nature of the climate, being answerable to the Iland of *Iapan*, the land of *China*, *Persia*, *Jury*, the Ilandes of *Cyprus* and *Candy*, the South parts of *Greece*, *Italy*, and *Spaine*, and of many other notable and famous countreis, because I meane not to be tedious, I leaue to your owne consideration.

Whereby also the excellent temperature of the ayre there at all seasons, much warmer then in England, and neuer so violently hot, as sometimes is vnder & between the Tropikes, or nere them ; cannot bee vnknowne vnto you without farther relation.

For the holsomnesse thereof I neede to say but thus much : that for all the want of prouision, as first of English victuall ; excepting for twentie daies, wee liued only by drinking water and by the victuall of the countrey, of which some sorts were very straunge vnto vs, and might haue bene thought to haue altered our temperatures in such sort as to haue brought vs into some greeuous and dangerous diseases : secondly the want of English meanes, for the taking of beastes, fishe, and foule, which by the helpe only of the inhabitants and their meanes, coulde not bee so suddenly and easily prouided for vs, nor in so great numbers & quantities, nor of that choise as otherwise might haue bene to our better satisfaction and contentment. Some want also wee had of clothes. Furthermore, in all our trauailes which were most speciall and often in the time of winter, our lodging was in the open aire vpon the grounde. And yet I say for all this, there were but foure of our whole company (being one hundred and eight) that died all the yeere and that but at the latter ende thereof and vpon none of the aforesaide causes. For all foure especially three were feeble, weake, and sickly persons before euer they came thither, and those that knewe them much marueyled that they liued so long beeing in that case, or had aduentured to trauaile.

Seing therefore the ayre there is so temperate and holsome, the soyle so fertile and yeelding such commodities as I haue before mentioned, the voyage also thither to and fro beeing sufficiently experimented, to bee perfourmed thrise a yeere with ease and at any season thereof: And the dealing of *Sir Walter Raleigh* so liberall in large giuing and granting lande there, as is alreadie knowen, with many helpes and furtherances els : (The least that hee hath graunted hath beene fiue hundred acres to a man onely for the aduenture of his person:) I hope there remaine no cause wherby the action should be misliked.

If that those which shall thither trauaile to inhabite and plant bee but reasonably prouided for the first yere as those are which were transported the last, and beeing there doe vse but that diligence and care as is requisite, and as they may with eese : There is no doubt but for the time following they may haue

victuals that is excellent good and plentie enough; some more
Englishe sortes of cattaile also hereafter, as some haue bene
before, and are there yet remaining, may and shall bee God
willing thither transported : So likewise our kinde of fruites,
rootes, and hearbes may bee there planted and sowed, as some
haue bene alreadie, and proue wel : And in short time also they
may raise of those sortes of commodities which I haue spoken of
as shall both enrich them selues, as also others that shall deale
with them.

And this is all the fruites of our labours, that I haue thought
necessary to aduertise you of at this present : what els concerneth
the nature and manners of the inhabitants of *Virginia :* The number
with the particularities of the voyages thither made ; and of the
actions of such that haue bene by *Sir Walter Raleigh* therein and
there imployed, many worthy to bee remembred ; as of the first
discouerers of the Countrey : of our generall for the time *Sir
Richard Greinuile* ; and after his departure, of our Gouernour there
Master *Rafe Lane* ; with diuers other directed and imployed vnder
theyr gouernement : Of the Captaynes and Masters of the voyages
made since for transportation ; of the Gouernour and assistants of
those alredie transported, as of many persons, accidents, and thinges
els, I haue ready in a discourse by it self in maner of a Chronicle
according to the course of times, and when time shall bee thought
conuenient shall be also published.

Thus referring my relation to your fauourable constructions,
expecting good successe of the action, from him which is to be
acknowledged the authour and gouernour not onlyof this but of all
things els, I take my leaue of you, this moneth of Februarii, 1588.

F I N I S.

XI.

The Coniuerer.

THEY haue comonlye coniurers or iuglers which vse strange gestures, and often contrarie to nature in their enchantments: For they be verye familiar with deuils, of whome they enquier what their enemys doe, or other suche thinges. They shaue all their heads sauinge their creste which they weare as other doe, and fasten a small black birde aboue one of their ears as a badge of their office. They weare nothinge but a skinne which hangeth downe from their gyrdle, and couereth their priuityes. They weare a bagg by their side as is expressed in the figure. The Inhabitants giue great credit vnto their speeche, which oftentymes they finde to bee true.

The manner of makinge their boates. XII

XII.

The manner of makinge their boates.

THE manner of makinge their boates in Virginia is verye
wonderfull. For wheras they want Instruments of yron,
or other like vnto ours, yet they knowe howe to make them
as handsomelye, to saile with whear they liste in their Riuers, and
to fishe withall, as ours. First they choose some longe, and
thicke tree, accordinge to the bignes of the boate which they would
frame, and make a fyre on the growng abowt the Roote therof,
kindlinge the same by little, and little with drie mosse of trees,
and chipps of woode that the flame should not mounte opp to
highe, and burne to muche of the lengte of the tree.   When yt is
almost burnt thorough, and readye to fall they make a new fyre,
which they suffer to burne vntill the tree fall of yts owne accord.
Then burninge of the topp, and bowghs of the tree in suche wyse
that the bodie of the same may Retayne his iust lengthe, they raise
yt vppon potes laid ouer cross wise vppon forked posts, at suche
a reasonable heighte as they may handsomlye worke vppon yt.
Then take they of the barke with certayne shells: they reserue the
innermost parte of the lennke,* for the nethermost parte of the
boate. On the other side they make a fyre accordinge to the
lengthe of the bodye of the tree, sauinge at both the endes.   That
which they thinke is sufficientlye burned they quenche and scrape
away with shells, and makinge a new fyre they burne yt agayne,
and soe they continne somtymes burninge and sometymes scrap-
inge, vntill the boate haue sufficient bothowmes.   Thus God
indueth thise sauage people with sufficient reason to make
thinges necessarie to serue their turnes.

---

* Probably a typographical error for "barke."

XIII
Their manner of fishynge in
Virginia.

XIII.

Their manner of fishynge in Virginia.

THEY haue likewise a notable way to catche fishe in their Riuers, for whear as they lacke both yron, and steele, they fasten vnto their Reedes or longe Rodds, the hollowe tayle of a certaine fishe like to a sea crabb in steede of a poynte, wherwith by nighte or day they stricke fishes, and take them opp into their boates. They also know how to vse the prickles, and pricks of other fishes. They also make weares, with settinge opp reedes or twigges in the water, which they soe plant one with another, that they growe still narrower, and narrower, as appeareth by this figure. Ther was neuer seene amonge vs soe cunninge a way to take fish withall, wherof sondrie sortes as they fownde in their Riuers vnlike vnto ours, which are also of a verye good taste. Dowbtless yt is a pleasant sighte to see the people, somtymes wadinge, and goinge somtymes sailinge in those Riuers, which are shallowe and not deepe, free from all care of heapinge opp Riches for their posterite, content with their state, and liuinge frendlye together of those thinges which god of his bountye hath giuen vnto them, yet without giuinge hym any thankes according to his desarte.

So sauage is this people, and depriued of the true knowledge of god. For they haue none other then is mentionned before in this worke.

The brovvyllinge of their fishe
over the flame.

XIIII.

XIIII.

The brovvyllinge of their fiſhe ouer
the flame.

AFTER they haue taken store of fiſhe, they gett them vnto a place fitt to dress yt. Ther they sticke vpp in the grownde 4. stakes in a square roome, and lay 4 potes vppon them, and others ouer thwart the same like vnto an hurdle, of sufficient heigthe, and layinge their fiſhe vppon this hurdle, they make a fyre vnderneathe to broile the same, not after the manner of the people of Florida, which doe but schorte,* and harden their meate in the smoke onlye to Reserue the same duringe all the winter. For this people reseruinge nothinge for store, thei do broile, and spend away all att once and when they haue further neede, they roste or seethe fresh, as wee shall see heraffter. And when as the hurdle can not holde all the fishes, they hange the Rest by the fyrres on sticks sett vpp in the grounde a gainst the fyre, and than they finishe the rest of their cookerye. They take good heede that they bee not burntt. When the first are broyled they lay others on, that weare newlye broughte, continuinge the dressinge of their meate in this sorte, vntill they thincke they haue sufficient.

* Scorche ?

Their feetheynge of their meate in earthen pottes. XV.

G VEEN

XV.

Their feetheynge of their meate in
earthen pottes.

THEIR woemen know how to make earthen vessells with special Cunninge and that so large and fine, that our potters with lhoye* wheles can make noe better : ant then Remoue them from place to place as easelye as we can doe our brassen kettles. After they haue set them vppon an heape of erthe to stay them from fallinge, they putt wood vnder which being kyndled one of them taketh great care that the fyre burne equallye Rounde abowt. They or their woemen fill the vessel with water, and then putt they in fruite, flesh, and fish, and lett all boyle together like a galliemaufrye, which the Spaniarde call, olla podrida. Then they putte yt out into disches, and sett before the companye, and then they make good cheere together. Yet are they moderate in their eatinge wherby they auoide sicknes. I would to god wee would followe their exemple. For wee should bee free from many kyndes of diseasyes which wee fall into by sumptwous and vnseasonable banketts, continuallye deuisinge new sawces, and prouocation of gluttonnye to satisfie our vnsatiable appetite.

* theyr ?

Their fitting at meate.   XVI.

XVI.

Their fitting at meate.

THEIR manner of feeding is in this wise. They lay a matt made of bents one the grownde and sett their meate on the mids therof, and then sit downe Rownde, the men vppon one side, and the woemen on the other. Their meate is Mayz sodden, in suche sorte as I described yt in the former treatise of verye good taste, deers flesche, or of some other beaste, and fishe. They are verye sober in their eatinge, and drinkinge, and consequentlye verye longe liued because they doe not oppress nature.

XVII.
Their manner of prainge vvith Rat-
tels abowt te fyer.

XVII.

Their manner of prainge vvith Rattels
abowt the fyer.

VVHEN they haue escaped any great danger by sea or lande, or be returned from the warr in token of Ioye they make a great fyer abowt which the men, and woemen sitt together, holdinge a certaine fruite in their hands like vnto a rownde pompion or a gourde, which after they haue taken out the fruits, and the seedes, then fill with small stons or certayne bigg kernells to make the more noise, and fasten that vppon a sticke, and singinge after their manner, they make merrie: as my selfe obserued and noted downe at my beinge amonge them. For it is a strange custome, and worth the obseruation.

XV

danfes

XVIII.

Theirdanſes vvhich
they vſeatt their hyghefeaſtes.

XVIII.

Their danſes vvhich they vſe att their
hyghe feaſtes.

AT a Certayne tyme of the yere they make a great, and
solemne feaste wherunto their neighbours of the townes
adioininge repayre from all parts, euery man attyred in
the most strange fashion they can deuise hauinge certayne marks
on the backs to declare of what place they bee. The place where
they meet is a broade playne, abowt the which are planted in the
grownde certayne posts carued with heads like to the faces of
Nonnes couered with theyr vayles. Then beeing sett in order
they dance, singe, and vse the strangest gestures that they can
possiblye deuise. Three of the fayrest Virgins, of the companie
are in the mydds, which imbrassinge one another doe as yt wear
turne abowt in their dancinge. All this is donne after the sunne
is sett for auoydinge of heate. When they are weerye of dancinge. they goe oute of the circle, and come in vntill their dances
be ended, and they goe to make merrye as is expressed in the
16. figure.

XIX
The Tovvne of Pomeiooc.

XIX.

The Tovvne of Pomeiooc.

THE townes of this contrie are in a maner like vnto those which are in Florida, yet are they not soe stronge nor yet preserued with soe great care. They are compassed abowt with poles starcke faste in the grownd, but they are not verye stronge. The entrance is verye narrowe as may be seene by this picture, which is made accordinge to the forme of the towne of Pomeiooc. Ther are but few howses therin, saue those which belonge to the kinge and his nobles. On the one side is their tempel separated from the other howses, and marked with the letter A. yt is builded rownde, and couered with skynne matts, and as yt wear compassed abowt with cortynes without windowes, and hath noe lighte but by the doore. On the other side is the kings lodginge marked with the letter B. Their dwellinges are builded with certaine potes fastened together, and couered with matts which they turne op as high as they thinke good, and soe receue in the lighte and other. Some are also couered with boughes of trees, as euery man lusteth or liketh best. They keepe their feasts and make good cheer together in the midds of the towne as yt is described in the 17. Figure. When the towne standeth fare from the water they digg a great ponde noted with the letter C wherhence they fetche as muche water as they neede.

X X.

The Tovvne of Secota.

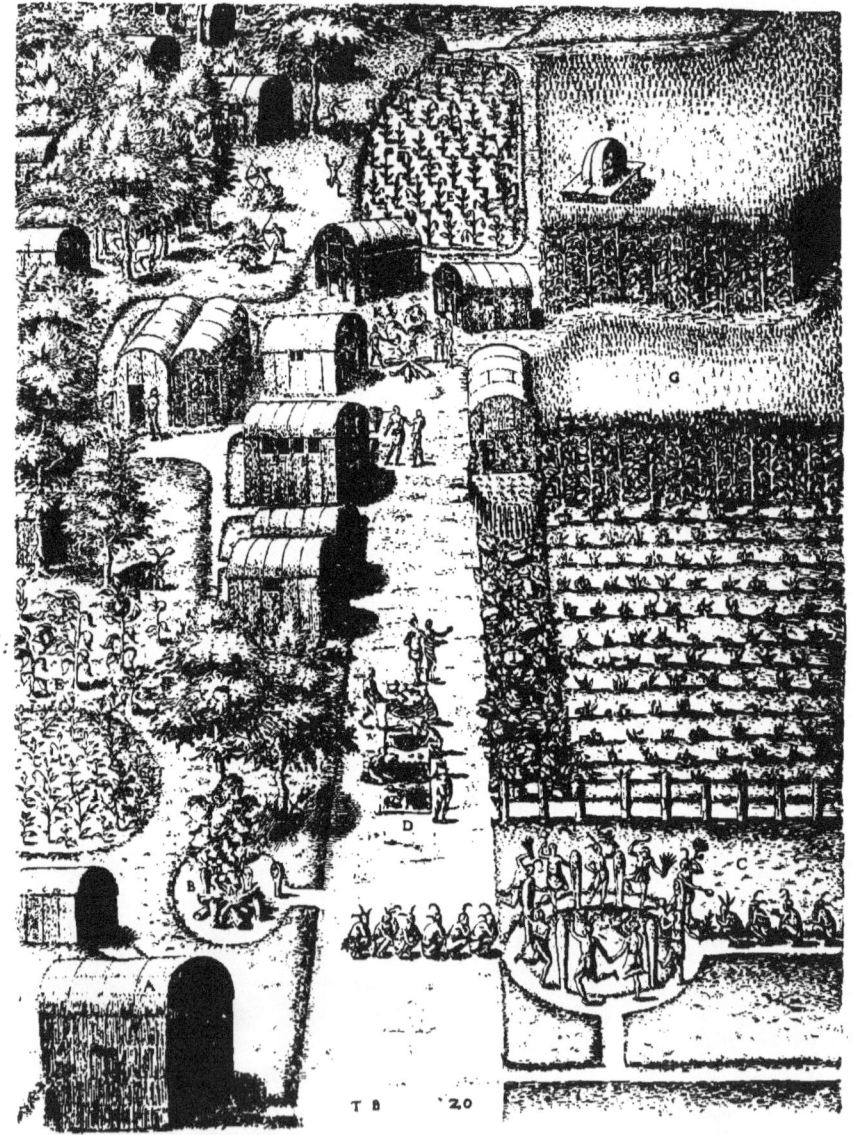

XX.

The Tovvne of Secota.

THEIR townes that are not inclosed with poles are commonlye fayrer then suche as arc inclosed, as appereth in this figure which liuelye expresseth the towne of Secotam. For the howses are Scattered heer and ther, and they haue gardein expressed by the letter E. wherin groweth Tobacco which the inhabitants call Vppowoc. They haue also groaues wherin thei take deer, and fields wherin they sowe their corne. In their corne fields they builde as yt weare a scaffolde wher on they sett a cottage like to a rownde chaire, signiffied by F. wherin they place one to watche, for there are suche nomber of fowles, and beasts, that vnless they keepe the better watche, they would soone deuoure all their corne. For which cause the watcheman maketh continual cryes and noyse. They sowe their corne with a certaine distance noted by H. other wise one stalke would choke the growthe of another and the corne would not come vnto his rypenes G. For the leaues therof are large, like vnto the leaues of great reedes. They haue also a seuerall broade plotte C. whear they meete with their neighbours, to celebrate their cheefe solemne feastes as the 18. picture doth declare: and a place D. whear after they haue ended their feaste they make merrie togither. Ouer against this place they haue a rownd plott B. wher they assemble themselues to make their solemne prayers. Not far from which place ther is a lardge buildinge A. wherin are the tombes of their kings and princes, as will appere by the 22. figure likewise they haue garden notted bey the letter I. wherin they vse to sowe pompions. Also a place marked with K. wherin the make a fyre att their solemne feasts, and hard without the towne a riuer L. from whence they fetche their water. This people therfore voyde of all couetousnes lyue cherfullye and att their harts ease. Butt they solemnise their feasts in the night, and therfore they keepe verye great fyres to auoyde darkenes, and to testifie their Ioye.

Ther Idol Kivvafa.

XXI.

XXI.

Ther Idol Kivvaſa.

THE people of this cuntrie haue an Idol, which they call KIWASA: yt is carued of woode in lengthe 4. foote whose heade is like the heades of the people of Florida, the face is of a flesh colour, the breſt white, the rest is all blacke, the thighes are also spottet with whitte. He hath a chayne abowt his necke of white beades, betweene which are other Rownde beades of copper which they esteeme more then golde or ſiluer. This Idol is placed in the temple of the towne of Secotam, as the keper of the kings dead corpses. Somtyme they haue two of thes idoles in theyr churches, and somtine 3. but neuer aboue, which they place in a darke corner wher they shew terrible. Thes poore soules haue none other knowledge of god although I thinke them verye Desirous to know the truthe. For when as wee kneeled downe on our knees to make our prayers vnto god, they went abowt to imitate vs, and when they saw we moued our lipps, they also dyd the like. Wherfore that is verye like that they might easelye be brougt to the knowledge of the gospel. God of his mercie grant them this grace.

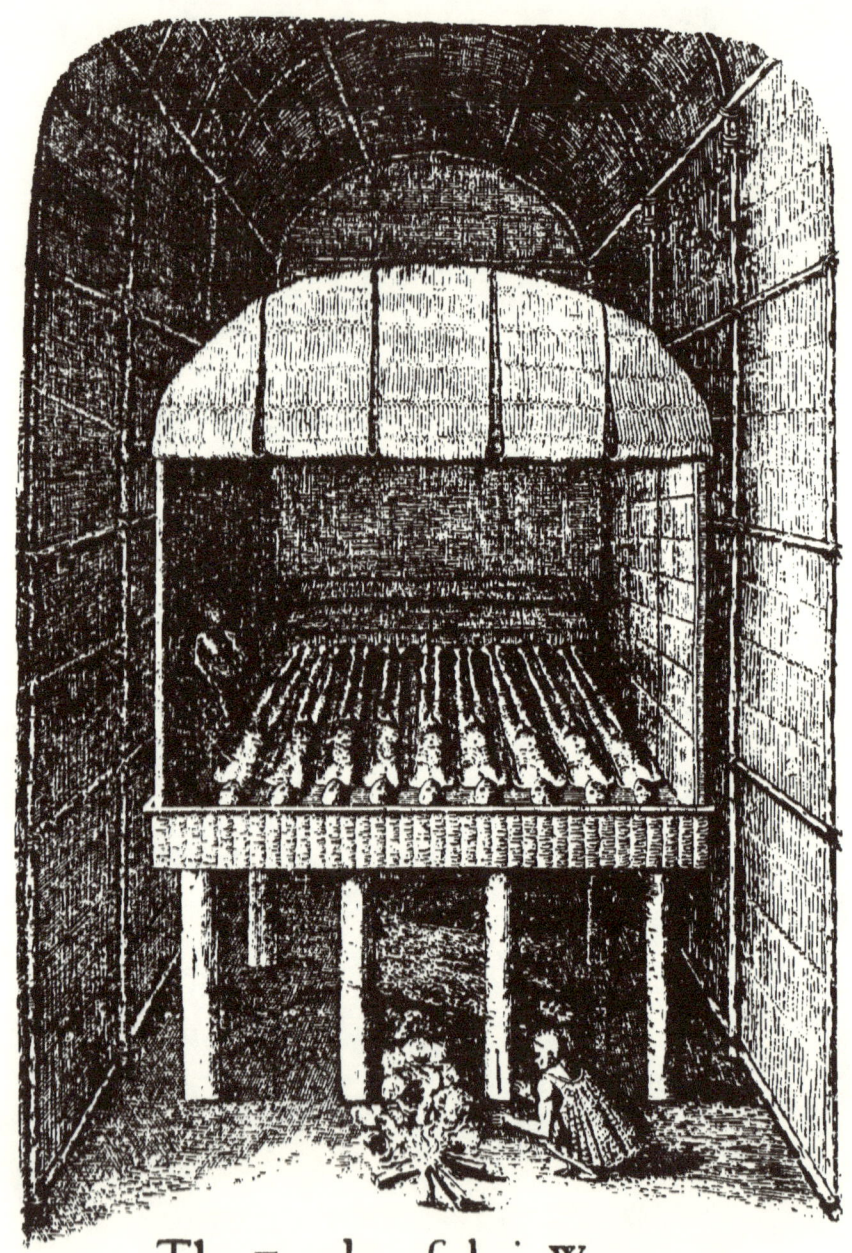

The Tombe of their Werovvans
or Cheiff Lordes. XXII.

XXII.

The Tombe of their Werovvans or
Cheiff Lordes.

THEY builde a Scaffolde 9. or 10. foote highe as is expressed in this figure vnder the tombs of their Weroans, or cheefe lordes which they couer with matts, and lai the dead corpses of their weroans theruppon in manner followinge. first the bowells are taken forthe. Then layinge downe the skinne, they cutt all the flesh cleane from the bones, which they drye in the sonne, and well dryed they inclose in Matts, and place at their feete. Then their bones (remaininge still fastened together with the ligaments whole and vncorrupted) are couered agayne with leather, and their carcase fashioned as yf their flesh wear not taken away. They lapp eache corps in his owne skinne after the same is thus handled, and lay yt in his order by the corpses of the other cheef lordes. By the dead bodies they sett their Idol Kiwasa, wherof we spake in the former chapiter: For they are persuaded that the same doth kepe the dead bodyes of their cheefe lordes that nothinge may hurt them. Moreouer vnder the foresaid scaffolde some one of their preists hath his lodginge, which Mumbleth his prayers nighte and day, and hath charge of the corpses. For his bedd he hath two deares skinnes spredd on the grownde, yf the wether bee cold hee maketh a fyre to warme by withall. Thes poore soules are thus instructed by nature to reuerence their princes euen after their death.

The Marckes of sundrye of the XXIII.

Cheif mene of Virginia.

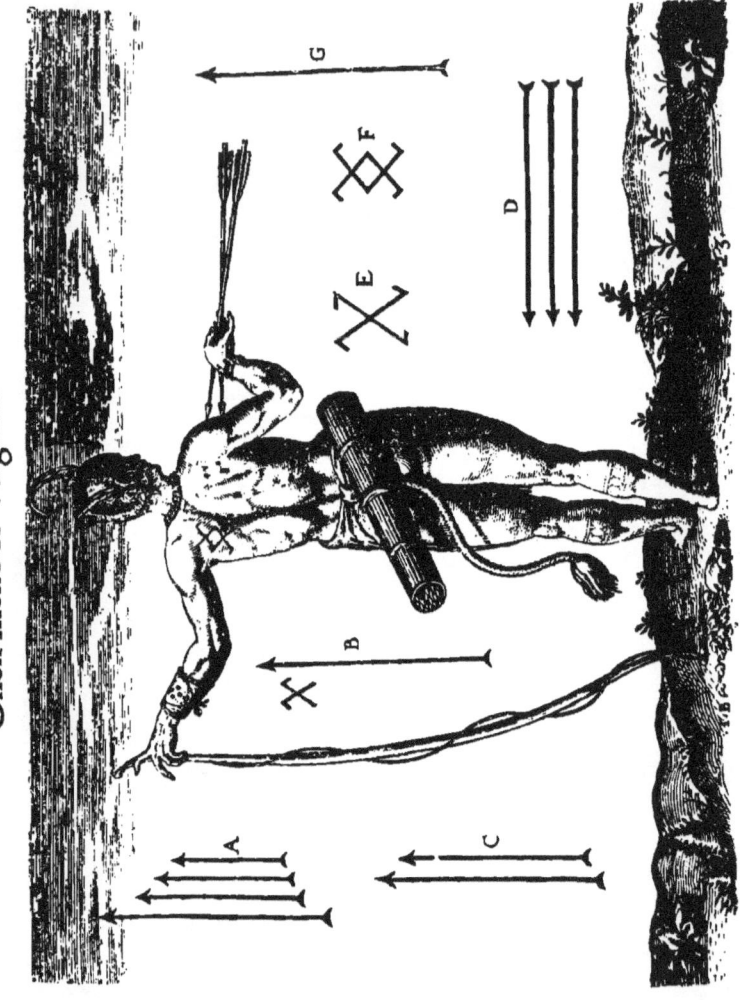

XXIII.

The Marckes of fundrye of the Cheif mene
of Virginia.

THE inhabitants of all the cuntrie for the most parte haue marks rased on their backs, wherby yt may be knowen what Princes subiects they bee, or of what place they haue their originall. For which cause we haue set downe those marks in this figure, and haue annexed the names of the places, that they might more easelye be discerned. Which industrie hath god indued them withal although they be verye simple, and rude. And to confesse a truthe, I cannot remember that euer I saw a better or quietter people then they.

The marks which I obserued amonge them, are heere put downe in order folowinge.

The marke which is expressed by A. belongeth to Wingino, the cheefe lorde of Roanoac.

That which hath B. is the marke of Wingino his sisters husbande.

Those which be noted with the letters, of C. and D. belonge vnto diverse chefe lordes in Secotam.

Those which haue the letters E. F. G. are certaine cheefe men of Pomeiooc, and Aquascogoc.

SOM PICTVRES
OF THE PICTES
WHICH IN THE OLDE
tyme dyd habite one part of the
great Bretainne.

THE PAINTER OF WHOM I HAVE
had the first of the Inhabitants of Virginia, gaue me allso thees
5. Figures following, fownd as he did assure me in a oolld English
cronicle, the which I wold well sett to the ende of
thees first Figures, for to showe how that the
Inhabitants of the great Bretannie haue
bin in times past as sauuage as
those of Virginia.

G

The trvve picture of one
Picte I.

T B I

The trvve picture of one

Picte I.

IN tymes past the Pictes, habitans of one part of great Bretainne, which is nowe nammed England, wear sauuages, and did paint all their bodye after the maner followinge. They did lett their haire growe as fare as their Shoulders, sauinge those which hange vppon their forehead, the which they did cutt. They shaue all their berde except the mustaches, vppon their breast wear painted the head of som birde, and about the pappes as yt weare beames of the sune, vppon the bellye sum feerefull and monstrous face, spreedinge the beames verye fare vppon the thighes. Vppon the two knees som faces of lion, and vppon their leggs as yt had been shelles of fish. Vppon their Shoulders griffones heades, and then they had serpents abowt their armes: They caried abowt their necks one ayerne ringe, and another abowt the midds of their bodye, abowt the bellye, and the saids* hange on a chaine a cimeterre or turkie soorde, they did carye in one arme a target made of wode, and in the other hande a picke, of which the ayerne was after the manner of a Lick, with tassels on, and the other ende with a Rounde boule. And when they had ouercomme some of their ennemis, they did neuer felle to carye awey their heads with them.

---

* "And the saids" probably a typographical error for "at the side." A few lines lower down, "picke" and "lick" are apparently *pike* and *lance*.

The trvve picture of a vvomen
Piƈte I L

The trvve picture of a vvomen

Picte II.

THE woemen of the pictes aboue said wear noe worser for the warres then the men. And wear paynted after the manner followinge, hauinge their heads bear, did lett their hairre flyinge abowt . their Showlders wear painted with griffon heades, the lowe parts and thighes with lion faces, or some other beaste as yt commeth best into their fansye, their brest hath a maner of a half moone, with a great starre, and fowre lesser in booth the sides, their pappes painted in maner of beames of the sonne, and among all this a great litteninge starre vppon their brests. The saids of som pointes or beames, and the hoolle bellye as a sonne, the armes, thighes, and leggs well painted, of diuerses Figures : They dyd also carye abowt theyr necks an ayern Ringe, as the men did, and suche a girdle with the soorde hainginge, hauinge a Picke or a lance in one hande, and twoe dardz in the other.

The trvve picture of a yonge
dowgter of the Pictes I I I.

The trvve picture of a yonge dowgter of the

Pictes III.

THE yong dougters of the pictes, did also lett their haire flyinge, and wear also painted ouer all the body, so much that noe men could not faynde any different, yf they had not vse of another fashion of paintinge, for they did paint themselues of sondrye kinds of flours, and of the fairest that they cowld feynde. being fournished for the rest of such kinds of weappon as the woemen wear as you may see by this present picture a thinge trewlly worthie of admiration.

The trvve picture of a man of nation neigbour vnto the Picte I I I I.

The trvve picture of a man of nation

neigbour vnto the Picte IIII.

THER WAS in the said great Bretainne yet another nation
nigbour vnto the Pictes, which did apparell them selfues
with a kind of cassake other cloath Ierkin, the rest of the
bodye wear naked. They did also wear longe heares, and their
moustaches, butt the chin wear also shaued as the other before.
They dyd were alardge girdle abowt them, in which hange a croket
foorde, with the target, and did carye the picke or the lance in
their hande, which hath at the lowe end a rownde bowlle, as you
may see by this picture.

The trvve picture of a vvomen
nigbour of the Pictes   V.

The trvve picture of a vvomen

nigbo ir of the Pictes V.

THEIR woemen wear apparelled after this manner, butt that their apparell was opne before the brest, and did fastene with a little lesse, as our woemen doe fasten their peticott. They lett hange their brests outt, as for the rest they dyd carye suche weappens as the men did, and wear as good as the men for the warre.

A TABLE
OF THE PRINCI-
PALL THINGES THAT
are contained in this Hiſtorie,
after the order of the
Alphabet.

FINIS.

AT FRANCKFORT,
INPRINTED BY IHON WE
chel, at Theodore de Bry, owne
coaſt and chardges.

M D X C.

www.ingramcontent.com/pod-product-compliance
Lightning Source LLC
Chambersburg PA
CBHW020952030726
47496CB00005B/1475